Praise fc
Cookt

"There's a feisty new amateur sleuth in town and her name is Jenna Hart. With a bodacious cast of characters, a wrenching murder, and a collection of cookbooks to die for, Daryl Wood Gerber's *Final Sentence* is a page-turning puzzler of a mystery that I could not put down."

—Jenn McKinlay, *New York Times* bestselling author of the Cupcake Mysteries and Library Lovers Mysteries

"In *Final Sentence*, the author smartly blends crime, recipes, and an array of cookbooks that all should covet in a witty, well-plotted whodunit."

—Kate Carlisle, *New York Times* bestselling author of the Bibliophile Mysteries

"Readers will relish the extensive cookbook suggestions, the cooking primer, and the whole foodie phenomenon. Gerber's perky tone with a multigenerational cast makes this series a good match for Lorna Barrett's Booktown Mystery series . . ."

—*Library Journal*

"So pull out your cowboy boots and settle in for a delightful read. *Grilling the Subject* is a delicious new mystery that will leave you hungry for more."

—Carstairs Considers Blog

Books by Daryl Wood Gerber

The Cookbook Nook Mysteries

Final Sentence
Inherit the Word
Stirring the Plot
Fudging the Books
Grilling the Subject
Pressing the Issue
Wreath Between the Lines
Sifting Through Clues
Shredding the Evidence
Wining and Dying
Simmering with Resentment

The French Bistro Mysteries

A Deadly Éclair
A Soufflé of Suspicion

The Fairy Garden Mysteries

A Sprinkling of Murder
A Glimmer of a Clue
A Hint of Mischief

More Books by Daryl Wood Gerber

Suspense

Girl on the Run
Day of Secrets
Desolate Shores
Fan Mail
Cold Conviction

Writing as Avery Aames

The Long Quiche Goodbye
Lost and Fondue
Clobbered by Camembert
To Brie or Not to Brie
Days of Wine and Roquefort
As Gouda as Dead
For Cheddar or Worse

SIMMERING WITH RESENTMENT

A Cookbook Nook Mystery

Daryl Wood Gerber

BEYOND THE PAGE
PUBLISHING

Simmering with Resentment
Daryl Wood Gerber
Copyright © 2022 by Daryl Wood Gerber
Cover design and illustration by Dar Albert, Wicked Smart Designs

Beyond the Page Books
are published by
Beyond the Page Publishing
www.beyondthepagepub.com

ISBN: 978-1-954717-91-6

To all of my readers. Thank you for being so supportive over the years. You make my life rich, and your enthusiasm makes me want to keep writing.

Acknowledgments

"Be strong, be fearless, be beautiful.
And believe that anything is possible when you have the
right people there to support you." —Misty Copeland

I have been truly blessed to have the support and input of so many as I pursue my creative journey.

Thank you to my family and friends for all your encouragement. Thank you to my talented author friends, Krista Davis and Hannah Dennison, for your words of wisdom. Thank you to my PlotHatcher pals: Janet (Ginger Bolton), Kaye George, Marilyn Levinson (Allison Brook), Peg Cochran (Margaret Loudon), Janet Koch (Laura Alden), and Krista Davis. You are a wonderful pool of talent and a terrific wealth of ideas, jokes, stories, and fun! I adore you. Thanks to my Delicious Mystery author pals, Roberta Isleib (Lucy Burdette), Krista Davis, and Amanda Flower. I treasure your creative enthusiasm via social media.

Thank you to Facebook fan-based groups Delicious Mysteries, Cozy Mystery Review Crew, Save Our Cozies, Sisters in Crime Guppies, and so many more. I love how willing you are to read ARCs, post reviews, and help me as well as numerous other authors promote whenever possible. We need fans and friends like you. Thank you to all the bloggers like Dru Ann Love and Lori Caswell, who enjoy reviewing cozies and sharing these titles with your readers.

Thanks to those who have helped make this eleventh book in the Cookbook Nook Mystery series come to fruition: my publisher, Beyond the Page, my editor, Bill Harris, my agent, John Talbot, my cover artist, Dar Albert, and my biggest supporter, Kimberley Greene. Thanks to Madeira James for maintaining constant quality on my website. Thanks to my virtual assistant Christina Higgins for your novel ideas. Honestly, without all of you, I don't know what I would do. You keep me grounded.

Last but not least, thank you librarians, teachers, bookstore owners, and readers for sharing the delicious world of a Cookbook Nook in fictional Crystal Cove, California, with your friends.

Cast of Characters

Bailey Bird Martinez, Jenna's best friend
Brianna Martinez, daughter of Bailey
Bucky Winston, husband of Cinnamon Pritchett, firefighter
Cary Hart, Jenna's father
Cinnamon Pritchett, chief of police
Darinda Weatherly, bride-to-be
Eddie Milsap, former assistant and now manager of Bait and Switch
Flora Fairchild, owner of Home Sweet Home
Gracie "Gran" Goldsmith, works at Cookbook Nook
Gunther Hildenbiddle, owner of California Catch
Harmony Bold, wedding planner
Ilya Bakov, jewelry store owner
Jake Chapman, friend
Jenna Hart, owner of Cookbook Nook and Nook Café
Jim Daley, insurance agent
Katie Casey Landry, aka Chef Katie
Keller Landry, Katie's husband
Lola Bird, Bailey's mother and owner of Pelican Brief
Marlon Appleby, deputy
Matias Lajoie, owner of Tradewinds
Min-Yi, daughter of Katie
Pepper Pritchett, mother of Cinnamon and owner of Beaders of Paradise
Rhett Jackson, fiancé of Jenna and owner of Intime
Sarita Strachline, former restaurant owner and convicted arsonist
Shay and Sela Strachline, daughters of Sarita and Todd
Tina Gump, culinary student and nanny to Brianna
Tito Martinez, reporter and husband to Bailey
Todd Strachline, Sarita's ex-husband and local accountant
Ulrich Hildenbiddle, Gunther's son
Vera Hart, aunt to Jenna and co-owner of Cookbook Nook
Wren Weatherly, owner of Home Décor
Z.Z. Zoey Zeller, mayor and realtor

Chapter 1

"Who are you, and what have you done with my pal Jenna?" Bailey Bird, my best friend since high school, fisted her hands on her hips and scowled at me.

"I'm still me." I pulled white toile from a box and arranged it at the base of the Cookbook Nook's display window.

"No. You're not. You're immersed in weddings and dresses and flower arrangements, and, like, honestly you're scaring me."

"Boo!" I teased as I added a white floral recipe box and set it just so.

"You're in full-on Bridezilla mode," Bailey said. Her cheeks were nearly the same color as her cropped hot-pink sweater. "Bridezilla," she repeated in a vampiric tone.

Bailey and I were tweaking the window display to lure more customers to the shop. We had gone with an all-white theme. White linens, white aprons, white plates, and elegant crystal with white rims. For the featured cookbooks on the main table, we'd already set out a handful with recipes that would make a professional or amateur wedding planner salivate. *Wedding Cakes with Lorelie: Step by Step* was visually stunning and included charts for how to increase the size of the cakes. Of course, a go-to cookbook was always *Martha Stewart's Wedding Cakes: More Than 100 Inspiring Cakes — An Indispensable Guide for the Bride and Baker.*

"I'm no more a Bridezilla than you were." I hadn't spent my youth thinking about weddings. When I married my first husband, David, years ago—may he rest in peace—he'd suggested *less is more.* With a little cajoling, I'd agreed. We only invited family and a few guests. I wore a simple ecru cocktail dress and carried a bouquet of daisies, my mother's favorite flower. Now? When I married Rhett Baxter, I wanted to do it properly. The gown. A weekend of festivities. The whole shebang. "We only have three weeks left." Three weeks and four days, to be exact, but who was counting?

Our wedding would take place on the last Saturday in June. Our honeymoon would occur later, in the fall, when we could go leaf-peeping and wine tasting in the upper northwest. I tucked a stray hair behind my ear, irritated that I'd forgotten to don a hair band. I was growing my hair a little longer so I could wear an updo for the event, but it was invariably falling into my face.

"I've got to keep my eye on the prize," I said. Specifically, spending the rest of my life with Rhett. "To do that, I have to organize all the events."

"You have a wedding planner."

"Yes, but you know me. I'm very hands-on."

Family was coming in. My sister, her husband, and children would stay with our father. My brother, who I hadn't seen in over two years, would lodge with a buddy. Rhett's parents and sisters had rented rooms at the Crystal Cove Inn.

"Plus, I have to keep this shop running smoothly throughout," I added.

A few years ago, my aunt, who had made a fortune in the stock market, asked me to help her open the Cookbook Nook, a culinary bookshop located in the quaint Fisherman's Village shopping complex, which she owned. The bookshop was her passion project. Eager to change my course, I left my advertising job in San Francisco and moved home. I adored the store. I appreciated the layout with the moveable bookshelves filled with cookbooks as well as fiction featuring food. And I loved all the other things we sold in the shop — colorful aprons, spatulas, cookie jars, salt and pepper shakers, and cooking gear for kids. My mind was always whirring with new items that we could stock to please our steady stream of customers, in particular, our regulars.

"Hand me that wedding plate." I extended my right arm.

"You see? You're giving orders like a general." Bailey giggled. "Next thing you know, you'll be sending all units into battle."

"With Bride's Dream Expo in town for the rest of this week and into next week, it might feel like we're at war," I joked. "Talk about a pack of Bridezillas!"

At the beginning of June every year, the expo came to Crystal Cove. Designers, photographers, florists, hoteliers, caterers, and more would be on hand to show googly-eyed brides-to-be exactly what they wanted — or rather *needed* — in their weddings.

"The plate?" I asked.

"Say please."

"Pretty please?" I sang sweetly.

Bailey gave me the requested wedding plate as well as the matching cup and saucer. Not long after we opened the Cookbook Nook, we'd hired her. She'd turned out to be a top-notch salesperson, adept at engaging customers, and equally adept at making me laugh.

"Speaking of the expo," Bailey said, "I can't wait to go."

"Are you getting married again?" I winked.

Bailey was blissfully in love with her husband, Tito Martinez, a terrific reporter for the *Crystal Cove Courier*. "You're going this afternoon, right?"

"I am."

"When is your final dress fitting?"

"A week from tomorrow."

Luckily, Harmony Bold, wedding planner extraordinaire, was helping me navigate my nuptials. This afternoon, she was escorting Rhett and me to the expo so we could take a last-minute peek at everything, in case we wanted to add to our event, although practically every item we had on our to-do lists other than finalizing entertainment had been completed.

"Enough about me." I twirled a hand. "Let's focus on finishing this."

"*Psst,*" Bailey rasped. "Heads up. Incoming customers. Nine o'clock."

A group of women in their early twenties sauntered into the shop. Each was carrying a Bride's Dream Expo cream-colored canvas tote bag.

"Welcome," I chimed. "Have fun browsing."

"Whew, is it hot outside!" said the one wearing a Minnie Mouse wedding hair band with adorable white ears and veil. I bet I knew where she was planning on honeymooning. "It's so nice to get out of the sun."

"Is it always this hot in Crystal Cove?" one of her companions asked, cooling herself with a Bride's Dream Expo fan. She was wearing skinny jeans and a long-sleeved, scoop-necked T-shirt with the words *Marry Me* scrawled across the front.

"No," I said. "This is an anomaly."

Crystal Cove was a lovely tourist destination on the coast of California south of Santa Cruz. The town was settled in the 1850s, although it wasn't officially founded until 1883. It consisted of three crescent-shaped bays, a range of modest mountains, which defined the eastern border of the town, and usually boasted moderate Mediterranean temperatures.

"The weatherman says it will cool down tomorrow," I added. "And a rare summer rainstorm might be in the forecast."

The women proceeded into the shop, chatting about how pleased they were that the expo entrance fee was a measly fifteen bucks.

"By the way" — Bailey sidled over to me — "Tito thought your wedding invitation was quite nice."

"Glad to hear it."

Tito had no compunctions about offering his opinion. On anything. When I'd first met him, I'd thought he was a pompous, in-your-face bulldog. Good for a reporter, not for a friend. Now, however, I liked him a lot. He was quite a charming and humorous guy and treasured Bailey and their daughter with all his heart. That made him a star in my eyes.

"He liked the gilded gold border."

Tigger, my rescue ginger cat, mewed from the top of his cat condo, agreeing on the assessment of the invitations. And why shouldn't he? He'd had the final say, after all. Rhett and I had laughed about his participation in the selection. When we were deciding on designs, Tigger galloped across the dining room table, scattering all the invitations to the floor. The one that remained on top was the one Rhett and I settled on. It was simple, yet elegant. Like our relationship.

"How is Tito?" I asked.

"As happy as a clam." He'd served as the editor at the *Courier* for a New York minute and, hating the responsibility, had ceded the job to another reporter who had jumped at the chance. "He's working on a new story about graft in politics."

"I'll bet our illustrious mayor isn't happy about that."

"The story deals with politics in Silicon Valley, not here. He'll also be doing some fluff pieces for the expo."

"He loves doing those," I teased.

"Not." She snorted.

"Silverware, please." I removed the silverware I'd installed in the display—not elegant enough—and jutted out my hand.

Bailey placed a Lenox Gorham fork, knife, and spoon in my palm. "Ahem." She cleared her throat on purpose. "Why didn't I know that you'd secured CC Vineyards for your venue until your aunt told me?"

"Because we didn't know ourselves until last week, and then I forgot to tell you. Harmony pulled out all the stops to get it. Did you know there's a two-year waiting list for it?"

"I know!"

"Well, there was a cancelation!" I whooped with glee.

"Lucky you." Bailey and Tito had gotten married at Baldini Vineyards, a local site with an ocean view. The CC Vineyards' view was quite similar, but the terrace was much less formal and more in keeping with Rhett's and my taste. Soft greens, creamy whites, and burgundies were going to be our color palette. "Are you still planning to have the out-of-towners' dinner at Intime?" Bailey asked. She stood, lifted a silk bridal bouquet from the main display table, and brushed it against my ear.

"Stop." I shooed her away. "Put that down." For a bit of pizzazz, we'd set a dozen silk wedding bouquets around the shop. All the brides that were coming in were drawn to them.

Bailey obeyed and plucked her short spiky hair sassily. "So . . . are you . . . the dinner . . . at Intime?"

"Absolutely." Intime was the French bistro that Rhett owned with partners. From the day it opened, it had garnered rave reviews and repeat customers. "Rhett has been working on the perfect menu. Onion tart appetizers. A choice of steak au poivre or rotisserie chicken. A selection of crème brûlée, chocolate soufflé, and profiteroles for dessert."

"Yum. I'm gaining pounds imagining it." Bailey was as slim as a reed. I doubt she'd ever put on weight. Her little girl kept her hopping.

"Yoo-hoo! I'm here." Aunt Vera, clad in a silver caftan, waltzed into the shop. She set her turban on the sales counter and smoothed the red hair that was fringed around her face. "Is my client here yet?" She scanned the store.

"Not that I know of."

My aunt was my father's older sister and had been like a mother to me since my mother had passed away. In addition to managing the shop with me, Aunt Vera offered tarot card and palm readings.

"Do you see her?" I asked.

There were only a few customers browsing the cookbooks and assorted kitchen items we stocked.

"Him," she corrected me.

Chapter 2

"Him, who?" I asked, surprised. My aunt didn't have many male clients.

"Jake," she replied.

Jake Chapman, one of my father's oldest friends, wasn't a woo-woo kind of guy. In fact, he prided himself on being a laid-back, down-to-earth man.

"You know he's sweet on Z.Z.," my aunt said. "I think he's trying to figure out their course."

"Should Z.Z. be worried?" I asked.

"Doubtful. He's head over heels for her." She rounded the sales counter and busied herself with receipts. "I can see you've sold quite a lot of merchandise already. Not bad for a Wednesday."

"We've been jam-packed." I rose to my feet, brushed off my knees, smoothed the skirt of my butter-yellow sundress, and slipped into my yellow polka-dot flip-flops. Almost daily, I donned sandals. My toes enjoyed the fresh air. "It's only slow now because the future brides are eating lunch."

"By the by"—my aunt beckoned me—"am I invited to join you for the taste testing?"

Before attending the expo, I'd arranged for a wedding cake taste test. I smirked. "Who told you that was on the agenda?"

"Katie can't keep a secret from me."

Chef Katie, another of my lifelong friends, managed the Nook Café, an adjunct of the Cookbook Nook. Rhett and I had hired her to do the catering for the wedding. She and I had settled on the entrée selections. I couldn't wait to see what she planned for the appetizers. Meanwhile, she was trying out a number of wedding cake recipes.

I patted my aunt's hand. "Yes, you're invited. Bailey, too, and Gran if she makes it in. She phoned earlier to say one of her grandchildren had the sniffles, and she needed to take the girl to the doctor." Gran—aka Gracie Goldsmith—worked at the shop a couple of days a week *to keep herself out of trouble,* she clowned.

"Hello!" Harmony Bold warbled as she swept into the shop looking ready for action in a ruby red sheath, her navy blue portfolio tucked under her arm, her long hair swept into a chic chignon. "I'm starved." Tigger sprinted to her. She bent to pet him. "Hello, sweet boy. Aren't you the most adorable cat in the whole world? Yes, you are." Standing, she eyed Bailey, my aunt, and me. "Is Katie ready for us, do you think?"

"Am I ever!" Katie appeared in the breezeway that connected the shop to the café, wheeling a trolly filled with mini wedding cake selections. The hem of her pink-checkered dress peeked from beneath her chef's coat.

"Hold on." I raised my hand. "I thought we were coming to the café's kitchen for the tasting."

"Hoo-boy, not a chance." She wasn't wearing her toque. Her curls bounced as she shook her head. "The café is packed to the gills with women of all ages. We offered a specialty first-day-of-the-expo luncheon and needed to have two seatings to accommodate them all. The kitchen is abuzz with activity."

"Ca-ching," Bailey whispered in my ear.

"Ca-ching, indeed." I gave her a thumbs-up.

A little over a year ago, my aunt found it in her heart to make Katie and Bailey limited partners in the Cookbook Nook and Nook Café. She knew they had families to raise and realized salaries alone couldn't bring in the requisite income.

"Hello! Could someone ring us up?" the young woman in Minnie Mouse headdress asked.

"Of course." My aunt hurried to them.

Katie pushed the trolly next to the vintage table where my aunt gave her readings and where, weekly, we put out a new foodie-themed jigsaw puzzle that our customers enjoyed piecing together. Rather than move this week's vintage puzzle featuring a bride and groom cutting a wedding cake, Katie unfurled a tablecloth she'd tucked on the trolly's lower shelf and spread it over the puzzle. Then she set out a selection of plates, napkins, and forks, and the six mini cakes, each sliced into morsel-sized portions.

"Lemon raspberry," she said, pointing to the rightmost cake. "A favorite for most weddings." She held a finger above the next one. "Banana mocha."

Bailey scrunched her nose. "C'mon. That's not a thing."

Harmony said, "Yes, it is. I told Katie about it. It was a huge hit at the Naylors' youngest daughter's wedding." The Naylors, one of the founding families of Crystal Cove, were royalty to locals.

Katie chortled. "Next, chocolate with decadent chocolate ganache."

My mouth started watering.

Katie continued. "Carrot cake with cream cheese frosting, a fan favorite. Vanilla, of course, with a lemon curd filling, and lastly, spiced pear cake with salted caramel icing."

Bailey fake-swooned. "I want that one. The whole thing."

"None of them have nuts, and any of them can be made gluten-free." Katie added, "If you can't decide on one, Jenna, you could do a layer of each."

"I could?"

"For example, chocolate, vanilla, and lemon-raspberry—"

"Won't the flavors mingle together? How do you cut that?" I tilted my head trying to picture it.

"It works. Trust me." Katie looked at Harmony, who concurred. "No matter what, you should have at least one option for those with allergies."

Bailey held up a hand. "What about making a cupcake tower? I saw one on the Food Channel that was spectacular. Four tiers. The top, of course, is the official wedding cake. But that way—"

"Everyone can choose the cake they want without flavors smooshing." I applauded gleefully. "Love it. It's a win-win." I addressed Katie. "Can you do that?"

"I'm Chef Katie. I can do anything." With mock smugness, she blew on her fingertips and polished them on her lapel.

Harmony knuckled Katie's arm. "Okay, ladies, dig in. Let's sample these."

Katie said, "But you might want to taste the chocolate last. It could overpower all the rest."

"Noted." I dished up a slice of the pear cake with salted caramel icing and took a bite. "Oh, wow! I adore this one. Rhett will love it, too." Rhett had granted me final say on cake choices, but I knew his tastes well enough to vote wisely on his behalf.

As Minnie and her entourage left the shop, two women—a mother and daughter, I presumed, given their similar brunette hairstyles, apple cheeks, and startling blue eyes—strolled into the store. They, too, were carrying Bride's Dream Expo tote bags. The exposition organizers were handing them out to all registrants.

The younger woman eyeballed the cakes. "Those look scrumptious. Don't they, Mom?" She gazed at the group of us. "Who's the bride-to-be?"

Harmony pointed at me. "Jenna."

I raised a hand.

"Congratulations," the daughter said.

"Who's doing the catering?" her mother asked.

"The Nook Café!" Katie fearlessly stepped toward them. "Right next door. Best food in town, if I do say so myself."

The mother exchanged a look with her daughter. "Do you have a card?"

Katie pulled one from her pocket. "Always." She sneaked a peek over her shoulder at me and winked.

"Are you reasonably priced?" The mother studied the card. Her daughter peered at it, as well.

"It depends. Are you reasonably selective?" Katie said, then added, "Kidding," and chortled heartily.

The mother glanced at her daughter and back at Katie. "We'd like to think so."

Katie assessed the older woman. "When are you getting married?"

"Not me," the mother said. "Her." Fondly, she gripped her daughter's elbow. "To the most delicious man in the world. He's a dentist. With an excellent reputation. And he adores my girl."

The daughter blushed.

"Thanks for this." The mother pocketed Katie's card. "We'll be in touch. Right now, we have to find a gift for the future mother-in-law." The two sauntered to the shelves that held dessert cookbooks.

I elbowed Harmony. "Follow them. Give them your card, too."

"No. That's alright. I have plenty of brides to tend to."

"Jenna!" Flora Fairchild rushed into the shop. "You won't believe it!" She was panting hard, and her face was white with panic. She hadn't come to buy anything. She wasn't carrying a purse, and she was still wearing her shop apron. "You won't believe who has come to town."

"Who?" I asked, adrenaline skyrocketing.

"Sarita Strachline!"

Chapter 3

I gulped. Sarita? Why was she here? Did Rhett know? In a flash, I retreated to the storage room at the back of the shop. I needed to breathe. Collect myself. Packed with books and filing cabinets and boxes filled with items we offered for sale, the storage area, which also served as our office, wasn't the most spacious place to find calm, but I had to try.

Bailey followed me in. "Why did you yelp?" She made sure the drapes closed after her.

"Because . . . Because . . ." I fetched a cup of water from the water-cooler and sat at the desk. Tigger stole in and sprang into my lap, picking up on my anxiety. His purr sounded like a diesel in idle. "It's okay, buddy," I cooed. "I'm fine."

"Who is Sarita Strachline?" Bailey leaned against the edge of the desk.

"She . . ." I inhaled and exhaled, willing my shoulders to relax. "She owned the restaurant. The Grotto. She's the one—"

"Who burned it down? The woman who hightailed it out of town and left Rhett to take the fall?"

"Yep."

"A short while after you and Rhett started dating, you convinced the police—"

"To reopen the case."

Before Rhett and I met, he'd been the chef at the Grotto, a popular fish-themed restaurant that had been located on the second floor of Fisherman's Village until a deliberately set fire burned the place down. Luckily the other shops hadn't suffered significant damage. Rhett had arrived as the blaze was building. Anxious to retrieve his collection of his mother's recipes, he'd rushed in. He'd escaped within an inch of his life. At first, due to his presence at the scene, the police thought he'd started it. However, they didn't arrest him for the crime because there wasn't enough evidence to hold him. No propellants at his house or in his car. No telltale signs on his clothing. Despite being let go, suspicion hung around him like a dark cloud for more than a year, so he quit being a chef and opened Bait and Switch Fishing Supply and Sport Store. It wasn't until recently that he'd found the courage to start his own restaurant,

Intime. Investors had made him an offer he couldn't refuse. To seed the venture, he sold half of the sporting goods store to his former assistant manager.

"Come to think of it, wasn't it Cinnamon Pritchett you convinced?" Bailey asked.

"Yep."

Chief Cinnamon Pritchett had dated Rhett at one time. After she and I became friends, I begged her to reopen the case and take a hard look at the Grotto's owner, Sarita Strachline, speculating as Rhett had that before Sarita had set the blaze, she'd stolen the art that she'd hung in the restaurant so she could keep the art but pocket the insurance payout for loss. As it so happened, Rhett and I were right. Sarita had stolen the art. With the help of the New Orleans Police Department, Cinnamon located Sarita in Louisiana, discovered the cache of art, and solved the crime.

"The insurance company demanded she give back the money she'd recouped for the loss, but she'd spent some of it," I went on. "Her children were devastated. Her ex-husband, Todd, a local accountant—Sarita and he divorced long before the fire—claimed ignorance on all counts."

"I haven't met him, but I hear he's got a good reputation."

"I haven't met him, either, but that's what I've heard, too." My aunt did all of our books. We had no need for a second accountant. I drummed the desk. "What's Sarita doing out so early? And more importantly, why would she dare show her face here? After all the pain she caused?"

"Maybe Flora knows," Bailey said. "Flora knows everything."

Flora Fairchild, who owned Home Sweet Home, a darling shop that offered potpourris, handmade items, and a wide selection of collectibles, was a gossip through and through. She rooted around in everybody else's business, and she relished being an alarmist. Chicken Little had nothing on her.

Bailey rested a hand on my shoulder. "Let's ask."

"I have to tell Rhett."

"After we get the skinny." Bailey offered me a hand. "C'mon, pal. On your feet. Buck up."

We passed through the drapes into the shop. Flora was standing with my aunt and Harmony at the vintage table, one hand toying with the single braid she'd plaited in front of her shoulder and staring at the cakes as if she wanted an invitation to taste them.

"Flora." I crossed to her. "Where did you see Sarita?"

"On the Pier." Flora released her hair and fiddled with the beading on her apron.

Crystal Cove stretched from the lighthouse at the northernmost end of town to the Pier at the southernmost end. In between we had parks, an aquarium, the community college that offered a specialized degree in the study of grapes, and lots of eateries and shops.

"I was making a delivery," Flora added. "She was climbing onto her sailboat."

The Pier boasted carny games, a theater, boutique shops, and restaurants. In addition, it was the launching site for fishermen and sailors.

"It was a beautiful boat." Flora spread her arms. "A thirty-foot Pearson with wispy blue stripes." Flora knew a lot about boats. Her parents were quite the sailors. "She dubbed it the *Second Wind*."

"*Second Wind*." Bailey cozied up beside me. "Considering Sarita's history, that's a pretty cheeky name, if you ask me."

"Definitely cheeky," Flora said. "But that's how she always was."

"You knew her?" I asked.

"Once upon a time." She wriggled her fingers. "I'm always amazed how people can pull the wool over someone's eyes. We all thought she was nice back then."

"We?" I asked.

"The book club we belonged to. She made the most flavorful brownies." Flora leaned in. "Between you and me, I'm not sure she ever read the books on our list, but she liked coming to the events to show off her baking skills."

"Jenna," my aunt said, "we saw that boat on Sunday when we were shopping for Rhett. Remember?"

"I do." We'd gone to the Pier because I wanted to buy my future husband a really special wedding gift. He had his heart set on learning to windsurf. Bait and Switch had been putting on a stunning display of equipment that day. A dozen sailboats had been tethered at the far end of the Pier. "Flora, do you know when Sarita got out of jail?"

"Last Saturday," Flora said. "Early parole, I hear. I asked around."

Of course she had.

"Apparently she was a model inmate."

She was a premier con woman, for sure, I mused. "And why did she come back to town?"

"She has two daughters," my aunt said.

Flora nodded. "True, but that's not why she came back. She plans to start over again here."

"Here?" I gulped. "Start over here? Meaning she's planning to live in Crystal Cove permanently? Oh, no." I exchanged a worried glance with Bailey.

"I heard she worked as a short-order cook while she was in jail," Flora said, "but I don't think she intends to open another restaurant."

"How can you be certain?"

"There's talk that she's considering investing in another business. It's hush-hush." Flora drummed her fingertips on her chin. "I can't recall who told me that. Perhaps Faith." Faith was Flora's twin sister.

I could barely breathe, unable to tamp down the panic I was feeling.

"Now, now, dear." My aunt slung an arm around my shoulders. "Sit." She forced me into a chair beside the table and deftly pulled a pack of tarot cards from her caftan pocket. She shuffled once and handed me the deck. "Cut the cards."

"Aunt Vera, not now. I have to tell Rhett about this. He'll be—"

"Do it!" she ordered. "Humor me."

I glowered at her. Humor her, indeed. She knew I wasn't a believer in the tarot. Sure, I understood the meanings of the cards, but I didn't believe that a card could determine one's future. However, I wouldn't deign to dampen my aunt's enthusiasm for the art. She had the innate ability of turning a negative card into something positive for a client. In particular, she was partial to single-draw readings because she could craft a quick, whimsical, and positive tale.

I cut the deck and handed it back. "Here you go. What bright light do you see at the end of the tunnel?"

She flipped over the top card and frowned.

"What's wrong?" I leaped to my feet, trying to get a glimpse of the card. When I did, my heart juddered. The Ten of Swords featured a man lying facedown with ten swords in his back. It was a startling card and an indicator that the subject of the reading— namely *me*—would suffer an unwelcome surprise.

Bailey spied the card and brandished a hand. "It doesn't mean a thing, girlfriend. Nada. Forget about it."

"She's right, dear." My aunt shimmied her shoulders. "It means nothing. It was a single draw. No big deal." Her gaze wavered; she was lying through her teeth.

Besides, the prediction had already come true. Sarita Strachline, as unwelcome a surprise as I could imagine, was back in town. Shoot me now.

"Time to go to the expo, Jenna." Harmony tapped her watch. "Lose the doom and gloom and slap on a grin."

Bailey knuckled my arm. "Cheer up. This is not dire."

I glared at her.

"It's not," she protested.

"Pollyanna," I muttered.

"If the label fits." She gave me a fierce, supportive hug.

"Before you go," Katie said, "which cakes will you choose, Jenna?"

I didn't have a clue. My stomach was roiling. "I'll give you my decision later, okay? They're all . . . wonderful."

Katie grimaced. She could read me as well as Bailey could.

"Harmony," I said, "I need to fetch my purse."

"Jenna, dear." My aunt tried to corral me.

"Relax. I'm fine." I bussed her on the cheek and forced a cheery lilt into my tone. "Don't worry. I'm not taking this reading to heart. Everything will be fine. Fine and dandy. Fine and super dandy."

And I believed it until Tigger yowled at the top of his lungs.

Chapter 4

Bride's Dream Expo was taking place in a gigantic white tent set in the parking lot that abutted the community college as well as Aquarium by the Sea. A check-in desk stood to the right of the entrance. Attendees flowed beneath the entryway's arch of pink, lavender, and white balloons. Each attendee sported a badge and was carrying an expo tote bag. A separate exit stood to the left of the entrance.

Harmony collected our credentials and handed me mine as well as a tote. "They're nicely made," she said as she peeked inside. "Stuffed with swag."

Inside the tent, she pulled to a stop and consulted a site map. Crystal Cove Florists, which was in charge of our floral arrangements, had scored a prime location to the right. The venue's banner stood out with its multiple images of colorful arrangements. I moseyed to the venue to admire the bouquets, which ranged from sheer white to dusty rose to tropical blooms. Two women were studying the white-themed bouquets. Their conversation tickled me.

"Is this too white?" the taller woman asked.

"You can never have too much white," her friend replied.

"But it's white-white."

"That's because white is white."

"Pearl white isn't white."

And on they went.

The owner, Posey, a cheery woman with rosy cheeks, rolled her eyes at me. I bit back a giggle. I could only imagine all the conversations she'd been privy to so far.

"Hi, Jenna," she said. "Getting excited about your big day?"

"I'm over the moon. Have you seen Rhett?"

"He's over there." She pointed. "In the photographers' section."

Dozens of photographers had rented booths. Rhett was standing near In the Moment Photography, the outfit that was going to photograph our wedding, talking to Z.Z. Zeller, Crystal Cove's mayor, and her boyfriend, Jake Chapman. It dawned on me that Jake hadn't shown up for his appointment with my aunt. Had he forgotten or changed his mind?

"Jenna!" Rhett hailed me. How handsome he looked in light brown linen slacks and white poplin shirt, the sleeves casually rolled up. His face was tan, his smile broad. The way he was ogling me made me weak at the knees.

"Harmony," I said to my wedding planner, "this way." I guided her through the throng until we reached Rhett, Z.Z., and Jake. I pecked Rhett on the cheek, but that wasn't good enough for him. He lifted my chin with a fingertip and gave me a lingering kiss.

"Missed you, too," I cooed, warmth creeping into my cheeks. I'd seen him before heading for work, but he'd been sound asleep. A restaurateur kept weird hours. He typically went to bed around two in the morning and awoke late.

"Isn't it wonderful?" Z.Z., a five-foot-tall force of nature, eagerly sought out events that would intrigue tourists year-round. "There are musicians, makeup artists, dress designers, and more. I can't imagine being a young bride and seeing all of this. How will they manage their budgets? I'd want one of everything."

Jake laughed and slung an arm around Z.Z.'s shoulders. "You are the queen of budgets. I'm sure you'd find a way to color within the lines."

"Oh, you," Z.Z. joshed, and knuckled him in the ribs.

Jake, who reminded me of an aging rodeo star, could easily take the hit. Though he was close to twenty years older than Z.Z., he was perhaps the sprightliest man alive, next to my father.

"Thousands are here today, and it's only the first day," Z.Z. said.

"But it's not overwhelming," Jake said. "It's real easy to navigate. You'll find all the photographers here. Florists, over there." He gestured with a gnarled hand. "Restaurants and caterers are at the back in the food court."

Harmony nodded, pointing to the areas he mentioned on her site map.

"You did it again, my love." Jake beamed at Z.Z. "I marvel at your organization skills."

"Don't give me any credit." Z.Z. patted his arm. "The Bride's Dream Expo event planner created the layout, not me."

"She's being modest," Jake said.

"Why are you here, Jenna?" Z.Z. asked. "I thought your wedding planning was in its final stages."

"It is, but Harmony tells me that sometimes brides want to see what's going on at an expo."

"Plus, we need to settle on the entertainment," Rhett said.

I'd been leaning toward the idea of having a string quartet. He was thinking more along the lines of upbeat disc jockey music.

"Harmony," Z.Z. said, "I hear your business is thriving. I've heard wonderful things about your attention to detail. My niece might be in the market next year . . ."

As the two of them discussed Z.Z.'s niece, I looped my hand around Rhett's elbow and said sotto voce, "When we're done here, we have to talk. Sarita Strachline is out of jail, and she's here. In town."

His gaze darkened. "How is that possible?"

"Early parole."

"I wonder what her ex-husband will think about that?" Rhett's voice had an edge to it. "Todd wasn't pleased when she bought him out prior to the arson. He was even angrier when she skipped town, and he learned she'd reaped the insurance payout, much of which she spent before she went to jail."

"She blew through it?"

"That's the story."

Z.Z. and Harmony ended their conversation, and Z.Z. said, "Is everything okay, you two?"

I forced a smile. "We're good. It's all good. Harmony, we should—"

"Hi, Jenna!" a woman trilled. "Fancy seeing you here."

The brunette woman with the startling blue eyes who'd come into the store earlier with her daughter strode toward us. At the same time her daughter emerged from one of the photography venues carrying a silk rose and a dozen brochures.

"Darinda, dear, over here!" the mother called.

"Wren Weatherly," Z.Z. said to the woman. "What a lovely surprise. I see you and Jenna have met. Wren"—Z.Z. motioned to Jake—"meet my fiancé, Jake Chapman."

"Fiancé?" I looked between them. "Since when?"

Z.Z. blushed. "Since this morning."

Rhett clapped Jake on the back. "Congrats."

I gawked at Jake.

He saw me gawking, and his cheeks blazed pink. Realization

about missing his appointment with my aunt must have sunk in. He said hastily, "My love, I forgot I have to see someone about . . . a th-thing," he stammered. "I'll call you later." He pecked Z.Z.'s cheek.

"Don't tell me you have cold feet already," Z.Z. kidded.

"Nothing like that. Bye, ladies. Bye, Rhett." He hurried away.

"Well, congratulations," Wren said. "And might I add that my daughter Darinda, a dental technician"—she swept her hand to introduce her—"is also a future bride."

"Congratulations!" Z.Z. chimed.

"That's not all I am, Mom," Darinda said under her breath.

Wren petted her daughter's cheek and continued. "We had the best time looking at the bridesmaid ideas." She had a dulcet voice and energetic smile. "There are candles and jewelry and . . . Oh!" The *oh* popped out of her. "Have you ever heard of bath bombs? They're these round things that fizz up in the bath and help regenerate your skin. After they dissolve, you find a little surprise in the middle, like jewelry or money. How fun is that?"

"I've seen those at Home Sweet Home," I said, having noticed a couple of baskets filled with them at Flora's shop. "But I've never tried them."

Wren grinned. "They're so much—"

"Mom." Darinda tapped her watch.

"Right. We have to sign up for the grand prize." Wren hitched her tote higher on her shoulder. "There's a ten-thousand-dollar grand prize for one lucky couple to help defray wedding costs."

"Who knew how expensive everything was?" Z.Z. said supportively.

"They'll announce the winner Monday afternoon," Wren continued, "right before the expo closes."

"Mom, we also have to meet with florists."

"Of course, sweetie. Let's go." To all of us, she said, "Forgive my daughter. She hates being late to anything. The excitement never ends, right? Don't miss the bath bombs." She steered Darinda past the booth for That's Amore Photography and out of sight.

"Wren's name sounds familiar," I said.

"She was one of the partners in the Grotto," Rhett said.

I gulped. What were the odds of meeting her on the same day I'd heard about Sarita returning to town?

Z.Z. *tsked* and lowered her voice. "Poor dear. She and her husband lost every penny because of the fire."

"Every penny?"

"The insurance policy for the place hadn't covered rebuilding it from the ground up."

"You're kidding!"

"When Sarita walked away, the Weatherlys were out of luck. A year later, Wren's husband . . ." She worked her lip between her teeth.

"Her husband committed suicide," Rhett explained.

I felt a sharp pain in my chest. "Poor thing."

"Wren worked hard to keep things afloat," Z.Z. continued. "Finally, she found a banker who would lend her enough capital to invest in a new business."

"Another restaurant?" I asked. I knew most, not all, of the restaurant owners in town. Many were regulars at the Cookbook Nook.

"No. She owns Home Décor," Z.Z. said.

"That's Flora's competitor."

"Not really. Home Décor is quite different from Home Sweet Home," Z.Z. continued. "The shop showcases furniture and wall hangings. Very upscale. Nothing cutesy about it."

Though Home Décor was next door to Crystal Cove Florists, I'd never even peeked inside. Home Sweet Home was my go-to place for gift items.

Harmony consulted her watch. "Rhett and Jenna, we have to get a move on if we want to see all the entertainers before they pack up for the afternoon."

Rhett's cell phone buzzed. He removed it from his pocket and groaned. "Oh, no."

Chapter 5

"What's wrong?" I squeezed Rhett's elbow.

"I have a mini emergency to deal with." He frowned. "Seems the AC at Intime is on the fritz. In this heat—"

"It's always something."

"Will you be upset if I leave to take care of the issue?" Rhett gazed intently into my eyes. "You'll still marry me, won't you?"

I grinned. "Of course. If I can select cake flavors without you, I can choose music."

"Nothing too sedate," he reminded me.

"Can the music for when I'm walking down the aisle be traditional? I mean, you don't want me doing a two-step or jig, do you?"

He hugged me. "Promise me not Bach."

"Bach, ick." I wrinkled my nose. "Mozart or Pachelbel."

"Fine."

For the next hour, Harmony and I interviewed a variety of musicians. A pianist and violinist duo was as close as I was going to get to a string quartet. Other similar groups were booked for a year. However, disc jockeys were plentiful. One, the Dancing DeeJay, won my vote. He favored playing oldies, and Rhett, despite being born in the eighties, loved music by Elvis, the Beatles, and the Rolling Stones. When he agreed to play Pachelbel's "Canon in D" for my entrance, I hired him.

"Let's grab a bite to eat," Harmony said. "My treat. I've only eaten cake today."

Come to think of it, that was all I'd eaten since breakfast, too. "Sure."

We wended our way past honeymoon package providers and sunset cruise purveyors to the food court, where many caterers and local restaurants had rented booths to show off their wares. Unlike the rest of the expo, the area was decorated in bold red, yellow, and blue. As an advertising person, I happened to know that bright colors stimulated appetites. Banners graced each booth. Upbeat rock music was being piped through speakers. Tables and chairs were arranged in the center.

Harmony and I circled the area before making our selections.

Bailey's mother's restaurant, the Pelican Brief, was offering kebabs of its delectable fried fish. Mum's the Word, a diner on the Pier known for its home cooking, was offering mini meatballs dipped in a special sauce. Shredding, a restaurant famous for its cutting-edge yet healthy dishes, was offering mini cups of Chinese coleslaw. Hot-Cha-Cha, a Brazilian café, was offering all things dessert: ice cream bombes, crêpes suzette, baked Alaska, and cherries jubilee. A crowd had gathered to watch the fiery presentations, which made me hopeful that a decent-sized group would have the same fascination when Katie did her flambé demonstration at the shop on Saturday. On demo days, we typically sold a ton of product.

"Step right up for the most remarkable fish on the planet!" a tall, bespectacled, older man in blue shirt, jeans, and blue apron announced like a circus barker. His banner read: *California Catch*. "Crispy pepper fish bites. The spicier the merrier."

A younger man, similar in bearing to the older man and clad in the same blue-themed getup, stood to his right. He, too, was holding a tray of fish bites in blue-checkered cups, each bite skewered with a toothpick.

Harmony tittered. "What a salesman Gunther is."

"Do you know him?" I asked.

"Sure do. Gunther Hildenbiddle." She smiled fondly. "He's a remarkable restaurateur. He and his son Ulrich are old friends of the family." Harmony's family, the Boldines—she'd shortened her name to Bold—owned a cluster of businesses on Buena Vista Boulevard. "Let's taste his wares."

She guided me to his booth. I'd seen California Catch on Seaview Road, the thoroughfare leading up into the hills. The line out the door was always long, but I'd never eaten there.

"Gunther," Harmony said as she approached him, "you're looking good."

"Don't kid a kidder." Gunther swept a hand along his salt-and-pepper hair. "I look older by the minute, young lady. Now you, on the other hand, look more like your mother every day, and that's saying something. She is one stunner of a woman."

Harmony's laugh sounded like bells.

"How is your mother?" he asked.

"Fine. Traveling with Dad. They're both as happy as clams."

"Good to hear."

Harmony gestured to me. "This is my friend Jenna Hart, a future bride."

Gunther grinned. "Well, aren't you a beauty, too?"

I felt my cheeks warm. "Thank you."

"Who's the lucky fellow?"

"Rhett Baxter," I replied.

"Good man. I hear his restaurant is dynamite. I'll get there one day. Soon, I hope." Gunther thrust his tray at us. "Here, try my spicy cod bites."

I took two checkered cups from the tray and handed one to Harmony. In the cup was a three-bite portion of fish plus a dollop of a red-colored sauce.

"Is this your specialty hot sauce, Gunther?" Harmony asked.

"Better believe it."

"It's divine."

I bit into one of the bites and hummed my approval. "Exactly the right amount of heat."

"All his recipes are his grandpa's," Harmony said.

Gunther nodded. "The old guy lived and died by the sea. Here. Try the bite-sized potato poppers." He set two poppers on plates and thrust them at Harmony. "They're mini potatoes scooped out and filled with mashed potatoes, bacon, and peppers. My son Ulrich's idea." He nodded to the younger man.

Ulrich offered a quick smile and continued hawking his wares.

Harmony took one of the poppers. "They look yummy." She grabbed napkins from a dispenser at Gunther's booth and handed me one. "California Catch is famous for its spicy food."

"Cayenne, chili powder, and white pepper." Gunther beamed. "You name it, I use it."

"He sells his own blends of spices at his restaurant. They're fabulous."

Gunther chuckled. "Maybe I need you to be my spokesperson, Miss Bold."

"Thanks, but no thanks. I've got plenty on my plate being a wedding planner." She said to me, "Gunther's first restaurant was Open Waters. Perhaps you've heard of it."

I nodded. "I remember that one. It's where my family and I went when I was in high school." My brother, sister, and I had been fascinated by the giant red octopus painted behind the bar as well as the beach-themed signs hanging on all the walls. My favorite had been *Flip-flops. It's a way of life.* I said, "Whatever happened to —"

Harmony shook her head sharply, warning me off asking why the restaurant had closed. "I'm surprised to see you here at the expo, Gunther." She rubbed his arm affectionately. "I didn't know you would cater a wedding."

"I'm just getting into the game now," Gunther said. "Here's my business card." He pulled one from his pocket. "But don't call me until next week. I'm off to a religious retreat at Mindful Nourishment."

"Ooh, I've heard of that," Harmony said. "It's a silent retreat in the Santa Cruz Mountains near Pasatiempo."

Gunther explained that the retreat was run by monks, and once the attendee had checked in, the monks left the guest alone. "No contact with the outside world," he said, "and a lot of meditation."

"I'm jealous," Harmony said. "I could use some time delving into my inner psyche."

"Being single gives a man plenty of time to ponder one's fate," Gunther said.

She knitted her brow. "You're not dating yet?"

"I had the love of my life, Harmony. You know that. When she . . ." He blinked as if fighting back tears. "I've decided to leave that love nonsense behind me." He addressed me. "Sorry, my dear Jenna. I don't mean to disparage marriage."

"*Disparage marriage.*" Harmony snickered. "That rhymes."

"Indeed it does. But love is for poets and dreamers, not me." Gunther sliced the air with the edge of his hand. "For now, I want to dig deep and peel away any layers of negativity before I do something horrible. You know, like" — he leaned toward us — "kill someone." He winked.

He was kidding, but his words sent a shiver through me.

Chapter 6

Harmony and I found an empty table at the center of the food court.

I sat down. "Will you fill me in about what happened to Gunther's wife? He seemed quite forlorn."

She set her portfolio and expo tote on the table and sat opposite me. "Bitter is a better word."

"Why is he bitter?"

"Sarita Strachline. I can't believe it!" a man crowed. "Sarita, is it really you?"

I spun in my chair and spied the ebony-haired woman who'd left Rhett to take the fall for the arson at the Grotto. Despite the perfection of her statuesque body, the outfit she had on—white ruffle blouse tucked into raggedy super-tight jeans and stiletto heels—would have looked better on a woman half her age. Her heavily outlined eyes and blood-red lips were over the top, too. Two teenaged girls in jeans and T-shirts accompanied her. The older, as statuesque as Sarita, cooled herself with a freebie fan that resembled a bridal bouquet. The younger, cute in a prepubescent freckly way, sucked on the straw of a one-liter lemonade inscribed with the *Dine by Design Catering* logo.

"Jenna." Harmony gripped my arm. "Are you okay? You look pale."

"It's her. Sarita."

"The one who set the Grotto—"

"Uh-huh."

"Oh, my. I'll get you some water. Be right back." She hurried off.

"Sarita, it is you!" Matias Lajoie, a weathered forty-something, and the owner of Tradewinds, a popular boat purveyor at the Pier, grabbed Sarita in a muscular hug and held her at arms' length.

She stiffened.

He released her. "How long has it been? Fourteen years? Fifteen? Are these your daughters?" He regarded the girls with a crooked smile. "Neither of you is ready to get married. That can't be why you're here. Don't tell me—" He assessed Sarita again. "Don't tell me you're at the expo because you're betrothed." Theatrically he slammed a hand on his chest. "Don't break my heart again."

"No." Sarita slipped a hand around each of her daughter's elbows. "We were at the aquarium, and the girls cajoled me into seeing what the expo was like, so we bought day passes. Girls, this is Mr. Lajoie. An old friend."

"Friend?" Matias snorted. "Before you two were born, your mother and I were—"

"Matias!" Sarita barked.

Matias reached out and cupped Sarita's face. She didn't shy away. "We have to get together soon. My card." He pulled one from his shirt pocket and slipped it into her oversized tote. "Call me."

Seconds after Matias moved on, a tall athletic man in cargo shorts and pale gray polo shirt stomped to Sarita. His dark eyes were smoldering. His flat nose flared with anger. "Why did you make me come inside this place?"

Apparently Sarita inflamed many hearts and souls.

"I was already on my way to the aquarium," he went on.

"Calm down," Sarita said. "I left you a pass. You didn't have to pay to enter."

He threw his arms wide. "I just heard a rumor that you bought that boat you're staying on."

"That's a lie. I told you, I'm renting it."

Not from Matias, I thought, *who had seemed stunned to run into her.*

"Either way, how can you afford it?" the man demanded.

"None of your business."

"Tell me."

She huffed. "I got a loan from a friend."

"From whom? Ilya Bakov?"

Sarita pursed her oversized lips.

"I'll find out, Sarita." He sliced the air with a hand. "I. Will. Find. Out."

"Good luck with that." Sarita released her daughters, who were fidgeting like they wished they could disappear. "Ilya is on a cruise to the Mexican Riviera."

The man shot out his left arm. "Did Matias give you the loan? I saw you with him just now. Are you dating him?"

Sarita raised her chin defiantly. "You and I are no longer married, Todd."

Aha, so he was Todd Strachline, the accountant.

"And FYI, I can date whom I please." Sarita preened the ruffle on her blouse. "We're done here. Girls, go with your father. I'll see you on Sunday, and we'll do something fun."

Todd gripped Sarita's arm. "Listen up."

"Let me go!" she growled.

"Dad!" the elder daughter cried. "Stop. Don't hurt her."

Todd released Sarita like she was a hot poker and took a step backward, hands up.

Harmony returned to the table and handed me a bottle of water. "Drink." She'd already removed the cap. "Maybe you're overheated."

"Thanks," I whispered.

"What are you staring at?"

I quickly explained my fascination with Sarita Strachline and her family drama.

Harmony twisted in her chair to observe the squabble. Todd wasn't holding on to Sarita, but he was still railing at her, sparing no barbs. Didn't he realize everyone around was a witness to their dispute? I noticed a few onlookers holding up their cell phones. Soon everyone in Crystal Cove and beyond would be able to view it.

Sarita slapped her ex-husband. Not hard. A quick tap to break the tension. Even so, her daughters squealed, and Todd's face tinged pink with embarrassment. He told the girls they were leaving. Sullenly, they shuffled toward the exit. Sarita watched them go, her smirk reminding me of a jackal's after it had dominated its prey.

I released the breath I'd been holding.

"I know a bit about their history," Harmony said.

"The Grotto fire?"

"That, plus, rumor has it, Todd vowed to burn the house down if Sarita won the children in the divorce. She didn't win them because she decided to settle with him. If he agreed to cede the restaurant to her, she would deed the house to him and let him have the girls, believing they needed the continuity of a home. A few months later, up the Grotto went in smoke." She *poofed* her hands. "She fled town with all the art and cash."

"And left her daughters behind?"

"Ta-ta, sweet things."

I thought of what Rhett had said about Sarita having spent all the cash. "Is Todd's house nice?"

"Nice enough, but he was fuming. Don't get me wrong. Everyone in town thought Sarita was a piece of work and thought Todd and the girls were better off without her, but I understand Todd's frustration."

"Those poor girls," I said. "They're probably ruing the fact they'd asked their mother to come here. It's so public."

"Yes, but think of all the sympathy texts they'll receive from their friends. A TikTok moment can't be bought." Harmony polished off her chicken bites from California Catch, blotted her fingertips on her napkin, and stuffed the napkin in the cup. "Look at the time." She rose to her feet, looped her tote over her forearm, and grabbed her portfolio. "Are we good? We've secured the disc jockey. Did anything else strike your fancy? Something you absolutely must see before we leave?"

"I don't think so, but I don't have to go back to the shop for a bit, so if it's okay with you, I'll take one more walk through. For fun. Perhaps do some networking and hand out a few Cookbook Nook business cards."

"Great idea."

"I'll take that to the trash." I held my hand out for her cup. She gave it to me and hugged me with one arm. "Have fun."

As I was disposing of the trash, a shadow loomed on my right. I pivoted and found myself inches from Sarita Strachline. A very angry Sarita Strachline.

"You!" She trained a finger at my nose. "I saw you listening in on my conversation. Why were you . . . Hold on." She took a step back, her eyes wide. "I know you. You're Jenna Hart. The witch who ruined my life."

"I did no such thing."

"You and your boyfriend sicced the cops on me."

"Because you set your restaurant on fire and let the police blame Rhett."

I turned to go, but she gripped my shoulder and spun me back. I flicked her hand. Hard. She released me.

"FYI, Rhett Baxter was an inferior chef," she sneered.

"However you felt about him, he should not have been a suspect in your mess." I glowered at her. "Why are you out of jail? You didn't serve a full sentence."

"Overcrowding. They're releasing felons with a record of good behavior." Sarita smirked. "I was a stellar prisoner. I figured out how to behave right from the get-go."

"I'll bet." I held her gaze for a long moment before attempting to push past her.

Yet again, she grabbed me. "Listen up."

I jerked free and whirled on her. "No, you listen up. Don't. Touch. Me."

"Or what?"

"Or I will have the police haul you in for intimidation."

She honked out a laugh. "There's no such thing."

"There is, too, and the charge is either felony or misdemeanor." I might not wear a police uniform, but for the past few years, having had my own run-ins with the law as well as finding myself assisting in homicide investigations—assisting because I'd either stumbled on a body or someone I cherished had been accused of murder—I'd boned up on legal terminology.

"Well, be forewarned." Sarita bared her teeth. "Intimidation isn't all I can do. Do you hear me?"

Out of the corner of my eye, I spied Sarita's elder daughter stealing to the table where she'd been sitting with her mother. She'd left her expo tote bag hanging on a chair.

"Huh, do you?" Sarita continued haranguing me. "Back off, witch. Back. Off."

The daughter froze. The fear that had registered on her face was palpable.

Chapter 7

It was difficult to erase Sarita's words from my thoughts as I returned to the Cookbook Nook to fetch Tigger. The venomous way she'd stared at me had shaken me to my toes. *Intimidation isn't all I can do.* What was she threatening to do? Did Rhett and I have to watch our backs?

Distracted, I didn't notice the fire truck in the parking lot of Fisherman's Village until I was almost at the shop's front door. Adrenaline surged within me. Had something happened to my aunt? To Bailey? To someone at the café? The truck's light wasn't flashing. The rear doors were closed. I didn't see anyone on a gurney. But the driver's door was hanging open.

I raced to the front of the vehicle and lurched to a stop when I saw Bucky Winston, the buff fireman who was married to Cinnamon. "What's going on?"

Before he could answer, I heard the sound of kittens mewing.

Bucky grinned and indicated a box by his feet. "This is what's going on."

The box was riddled with holes and had no top. I peered inside and spied a cluster of kittens. There were orange ones and gray ones, which led me to believe the sassy mother must have entertained two males while she was in heat.

My heart rate returned to normal. "Gee, what a big litter." I did a quick count. Six kittens.

"There are more than those," Bucky said.

Beyond him stood Cinnamon in her tan uniform, sans hat. She was cuddling a ginger kitten that reminded me of Tigger the day I'd found him. When I'd first met Cinnamon in her official capacity, she'd reminded me of a genial camp counselor with her blunt hair, athletic body, and perky walk. But then she spoke, and I knew not to ever underestimate her. She could be stern and imposing. Even though we'd become close friends since then, I'd only seen her weak and needy one time, when she was pregnant and in the hospital battling dehydration. Since losing the baby, she had once again buttoned down her emotions. Until now. She was cooing like an honest-to-goodness cat lover.

Bucky finger-combed his hair, the motion making his sizeable biceps flex. "Actually it's perfect timing running into you, Jenna. I need your help. These beauties were left on the fire station's doorstep. If you could—"

"I can't adopt a bunch of kittens."

Bucky chortled. "Nah. I don't want you to adopt them. I want you to help me with an ad campaign for our adoption day. Advertising is your specialty."

Was my specialty. Not to mention, when I'd worked in advertising, my accounts primarily were touting food products and women's face creams. "I've never tried to hawk kittens. But I suppose I could help. How old are they?"

Cinnamon said, "About five weeks, we think."

Old enough to be weaned, I thought, relieved.

"I think we should call it a fire sale. Get it?" Bucky chuckled. "They all look like they're on fire."

Studying them more closely, I agreed with him. The ginger cats were a fiery orange, and the gray cats each had a blaze of white on their foreheads or chests.

"I've already named the little darlings." He rattled them off. "Blaze, Bolt, Lightning, Firecracker, Sparks, Flame, Ember, Phoenix, Scorch, and Spitfire."

"That's ten," I pointed out.

"Two guys at the station already took one each. Blaze and Bolt. And Cinnamon's mom—"

"Help!" Pepper Pritchett scuttled out of Beaders of Paradise, the crafts shop in the complex, carrying a gray kitten in her arms. Upon closer inspection, I saw that its paw was caught in the beading of her hand-knitted summer sweater. "Help, please."

I got to her first and carefully extricated the claw from the needlework. "No harm to your garment. You might have to pull one thread through the hole."

"Phew! Thank you." Pepper held the kitten in front of her face. "As for you, you little rascal, listen up. If I adopt you, we need to have rules about my clothing."

And wrapping paper and yarn and anything else a cat might want to tear into, I mused. "If you ask my father, I'll bet he'd make a cat scratching post for you."

Pepper brightened. "Or a kitty condo like yours?"

"That might take some persuasion."

"I've got my wiles." Once upon a time before either Cinnamon or I were born, Pepper, a contemporary of my father's, had been in love with him. For years, she had loathed my mother for stealing him. When she finally made peace with that reality, she warmed to me. "What's this one's name again, Bucky?"

"Phoenix."

"Ooh," Pepper crooned. "You've risen from the ashes, like me." No one pressed her on the reference. She'd had a few challenges in the past year or so. "Yes, it suits you." She cradled the kitten and kissed its nose. "Phoenix it is."

Cinnamon grinned at me. "Aren't they all fabulous names? Isn't Bucky clever?" The moment she'd met him, she was smitten. Bucky glowed under her praise.

"The cleverest," I said.

"So can you help with the campaign, Jenna?" Bucky asked, looking quite vulnerable for such a virile man. "We'd like to have the adoption day on Saturday."

"Sure." Ideas were already swirling in my mind. "I'll give you some artwork tomorrow. In the meantime, who will tend to all of them?"

"All the guys at the fire station." Bucky puffed his chest. "We're not putting out any fires, and we're tired of making sourdough bread, so we'll have plenty of time to play with them. We only came here because Cinnamon's mom"—he nodded in Pepper's direction—"wanted her choice of the litter."

"Do you have any clue who left them?" I asked.

"Nope, and we're not going to try to find out. What's done is done." He lifted the darkest gray cat. "This is Scorch."

The cat chirruped.

"Sounds like feeding time. Have fun." I knuckled Bucky's arm fondly. "If you want my two cents, you might consider getting a wire crate with a roof for them. That box won't contain them and keep them safe."

"Gotcha."

I bid them all good night and went into the shop to fetch Tigger.

My aunt was at the sales counter, finalizing receipts. "Hello, dear. Did you have a good time at the expo?"

"It was interesting, to say the least. I saw Jake and Z.Z. there. Did he come in for his reading?"

Her forehead crinkled. "No, as a matter of fact."

"Huh," I mumbled. I could have sworn that was where he'd been headed when he'd left the expo. "Did you know they're betrothed as of this morning?"

Her eyes widened in shock. "No kidding. Well, that explains Jake's need for a reading, then."

"Except he didn't come here after I saw him."

"A busy man can have two appointments in one day," she gibed. "If he needs me, he knows where to find me. Speaking of appointments, I'm off. I have a hot date to watch the sunset. Will you lock up?"

"Yes."

I didn't give Tigger a chance to greet the kittens. If I did, I might wind up having to take one home, and Rhett and I didn't need another mouth to feed. Not with a wedding to plan.

As I stepped inside the house, Tigger wailed for no apparent reason. The sound made me think of Sarita again and the threat she'd directed at me. Rattled and on edge, I retreated to the kitchen, poured myself a glass of chardonnay, and took a sip. Rather than down the rest of the wine in one gulp, I said to Tigger and Rook, Rhett's and now *our* Labrador retriever, "C'mon, you guys. We're going for a walk on the beach."

Rook zipped to me, his tongue lolling out of his mouth. He adored walks. Given the chance, he'd walk morning, noon, and night. Rhett dutifully exercised the pooch before leaving for work, and we had a doggie door to the patio, but Rook was always eager for an evening stroll.

I kicked off my sandals, strapped on the sling pet carrier, placed Tigger in it, and grabbed Rook's leash. Together, we traipsed between my aunt's house and the cottage that I used to live in toward the ocean. The warmth of the setting sun felt good on my face. The gritty texture of sand tickled my toes. I did my best to breathe in rhythm with the *whoosh-whoosh* of the water lapping the shore. "Calm. I need to find my calm," I grumbled under my breath. "Sarita, how dare you threaten me. How dare you!"

Rook whimpered and peered up at me, doing his best to discern what I was saying.

I smiled. "I'm good, boy. Don't worry."

We walked for an hour, passing bunches of locals and tourists along the way, many commenting on how gorgeous Rook was. When the air grew chilly, I made a U-turn and headed back.

What I found when I arrived home sent me into a tailspin.

Chapter 8

One panel of the multipaned living room window was broken. Smashed to smithereens. Upon closer inspection, I realized that someone had thrown something through it. I spun around to see if a snickering teen was lurking nearby but didn't see a soul. There were no neighbors out and about, either.

The front door was still bolted. I unlocked it, stepped into the foyer, and inspected the offending object. A brick. With a note wrapped around it. It was lying on the area rug by the sofa. I didn't need to touch it to read it. In big, bold block letters, it said: *BACK OFF*.

My insides went cold. Had Sarita Strachline found out where I lived? Had she done this? Was she that unpredictable? Or worse, vindictive?

Rook strained at his leash, and Tigger squirmed in the pet carrier, but I wasn't about to set either of them free until I knew what was going on. I glanced out the window and saw Deputy Marlon Appleby's car parked at my aunt's house, meaning he was home and not on duty. When he and Aunt Vera eloped a bit ago, he moved in with her. I dialed his cell phone. He showed up to my place in less than a minute. My aunt accompanied him. She was still wearing the caftan she'd worn to work. Appleby, a large man with a moose-shaped jaw, had changed from his uniform into chinos and a Hawaiian shirt.

"Oh, Jenna dear. Whatever happened?" My aunt threw an arm around me.

Appleby inspected the brick and note and leveled me with his gaze. "Who have you ticked off this time, Jenna?" he jibed, though his eyes told a different story. He was truly concerned for me.

"Nobody. No—" My voice cracked. Tigger mewled. I petted his head. "*Shh.*"

"Jenna." My aunt removed her arm from my shoulders and faced me. "You seemed worried when you returned from the expo this afternoon. It wasn't because of the newborn kittens in the parking lot. Did something bad take place at the event? C'mon, out with it."

"Fine, I'll tell you." I huffed. "Sarita Strachline is back in town."

"I know. I was at the shop when you heard the news."

"She was at the expo with her girls." I told them about Sarita's dustup with her ex-husband. "She tracked me down afterward because she'd caught me listening in. When she realized who I was, she got in my face."

"In your—"

"She accused me of sending her to jail. She told me to back off."

"Back off," my aunt echoed.

Appleby motioned to the note on the brick. "I doubt she did this. It seems like something a kid would do."

"She has daughters," I said.

He scratched his jaw. "Nah, I don't see it." He studied the window.

My aunt did, as well. "Why don't you come stay with us? We can fix this with duct tape for now, and we'll call the emergency window repair people and ask for a rush job."

"I can't. I'm meeting Rhett for dinner at Intime in an hour. He's sending the staff home so the two of us can cook a private dinner. It's our . . ." Tears pressed at the corners of my eyes. "Our anniversary."

My aunt looked puzzled. "Of what? Your first date?"

"Of the first time he told me he loved me. Or at least he thinks it is." The memory of him declaring it to be so brought a smile to my face. "It was more likely the fourth or fifth time he'd said it, but why argue? If it's a date he can remember . . ." I knew it was silly to celebrate it, but I relished that he wanted to. I nuzzled Tigger. "Can the cat and pup stay with you until I get home?"

My aunt nodded and kissed my forehead. "Why don't we stick around until you've changed clothes?" she suggested, eyeing Appleby.

"Good idea," he said. "I'll tape up the window while we're here."

"I've got a bottle of wine opened on the counter in the kitchen." I pointed. "Help yourselves."

An hour later, though I appeared put-together in an aqua blue sheath, strappy sandals, a multicolored cashmere shawl, and a pair of aquamarine dangly earrings, I was still skittish as I pushed open the door to Intime. "I'm here!" I announced. My voice didn't sound shaky. I mustered a winning smile.

Rhett emerged from the kitchen in his chef's coat, white shirt, and cocoa-colored slacks. A lock of hair fell on his forehead. He swooped it off and kissed me warmly on the lips. "This way, my love." He ushered me into the state-of-the-art kitchen and handed me an Intime-emblazoned apron.

I removed my shawl and cross-body purse, set them on the serving counter, and donned the apron. "Love the ambiance. *Très* romantic."

Lit pillars and tapers in candlesticks were set on the two Viking stoves as well as on the tops of the baking racks, stainless steel counters, and shelving that was filled with sauté pans.

"Glad you like it."

A rendition of "Jailhouse Rock" ended, and the strains of "Best Thing That Ever Happened to Me" by Gladys Knight and the Pips started playing through the speakers.

"Aw, our song." I pecked his cheek. "I love you, too. What's on the menu?"

"I was thinking stir-fried shrimp with asparagus tips and white wine risotto. And peach flambé for dessert."

"Yum." I adored peaches, and it was the peak of the season. "What do you need me to do?"

"Dice onions and celery for the risotto." He pointed to the two fully stocked knife blocks. "Sharpen if you need to." Rhett hated dull knives.

"Done, Chef." I saluted. "If you'd pour me a glass of wine."

"Already poured." He withdrew a narrow carving knife from a block and aimed it at two Bordeaux glasses sitting on the prep table beside a sweet Hawaiian onion and four stalks of celery.

"A man after my heart."

"Always."

I gripped the lapels of his chef's coat and pulled him to me. "Did I say I love you already?"

"You did."

"Well, I'm saying it again, in case you weren't paying attention."

"I always pay attention." He grinned and kissed me tenderly. "Now, get to work."

"Aye, aye, Chef." I lifted my glass of wine and took a sip. Then I picked up a Wüsthof vegetable knife and cut off the ends of the onion. I peeled the onion's outer layers, sliced the onion in half, and, laying one piece broadside down on the cutting board, chopped it as Katie had taught me. I would never be a master chef, but in the past couple of years I had become a pretty good cook. I'd graduated from five-ingredient recipes to recipes of any length and any skill set. I enjoyed a challenge.

Rhett stepped to the opposite side of the prep table to prepare the cooked shrimp that he had preset in an ice bath. He pinched and removed the tails and diced the shrimp into bite-sized pieces. He offered me a taste. I accepted readily.

I hummed to the music as I worked. Rhett joined in. Neither of us would be hired to sing at a wedding, but we could carry a tune.

After a long while, Rhett set his knife down. "How was the rest of the Bride's Dream Expo?"

"Good." I didn't mention my set-to with Sarita or the brick through the window. I pushed the memories to the back of my mind. "Is the AC okay? Did you have to deal with any other problems?"

"The AC is fine. For some reason, it was low on refrigerant." He shrugged. "If it's not one thing it's another in the restaurant biz. Did you and Harmony find a band or DJ?"

"We did. The Dancing DeeJay. He's a bunch of fun. And he loves playing oldies."

"Will he be able to accommodate your walk down the aisle?"

"Yes."

Rhett heated oil in a sauté pan, crushed a couple of cloves of garlic and scraped them into the pan along with a tablespoon of butter, and turned the heat to low. In seconds, the savory aroma of garlic filled the kitchen. "Did you see anything else that inspired you?" he asked. "Have we changed our color palette? Swapped out our flowers? Did anybody talk you into a honeymoon trip other than the one we have planned?"

"Don't make fun." I pointed my knife at him. "Oh, I've been meaning to tell you, Katie and I have finalized the entrée selections, but we haven't pinned down the appetizers. She's working up a list of those. I'd like to include some spicy cod bites."

"What prompted that idea?"

"Harmony met an old family friend at the expo. Gunther Hildenbiddle. He owns California Catch. He was serving them."

"I know Gunther. Nice guy. He had a run of bad luck, but he seems to be holding his own now. Was he there to offer his services as a wedding caterer?"

"I think all the restaurateurs were, or certainly they were there to pitch their cafés and bistros as out-of-towner venues and sites for bachelor and bachelorette parties." Mission accomplished with the onions, I addressed the celery. Curling my fingers so my knuckles and not my fingertips were closest to the blade, I chopped with gusto.

"Oho," Rhett sniggered as he scooped up the onions and added them to the sauté pan on the stove. "Look who's been practicing."

I giggled. To be honest, I had been preparing for tonight's dinner. I wanted Rhett to be proud of me.

He sipped his wine and peered at me over the rim. "So . . ."

"So?" I echoed.

"What aren't you telling me?"

"*Hmm?*"

"Yeah, that's what I thought. You're holding back. Your voice is slightly high-pitched, and your right eye is twitching. What's going on?"

I didn't dare touch my eye with fingers that had recently cut an onion.

"Jenna, c'mon," he said. "No secrets between us. And you're keeping a big one. Talk."

I heaved a sigh. If the window repairmen hadn't fixed the broken pane by the time we arrived home, the duct tape on our living room window would be a dead giveaway that something bad had happened. I told him about finding the brick. "Appleby thinks a teen must have done it. You know how rambunctious they can be."

Rhett tilted his head. "The note said 'Back off'?"

"Yeah."

"That's a pretty specific warning."

"It was two words. It means nothing."

"Uh-uh. Your gut is telling you a teenager didn't do this." Rhett hooked a finger. "Tell me the rest."

"If I didn't know better, I'd think you were an investigator in a previous life."

"Rhett Holmes, at your service," he said in a British accent, and signaled for me to continue.

I bit the bullet and confessed to the run-in with Sarita at the expo.

His gaze darkened. "Go on."

"She was arguing with her ex-husband, Todd. I couldn't help overhearing them. There's definitely bad blood there."

"Not our problem." He moved to the stove and stirred the onions with a spatula. Over his shoulder, he said, "Or is it? How does this involve you?"

"She caught me listening in and lashed out at me."

"She what?" Rhett released the spatula and rounded the prep table. "Why didn't you lead with that?" He took me in his arms. "What did she say? Did she hurt you?" He caressed the back of my head.

"I'm fine, Rhett." I pressed apart. "She didn't raise a finger. However, she . . ." I hesitated. "She threatened me. She said I should back off."

"And later on, the brick with that exact phrase was thrown through our window."

"Yep."

"You told Appleby about Sarita, right?"

"I did."

"Didn't he think the two events were related?"

"No."

Rhett snorted. "Ever since he hooked up with your aunt, he's gone soft." His mouth quirked up on one side. "Love will do that to a guy."

I laughed, thankful that he was taking it in stride. "You aren't mad at me?"

"Why would I be?"

"Because I did listen in."

"Hard to close one's ears when it's a public spat," he countered, and kissed my cheek. "PS, I could never be mad at you."

I eyed my work station. "I'm done here. What else would you like me to do?"

"Go into the dining room and light the candle on our table."

"Our table?"

"Your favorite. By the window." He handed me a click-and-flame lighter and kissed my cheek. "Go."

Relieved that the story about Sarita was out in the open, I strolled into the dining room and drew in a deep breath. As Rhett's parents had for their restaurant in Napa Valley, he had chosen to make Intime resemble a classic French bistro, paneled with deep mahogany and mirrors hanging on all the walls that would catch the reflection of light from the candelabra-style chandeliers. Our table for two was covered with a white tablecloth and preset with silverware, a single white rose in a vase, and a white taper in a short crystal candlestick. Menus outlining our dinner lay between each setting. Rhett had thought of everything.

As I ignited the lighter, the music in the queue stopped.

Then something went *boom!*

Chapter 9

The restaurant rocked. My knees buckled. "Rhett!" I screamed, grabbing hold of the table. The candle tipped. I righted it and blew out the flame. "Rhett!"

I whirled around. Debris was spilling from the kitchen into the dining room. The stench of a mixture of gunpowder and something that reminded me of nail polish remover hung in the air. I sped to the archway and drew up short. My insides seized with panic. Rhett was prone on the floor, his head twisted to one side.

"Rhett!" I yelled. What had happened? Had the gas grill exploded? "Rhett!" He didn't stir.

Pots, pans, and shattered glass littered the floor. Flour was billowing like ash from a volcano. The faucet in the large sink by the prep table had broken; water was spewing upward. Candles had toppled. Suddenly, the contents of a trash bin ignited, which triggered the overhead safety sprinklers and stirred me to action.

I hurried to Rhett and tripped over something on the floor. I jolted when I spotted ball bearings by my feet as well as nestling around Rhett's body. I'd seen a documentary about homemade bombs. Similar items had erupted when the bomb had burst. Had someone set off a homemade bomb here? How? Why? I crouched beside him and gripped his wrist. His pulse was weak, his cheek scraped, and his ear bleeding. "Sweetheart, can you hear me?"

He moaned, but his eyes remained closed.

Tears clogged my throat. I wasn't sure I should move him, plus, I wasn't strong enough to do so. "I'm calling nine-one-one."

Doing my best not to slip on the ball bearings, I fetched my purse, which had flown halfway across the kitchen, and withdrew my cell phone. I stabbed in the number and reached the call center. The call taker asked what the emergency was. While telling her I believed Intime had been bombed, I removed my apron, soaked it in the fountain of water, and doused the fire in the trash bin. "My fiancé is hurt. He's alive." Rhett hadn't budged, but there was a rise and fall to his back. "But he needs help."

The woman said she was alerting the police and transferred me to another site. The new call taker—a young man by the sound of his voice—outlined the next few steps. He was sending the fire department and asked if I knew CPR. I did.

"I don't think he needs it," I said. "He's breathing."

He asked if I felt safe staying with the victim. I told him I didn't care if I was safe or not. I wasn't going anywhere until help showed up.

I knelt beside Rhett and stroked his hair, assuring him that I was there. What felt like an hour later, though it hadn't been more than two minutes, a siren pierced the night air.

Bucky and Nico, an equally muscular man, raced into the restaurant carrying a gurney.

"Didn't think I'd see you so soon again today, Bucky," I murmured.

"Yeah. Me, either. Where is he?"

"In the kitchen." I dashed ahead.

"Stop, Jenna." At social occasions, Bucky was affable, but when on duty, he was a no-nonsense guy. "Don't go in."

They rushed past me and set the gurney on the floor.

Despite Bucky's warning, I entered. No new fires had erupted. The one I'd doused in the trash bin had stayed doused, thanks to the overhead sprinklers. I repeated what I'd told the call center.

Carefully, Bucky and Nico turned Rhett onto his back. Bucky checked Rhett's eyes with a pen flashlight. "Might have a concussion," he said to Nico. "Looks like a secondary blast." Over his shoulder, he said to me, "That means the bomb was made with the intent to injure."

The words *intent to injure* gnawed at me. First the run-in with Sarita Strachline, then the brick through my window, and now a bomb? Had Sarita set it off? How would she have gained access to Intime?

"Rhett, can you hear me?" Bucky asked.

Rhett groaned out, "Uh-huh."

Bucky beamed a smile at me. "That's a good response. Real positive." He eyed Nico. "Okay, let's get him on the gurney and into the truck. We'll be taking him to Mercy Urgent Care, Jenna."

If they were taking him to Mercy, they couldn't think his injuries were dire, I told myself. Mercy was one of two emergency clinics in town. A full-fledged hospital was in Santa Cruz.

"Jenna," Bucky said, "why don't you stand outside the restaurant and wait for —"

"I won't leave him."

"Yes, you will!" Cinnamon Pritchett marched into the kitchen and stood with arms akimbo as she assessed the damage. "Out, Jenna. Now!"

"Cinnamon . . . I mean, Chief, please let me stay until they move Rhett."

She lasered me with a look. "Go. He's in good hands. I want you out of the area . . ." She motioned to the chaos in the kitchen, her message clear. In case there was a second bomb or the first hadn't fully discharged. "Officer Foster is outside."

Thwarted, I slogged to the sidewalk and wrapped my arms around my body. Two police cars and the fire department vehicle idled in front. Officer Foster, a fresh-faced female in her twenties, was establishing a perimeter with yellow crime scene tape. Cars were slowing to see what the big deal was. People were gathering across the street. The lights on top of the fire truck strobed the area. I swiveled toward the restaurant and caught a glimpse of myself in the window. Dirt smudged my face. My eyes looked haunted. Worry stewed inside me. Would they get Rhett out before another blast occurred? Were Cinnamon, Bucky, and Nico at risk?

A third police car pulled to an abrupt stop behind the other two. A two-man bomb squad team wearing protective gear hustled out. They spoke quickly to Foster before dashing into the restaurant.

"The lead guy is an expert," Foster informed me.

I was surprised we had one on the force. I couldn't remember Crystal Cove suffering a previous bombing incident.

Minutes later, Bucky and Nico exited the bistro with Rhett on a gurney, and I breathed easier. Rhett's eyes were closed, but his chest was rising and falling. The two men hoisted the gurney into the vehicle and strapped it in place. Then Bucky sat on a bench beside Rhett, and Nico hopped out and moved to the driver's side.

I started to mount the steps.

"Uh-uh, Jenna, you're not going with us," Bucky said.

"I need to be with him," I protested.

"Didn't you hear the man, Jenna?" Cinnamon restrained me, her gaze severe. "You stay right where you are. You'll get to the hospital soon enough. Let the emergency team take care of him first. For the moment, I need to hear your story." She handed me my shawl. "From the beginning."

The *whoop* of the fire truck made me jump. I watched it tear away from the curb and make a U-turn to head north on Buena Vista. The truck disappeared from view when it veered right on Seaview Road.

"Jenna." Cinnamon snapped her fingers in front of my face.

"Sarita Strachline." Angrily, I slung the shawl over my shoulders and tied the ends in a knot. "She's out of jail. Did you hear? I ran into her at Bride's Dream Expo. She threatened me."

"Threatened you?"

"She told me to back off."

"Why?"

"Because she knows Rhett and I are the ones who convinced you to reopen the case that sent her to jail."

"She can't hold you responsible for her incarceration. That's ridiculous."

"Is it?" I splayed my hands. "Without my input, she would still be living it up in New Orleans with not only the art she stole but also the money she'd recouped from the insurance company. What if she put the bomb in the restaurant?"

"How would she have gotten—" Cinnamon glanced at Intime and back at me. "Where's the staff?"

"Rhett let them have the night off. We were making a romantic dinner for two. It's sort of our anniversary."

"Sort of?"

"It's the day he first told me he loved me." I ran my upper lip between my teeth. My bravery started to dissolve.

Cinnamon placed a hand on my shoulder. "He's going to be okay."

"How can you be sure?"

She averted her gaze, as if she was studying the building. Yeah, that's what I thought. She couldn't make any promises.

"Let's start over," Cinnamon said. "Sarita. How would she have had access to Intime?"

"I don't know."

"How could she have known that you and Rhett would be here alone?"

"Maybe one of the staff let something slip when she was nearby."

"Where?"

"The Pier. A coffee shop." A chill coursed down my spine. No way would my paltry shawl keep me warm.

"Tell me everything you remember from the moment you arrived at the restaurant."

"Can I tell you at Mercy?" I jutted an arm in the direction the fire truck went. "I really want to see Rhett."

Cinnamon's face softened. "Wait here." She strode into the bistro. When she returned, she said the bomb expert along with Officer Foster would manage the situation at the restaurant. "Hop in." She climbed into the lead police car. I barely had time to fasten my seat belt before she made a U-turn. In minutes, we arrived at Mercy Urgent Care. She parked in a handicapped spot near the front of the facility, and we trooped inside.

Reception didn't seem as overwhelmed as it had the last time I was there, three or four months ago. Perhaps brides and families weren't into as many daredevil events as typical tourists were. No broken bones. No twisted ankles. The place smelled Lysol clean. Doctors and nurses were lingering instead of striding doggedly along the halls.

"Hi, Chief Pritchett," the woman at the desk said. "How may I help you?"

"Rhett Baxter was recently brought in. This is his fiancée."

The woman's face paled. "I'm so sorry." She aimed a finger. "In emergency."

"He'll be fine," I said, only half believing it.

Neither Cinnamon nor I was allowed into the operating room, nor could we get a peek at what the doctors were doing. A nurse directed us to bide our time in the waiting room. Wood-framed vinyl chairs and tables set with magazines lined two of the room's walls. A muted television with closed captioning was airing CNN. Two other people were in the room. They were talking in muted tones. Cinnamon offered to buy me a coffee from a vending machine. I declined. Nerves were making me twitchy enough.

"Sit," she advised.

I couldn't. I paced and noticed a frantic text from my aunt.

She wrote: *Are you alright? Where are you?*

I texted back: *Hospital. I'm fine.* The word *fine* echoed in my head. *Fine, fine, fine.*

I added: *Rhett in emergency.*

She responded: *Will he be okay?*

My reply was adamant: *Yes!!!*

She continued texting that Appleby had gone to Intime and would let her know anything he learned. I asked if she could watch the animals for the night. She wrote back that of course she would and I was to call if I needed her for anything. *Anything.*

An hour later, a thirty-something doctor I'd never met sauntered into the waiting room. His scrubs were pristine, which had to be a good sign, I told myself. No blood. And he didn't seem in a hurry. Did that mean Rhett was out of the woods? No stitches? No significant injuries?

The doctor removed his hat, shoved it into a pocket, and offered an earnest smile. His hair was wet with perspiration, the only detail revealing his angst. "Mrs. Baxter?" he asked.

I strode to him. "I'm Jenna Hart, Rhett Baxter's fiancée."

Cinnamon popped to her feet. "And I'm Chief Cinnamon Pritchett," she offered.

The doctor nodded to each of us. "Mr. Baxter is doing well. He's on medication and sleeping right now. In view of the severity of the incident, we were concerned about blast ear, which should be considered in any victim that has bleeding from the ear, but we think we can rule this out. Bleeding appears to have come from a laceration suffered in the fall. However, he does have tinnitus— that's a ringing in his ear." He rotated his hand by the side of his head. "It's minor. He isn't vomiting, which is a good sign, and he's not suffering any abdominal pain."

My lungs expanded, allowing in air. I could see Cinnamon relax slightly, too.

"However, he has suffered a concussion because his head hit the kitchen floor," the doctor went on, "so we'll be monitoring him through the night to make sure he doesn't lose consciousness. That requires waking him every hour. It's possible we'll need him to stay here for a few days."

"A few days?" I rasped.

"Yes. We'll be watching to see if he suffers any amnesia or depression or insomnia. Victims of blast injuries might not initially show signs of injury."

My spirit flagged. Depression. Amnesia. "Doctor, may I see him?"

"Like I said, he's sleeping."

"Yes, and I promise I won't wake him, but I want to touch his hand and let him know I'm here."

After he deliberated for a moment, he ushered us to Rhett's room and stepped to one side.

I tiptoed in and paused. Seeing the needle inserted into Rhett's arm and the IV fluid feeding into a vein in his hand made me queasy. "Oh, Rhett," I murmured, and inched closer.

Cinnamon followed me, saying nothing. A nurse who was to the right of Rhett's bed checking the monitor acknowledged us with a bob of her head.

The doctor cautioned, "Just a few minutes," and he left.

Rhett looked so vulnerable lying on the bed with the blanket tucked beneath his armpits. His cheeks had been swathed with ointment. A bandage covered the scrape on his nose. A swath of gauze had been wrapped around his head and ears.

Cinnamon's cell phone buzzed. She hooked her thumb, meaning she was going out to the hall to take the call.

I stroked Rhett's hand. His skin felt clammy. His breathing was ragged. "I'm here, sweetheart," I assured him. "I'm here."

A moment later, Cinnamon reappeared and flicked me on the arm. "Outside. Now."

I followed her. "What's up?"

"So we found the bomb. Under the stove. It was homemade and detonated by a timer."

"Homemade." I hummed, comprehending. "That explains the ball bearings."

"Ball bearings?"

I told her everything I'd noticed. "How did the bomb get there?"

"One of the staff," she suggested.

"No, I can't imagine any of them deliberately sabotaging the place or hurting Rhett. They adore him, and he trusts them implicitly. He and his business partners have vetted all of them."

The investors in Intime had also invested in Rhett's parents' restaurant in Napa. "Rhett did work with some of them at the Grotto. He—" I gulped as a notion flew into my mind. "You don't think one of the former Grotto employees was loyal to Sarita Strachline, do you? We have to question them. We—"

"Not *we*, Jenna," she said firmly. "The police will be investigating. Not you."

"I told you Sarita held a grudge against Rhett." I slapped the back of one hand against the other palm.

"How would she know how to make a bomb?" Cinnamon asked.

I scoffed. "Anybody with access to the Internet can figure it out. Heck"—I batted the air—"there are probably YouTube videos with step-by-step instructions. And everyone knows prisons are like schools for criminals." I glanced through the opened doorway at Rhett and back at Cinnamon. "Earlier, someone threw a brick through my window. Whoever threw it had wrapped a note around it that read *Back off.* Appleby saw it. I think Sarita Strachline did it."

"Jenna—"

"Those are the exact words she used when she accosted me at the expo."

"Don't you think that seems too on the nose?" Cinnamon stared at me. "Perhaps one of Intime's staff was at the expo and overheard her, and he or she threw the brick. Then set the bomb."

"No, it was Sarita," I said stubbornly. "She did this. She tried to kill Rhett."

"And you, Jenna. Don't forget, you were there, too."

Her theory pierced me like a lightning bolt. She was right.

Chapter 10

I returned to the waiting room, purchased a bottle of water from the machine, and paced as memories of Rhett and me together scrolled through my mind like a movie. The day we met. The way he'd flirted with me and I with him. Romantic dinners at his cabin. An all-day wine tour. Our first weekend trip. Our first night in our new home. Salty tears accompanied my musing. As I licked them off my lips, I tried to tell myself that he would be on his feet in no time. But would he? Should we postpone the wedding?

"Jenna!" Bailey raced into the waiting room carrying her daughter, who was the spitting image of her with her short spiky hair and button nose. "I got your text," she said breathlessly, adjusting the baby to her other hip and yanking the strap of her Baby on the Go tote bag higher on her shoulder. Both she and Brianna were dressed in pink jogging outfits. "How are you?" Despite the awkward reach with the baby in tow, she threw an arm around me and hugged me fiercely. "Did the doctors check you out? Are you okay?"

"I didn't need to be checked out. I didn't suffer any injuries."

"Have you seen Rhett?"

"Yes."

"Is he awake?"

"No, but they'll be waking him every hour to make sure he doesn't lose consciousness."

"That doesn't sound good."

I sighed. "The doctor said it was normal for someone who suffered a concussion."

"Poor Rhett. And poor you. I can't imagine what you're going through." Bailey bounced Brianna gently. "Tito is already at the scene of the crime getting the story. He texted that the blast looks pretty big."

"Rhett was thrown about six feet."

"Gee whiz." She inspected my face like a mama bear. "Are you sure you didn't suffer any cuts or bruises? You look fine, but are you really okay?"

"By sheer luck, I was in the dining room, but the explosion happened in the kitchen, and Rhett—" My voice snagged. I plopped into a chair near the television. A commercial for an antacid was playing between the news coverage. I wished I could down a container full. "Rhett went flying. He hit his head." I recounted all the other injuries the doctor said Rhett had suffered, certain I was forgetting something. I wished I'd taken notes. "They have to keep him for a few days. To observe. We won't know anything more until tomorrow or the next day."

"Of course." Bailey set Brianna on the floor and pulled some building blocks from the tote bag. "Here you go, my love." The baby had started to toddle but she preferred crawling. She needed toys to distract her. Bailey perched on a chair. "I've texted Tina to see if she can come get Brianna." Tina Gump, a former clerk at the shop, was now attending culinary school and working part-time as a nanny for Bailey. "I'll stay with you through the night if that's what it takes."

"No. You don't need to stay. Text Tina back. Tell her not to come." I smiled and sat beside my pal. "I'll nap here. Aunt Vera has the animals. If Rhett awakens, the nurse will come get me." I sipped from the water bottle I'd purchased from the vending machine. "Thirsty?" I asked her.

"No. Tell me what you think happened."

I recapped what I'd said to Cinnamon about the run-in with Sarita at the expo and returning home to find a brick through my window

"A brick? How infantile."

"That's what Deputy Appleby said. He was home and came over." I told her what I remembered about the blast. I could still smell the aroma of gunpowder and nail polish remover and hear the *thud* when Rhett hit the floor.

"Why a bomb?" Bailey said. "I mean, a bomb doesn't guarantee killing someone. Do you think she simply meant to scare you?"

"She meant to kill Rhett . . . us . . . in retaliation for siccing the cops on her." I was certain of it.

"Cinnamon is checking her out, right? Getting her alibi, yada-yada?"

"I'm sure she is. Or will." Doubt seeped into my thoughts. Would she? She'd dismissed the notion that Sarita would take the risk of hurting Rhett and me. But someone had. Who? Why? It wasn't random.

"Cinnamon is right," Bailey said. "You're lucky you weren't in the kitchen with —"

"I wish I had been." My voice cracked. "If I'd been there, maybe I could have helped him. Warned him. Sensed something."

"You are not Superwoman, and you don't have ESP!" Bailey's voice skated upward.

The elderly woman and two children sitting across the room gawked at us.

"We'll lower our voices, ma'am. Sorry." I said to the kids, "I hope your mommy is okay." I'd heard the doctor speaking to the older woman earlier about the children's mother. She'd tried to light a bunch of sparklers all at the same time. They'd exploded in her hand. Luckily, her daughter-in-law had a pail of water at the ready, the older woman had said, adding, *What had she been thinking?* her tone filled with judgment.

What had Sarita been thinking? I wondered, my mind refocusing on my own drama. Had she meant to kill Rhett and me? Or was she simply a despicable woman who'd wanted to scare us? I'd said to Cinnamon that it was easy to make a bomb. I'd been guessing. Was it easy? Could the police search bomb-making sites online and find out who had visited them? Would an examination of the search engine history on Sarita's computer show she had?

"Jenna." Bailey put a hand on my knee. "Breathe. Rhett will be fine."

I drew in a lungful of air and let it out slowly.

"That's the way," Bailey coaxed. "Do it again. Deep breaths."

The air-conditioning kicked on, jarring me and prying loose a piece of the puzzle I'd forgotten. "The AC." I twisted toward her. "Earlier today, Rhett had to leave the expo to go back to the restaurant to deal with an issue with the air-conditioning unit. Maybe that's how Sarita got in and put the bomb in place. She slinked in while Rhett was distracted with the technician. I have to call Cinnamon."

"No." Bailey rested a hand on my arm. "You can reach out to her tomorrow. For now, you need to remain calm and stay hopeful."

A chill cut through me. I leaped to my feet and wrapped my arms around my body. "I need to postpone the wedding."

"What? No!" Bailey popped up, too, and wagged a finger in my face. "Uh-uh. Everything is planned. No postponing anything. Rhett will come through this with flying colors, and all will be right with the world." She twirled a finger in front of her face. "Is he, you know, scratched or anything?"

"Yes. His nose. It's minor. And his cheeks, also minor. He cut his ear, too, but that's not the issue. What if he can't remember things? What if he can't remember me?"

"You?"

"Amnesia is a possibility."

"He'll remember you."

"What if he's depressed? He suffered a concussion."

"*Shh.*" She petted my shoulder. "Calm down. Rhett is Mr. Practical and as strong as an ox. He'll be one hundred percent okay."

"The restaurant." I covered my mouth with my hand as everything that had to be addressed cycled through my mind. "What are we going to do about Intime? I have to contact the insurance company and file a claim."

"Not tonight."

I paced the length of the waiting room, chewing on my thumbnail. "They'll have to send out an adjuster. We'll have to shut down the restaurant for repairs. Who knows how long that will take? And what about paying the staff's salaries?"

"They can file for unemployment."

"Some of them will quit. Rhett will hate letting any of them go. He's worked so hard to build his team—"

Brianna chirped. We both stared at her. She was staring at us with her big, beautiful, concerned eyes.

I crouched beside her and stroked her cheek. "I'm sorry I've been going off the rails, little one. I'm fine and your mommy is fine." I rose and hugged Bailey. "Go home. Thanks for being here."

"Do not cancel the wedding. Promise me. Be patient."

I made a raspberry sound.

"I know patience is not your forte," she teased. "But do it. This one time. Got me?"

I held up three fingers in a Girl Scout salute. "I won't do anything rash."

"That's the Jenna I know." She high-fived me and collected her daughter and the toys.

When she left, I fetched my bottle of water and drained it.

A half hour later, the next round of cheerleaders arrived. Dad and Lola strode in and made a beeline for me. The elderly woman and the children had gone, and a gaunt man had taken their place. He was staring blankly at the television, his hands worrying themselves in his lap.

Dad held out his hands to me. "Hi, sweetheart." Even dressed down in jeans and blue plaid shirt, the top button unbuttoned, he reminded me of the actor Cary Grant. All that was lacking was the accent.

I rose and allowed him to embrace me. He held me at arms' length to assess me. I broke free and finger-combed my hair.

Lola, so much like her daughter Bailey with the short-cropped hair and colorful sense of style, handed me a to-go box of food. "You didn't eat."

"I don't have an appetite."

"You've got to keep up your strength." She pressed the box into my hands.

I set it on a chair. "Don't mother me."

"How about I stepmother you?" She offered a supportive smile. She and my father had married a while back. My mother would have approved. She and Lola had been close.

"Water?" Lola asked, moving to the dispenser.

"I'm good." Any more water and I could float out of urgent care.

"I'll take a bottle," my father said. "We had Chinese food for dinner. I'm parched."

I motioned to the to-go box. "That doesn't smell like Chinese."

Lola said, "It's cheese and fruit. Something that won't spoil to tide you over."

"Thank you," I murmured, knowing I wouldn't eat it.

Lola, with her steady nature, was a perfect balance for my quasi-strict father. He was much less exacting now that he'd retired from the FBI and opened up a hardware store, a place that had odd hours because Dad didn't ever want to work nine-to-five *plus* again.

"How are you?" my father asked.

"I'll be fine when Rhett opens his eyes and says my name."

"Concussion," he murmured. I'd written him a text with the basics. "How far did he fly?"

"About six feet."

"Good thing he has a hard head."

I smiled, appreciating his levity.

"Tell me what you remember about the bomb." Prior to becoming an agent for the FBI, my father had served as a defensive tactics or, as many referred to it, DT, trainer. He knew every fighting technique. I was pretty sure he'd studied bombs and how to defuse them.

"The bomb expert said it was homemade. It contained ball bearings."

"Did you see any nails?"

I shook my head. "I can't recall." I told them about the smell and added that I'd been so concerned about Rhett I'd neglected to photograph the crime scene with my cell phone. "Would knowing how it was made make it easier to track down who constructed it?" I asked.

"Possibly." My father had all sorts of contacts who were still active at the FBI. "I'll put some feelers out."

"Let Cinnamon know what you're doing."

My father snorted. "Not a chance. I know she doesn't like you interfering. Can you imagine if she found out I was?"

My father and Cinnamon Pritchett had an unusual bond. In high school, after Cinnamon's father walked out on Pepper and her, she hooked up with a rough crowd. My father, at my mother's urging, became her mentor. With his guidance, Cinnamon turned her life around. Now she, like him, respected the letter of the law. She did not appreciate regular citizens like me or my father, now that he was retired, inserting themselves into an investigation. But sometimes, I reminded her it was necessary, and she should welcome input.

"If you do find something out," I said, "tell me, and I'll convey it to her."

He brushed a hand along my arm. "In the meantime, you should go home."

"Aunt Vera is watching the animals."

"I don't care about the animals. I care about you. You need to sleep."

"I can sleep in the chair."

Lola said, "Jenna, be reasonable. The hospital staff will inform you if there's any change."

A sob caught in my throat. I wrapped an arm around my midriff. "How long could he be unconscious?"

My father said, "If they're inducing a coma to reduce swelling, it could be a day or two."

"Inducing a . . ." I shivered. "The doctor didn't say anything about inducing a coma. He said they would wake him every hour." Tears pooled in my eyes and leaked down my face. I swiped them away. "I'm postponing the wedding." I hated sounding like a broken record.

"No," Lola said, with the same urgency as Bailey had. "He'll be fine."

"It's two weeks away!" I threw my arms wide.

"Three weeks and a few days," my father intoned.

I glowered at him.

He gathered me into his arms again and caressed my head like he used to when I was a girl. "Jenna-bear, calm down. Lola, tell whoever's in charge here that we're driving Jenna home now."

"My car is at the restaurant, Dad."

"We'll make sure someone brings it to your house." He held his hand out. "Keys."

I pulled them from my purse and delivered them to him.

"Let's go," he said and slung an arm around my shoulders.

I didn't protest.

Chapter 11

After my father dropped me at the house — I noticed the front window was already repaired — I walked to my aunt's place to fetch Tigger and Rook, but she wouldn't let me take them home. She insisted that I stay the night at her place, what with the brick incident and the bomb. I was too tired to argue.

First thing the next morning, I telephoned Mercy Urgent Care. Rhett was sleeping. The nurse who took my call told me the team attending to him had awakened him every hour, as scheduled — no induced coma necessary — and he was doing fine, but he needed his rest. My aunt suggested I go to work to take my mind off things. I returned to my house, walked Rook, fed him and Tigger, and showered and dressed in a floral dress and nectarine-colored flip-flops. I needed bright, fun clothes to boost my spirits.

Before leaving for work, I called the precinct. Cinnamon wasn't in. I left her a message laying out my theory about the air-conditioning issue at Intime. I even went so far as to suggest that Sarita Strachline might have paid an accomplice to pretend to be an air-conditioning service repairman so he could plant the bomb. It was a stretch, but if Sarita had an alibi, it was the only other idea I could come up with.

"Good morning, Jenna," Gran said as I arrived at the Cookbook Nook, her tone upbeat though her gaze showed her concern. She was at the sales counter tending to customers. I loved having her work in the store. She was more knowledgeable than any of us about cookbooks. She had been collecting them for years.

Based on the line of ten women waiting to check out, the sale on the *The Art of the Wedding: Invitations, Flowers, Décor, Table Settings, and Cakes for a Memorable Celebration* had been the lure. It was packed with a wide range of photographs, everything from a cozy wedding at a ranch to a high-end wedding at a mansion in the city.

Bailey was sitting at the children's table in the rear of the shop teaching three kids under the age of ten how to make papier-mâché bridal bouquets. We often set up projects so parents could roam the shop and know their children were occupied.

"Back in a sec," Bailey said to her protégés, and hopped to her feet. She strode to me.

I set Tigger on the kitty condo my father had built for him, but he wanted none of it. He'd picked up on my angst and needed to unwind. He hopped off and romped beneath the children's table to toy with whatever paper scraps landed on the floor.

"You look decent, considering." Bailey twirled a hand by my face. "Your coloring is good."

I tucked my hair behind my ears. "It's a wonder what a little blush can do."

"Love the floral getup."

"It's one my favorite dresses. It even has pockets." I eyed her outfit of turquoise top over pink capris and dangly pink crystal earrings. "Aren't you festive?"

"I dressed to boost my spirits, too." She licked her lips. "Did you stay the night at Mercy?"

"No. Dad and Lola made me go home."

"Any update on Rhett?"

I filled her in. "The nurse I spoke to this morning thought he was doing extremely well, but, you know, it's all relative." I gestured to the multitude of customers. "If you're okay out here with Gran, I'm going to work on the ad I promised Bucky."

"Ad?"

"For a kitten adoption on Saturday. Someone dropped off ten kittens at the fire station."

"We could adopt another cat," she said, knowing Tito loved them. His sister had given them their current American shorthair. Bailey, who hadn't had any pets growing up, treasured Hershey. "A kitten for Brianna would be perfect. Are they cute?"

"More than cute." Every kitten was, to be truthful. "They're being tended to at the station."

"I'll stop by and take a peek. Go." She nudged me toward the office. "I know you'll be brilliant. But if you need help, yell." She'd always been a good sounding board for me. We'd worked together at Taylor & Squibb.

For the better part of an hour, I threw together a bullet-point presentation of ad copy that I thought would work.

- *Wrap your arms around this little bundle of fur.*
- *It's raining kittens.*

- *Meet your lap warmer.*
- *"No, I won't be your BFF," said no homeless kitten ever.*
- *Fire up your heart. A kitten named [FILL IN THE BLANK WITH BUCKY'S NAMES] wants your love.*

Plus, I decided to make an individual poster for each cat, with name, age, a *hello* speech bubble, and what the cat enjoyed — *tummy rubs, running, tumbling, chewing on ribbon, etc.*

When I was done crafting the initial campaign, I sent an email to Bucky asking him for individual photos of the kittens and their accompanying names. Being the Johnny-on-the-spot first responder that he was, he answered in a matter of seconds. A short while later, I sent him a completed package of art that the local office supply shop could print. He offered me a free kitten for my services.

I wrote back: *Thanks, but no thanks. Hands full right now, as you well know.*

He responded: *How is Rhett?*

I typed: *Hanging tough.* What else could I write? I didn't have a clue.

For the next few hours I remained in the storage room. I organized shelves, planned out future orders, fielded texts and phone calls from Rhett's friends who had heard the news, and contacted his family. His mother was bereft. I told her Rhett was doing okay and not to worry. I said the same to one of Intime's backers who had reached out, quite concerned, adding that I would be touching base with our insurance agent and getting quotes for repairs. I would provide updates.

At noon, a woman trilled, "Jenna!"

I stopped what I was doing, closed the laptop computer, and pressed through the burgundy drapes.

Harmony Bold, looking fashionable in a soft blue lab coat over white cigarette pants, strode past the line of customers at the sales counter and clutched my arm. "Did I hear correctly? A bomb blew up at Intime? Rhett was hurt? What on earth —"

I filled her in, starting with the set-to with Sarita at the expo after Harmony left.

She moaned. "If only I'd stayed —"

"It wouldn't have made a difference. The woman is wacko." I

sighed. "Listen, considering what went down, I think I need to postpone the wedding."

"No, you don't."

"That's what I told her," Bailey chimed, joining us. "Rhett will look fine. Sure, he might have a few scratches, but he's so handsome no one will notice."

I threw her a peeved look. "It's not about how he looks, for heaven's sake. We don't know if he's out of the woods. We don't know if he'll have amnesia. What if he sees the incident as an omen, and he changes his mind about marrying me?"

"Get real!" Bailey squawked. "If anything, he'll be more protective than ever and will never want to let you out of his sight."

"Jenna," Harmony said in a soothing tone, "let's go to the café to chat about this. Can you spare a minute?"

"Sure, I—"

"Miss Hart," a man said.

I swiveled and saw Todd Strachline heading my way. He was carrying a flyer for the Fire Sale Kitten Adoptions, the one I'd crafted with a picture of a gray kitten and a speech bubble with the slogan: *I am homeless, not worthless. I do not need your pity. Just your love.* Todd's daughters, dressed for a day at the beach in short-shorts and tank tops, trailed him. The dark and aloof elder girl was holding a copy of *The Super Easy Teen Baking Cookbook: 60 Simple Step-by-Step Recipes.* The freckly younger girl had looped a bag from Beaders of Paradise over one arm and was carrying a white porcelain cookie jar with a wood-carved top that resembled a cat's ears. We often stocked jars that coordinated with the theme of the week, but all we could find for weddings were *Mr. and Mrs.* cookie jars or all-white cookie jars. I'd decided a cat-themed jar was a good year-round addition to our stock. We'd ordered three.

"Miss Hart," Todd repeated as he drew near.

Bailey squeezed my arm and returned to the kids' table.

"I heard about what happened at Intime," Todd said. "I'm so sorry. I—"

"Da-ad," the older girl said.

"Forgive me for my rudeness," Todd said. "Let me introduce my girls. Shay, my older daughter."

"She's fifteen," the younger one sang. "I'm Sela. I'm eleven." She had the squeaky voice of a tween.

Todd smiled indulgently. "Shay wants to be a baker when she grows up."

"I'm already a baker," Shay said, hitching her hobo purse higher on her shoulder with an exasperated huff.

"Yes, but you want to make your living doing so," her father revised. "Sela likes to eat what her sister bakes. Especially cookies."

The younger daughter tittered.

"That's an excellent cookbook you're holding," I said to Shay. "The reviews are fabulous. Lots of tasty treats. The recipes are precise. And there are some really good pictures."

"Cool," she said.

"And I love that cookie jar," I said to Sela.

"Me, too."

"Why don't you two keep roaming the store?" Todd gave the girls a nudge.

They appeared more than relieved to be given the freedom, whispering like conspirators as they shuffled away.

"I heard about the incident at Intime," Todd began at the point where he'd been interrupted. "How is your fiancé? How's Rhett?"

"He's alive." I wasn't sure what else to add.

"A bomb." Todd shook his head. "In Crystal Cove. It's hard to wrap my mind around that. Tongues are wagging."

"What are people saying?" I asked.

He lowered his voice. "Some believe my ex-wife did it. I can't believe she would, but she has changed over the years. Jail can harden a criminal."

Or hard-boil an already hardened criminal, I reflected.

"A couple of people were talking outside the beading shop." He hooked his thumb. "My girls were inside getting supplies. They like me to wait outside for them. You understand." He glanced in their direction and back at me.

How many rumors were already floating around town? I wondered. Were there other suspects?

"I believe Chief Pritchett is questioning their mother at this very moment," Todd added.

I was pleased to hear Cinnamon was on the case, as promised.

"I'm afraid Sarita needs therapy," Todd said. "For years, I told her to get into a group or something, but she . . ." He glimpsed his daughters again. "I hope they can weather whatever unfolds."

Chapter 12

"Children are resilient," I said to Todd, as if I was an expert.

"Yes, but . . ." His shoulders slumped. He sighed, resigned. "Shay, Sela"—he gave a slight whistle and signaled them—"let's pay for your items and head to the beach before there's nowhere to put our blanket." He ambled toward the sales counter.

Harmony petted my shoulder. "C'mon. Coffee. You look whipped. Let's go next door. Bailey, you don't need Jenna, do you?"

Bailey gave us a thumbs-up. "We've got this under control."

Harmony ushered me down the breezeway and into the Nook Café. The place was nearly as packed as the Cookbook Nook. The hostess asked us to wait until she cleared the table beyond her podium. It would be a noisy place to sit with all the comings and goings, she said. We told her we wouldn't mind.

"I'm telling you, Mother, it's not fair," Darinda Weatherly said plaintively as she entered the café through the main door, a digital camera hanging on a strap around her neck. Dressed in a red sheath and gaudy jewelry, she stood out from the other customers.

"Darinda, lower your voice," her mother hissed. Wren had worn a more sedate gray dress with a string of pearls.

Wren saw me staring in their direction and raised her shoulders in a what-can-I-do gesture. I offered a supportive smile.

"Nina Naylor got CC Vineyards on *my* date," Darinda continued, her tone still sorrowful. "My date. Because her filthy rich parents were willing to pay double what we offered."

"Darinda, please," Wren chided. Her cheeks flamed the same color as her daughter's dress.

"Look!" Darinda plucked a cell phone from her clutch purse and waggled it in her mother's face. "See? It's right there. In black and white. The vineyard turned down our offer. If we'd had enough —"

"Hush," Wren warned.

"I have your table ready, Jenna," the hostess said, grabbing two menus. "By the window with an ocean view. Follow me."

Katie had offered her two cents regarding the café's décor. She believed food should be the star and not the furnishings. Each of the tables was dressed with a simple white tablecloth and held a vase with a single white flower.

When we were seated, our perky waitress asked us for our beverage order and hurried away. Wren and her daughter passed by as the hostess took them to a table at the far end of the room, Wren looking miserable and Darinda muttering.

"The poor Weatherlys." Harmony followed them with her gaze. "I'm glad we booked CC Vineyards in time."

"I'm thrilled you were on top of things, and we were first on the cancellation list."

She opened her menu. "Aha! You see? You're still eager to get married. You don't want to postpone. You're just anxious."

"I'm also glad we didn't have to offer double for the spot."

"The Naylors shouldn't have done that," Harmony said. "It sets a precedent, but money talks."

The word *money* made me think of Sarita and how she'd spent almost all of the insurance money in a short amount of time. What had she spent it on? Had she needed to pay off an accomplice in the arson?

The waitress brought water and two cups of coffee.

As she left, Katie bustled to me. Her toque was slightly off-kilter, and the sleeves of her chef's coat were splattered with something yellow. "Jenna, I'm so sorry about Rhett. The bomb." She put a hand on my shoulder. "Bailey came in earlier for a to-go cup of tea and filled me in. I'm glad Rhett is going to be okay."

"He might not—"

"Tut-tut." She circled a finger in front of my face. "Let's feed you and rid your mind of any negative thoughts."

"Katie, I like you," Harmony said.

"Positive is as positive does," my pal intoned. "That is one of my uncle's favorite mottos." Katie's uncle, ever the adventurer, had rented his house to Katie and her husband for a song. "By the way, Jenna"—she poked the table with a fingertip—"I've been working all morning on the appetizers for the wedding. I'll bring some of those out for you to taste. Food always soothes the soul."

I wasn't sure that was true, but I consented. I could use some pampering. I set my cell phone on the table, faceup. I was hoping for some kind of update regarding Rhett's health, but there were no new messages from Mercy Urgent Care.

A few minutes later, Katie returned with a small plate of seared fish kebabs, two bites on each kebab with a grilled tomato between them. "A little birdie told me"—she eyed Harmony—"that you really enjoyed the kebabs from California Catch, so I decided to whip up a batch. Try one."

I lifted a kebab and bit off one of the bites. "Yum. Spicy."

"It's all about the hotness," Katie said. "Too hot, and you'll burn everyone's palate. Too mild, and they'd be blah."

"Did you purchase a jar of Gunther's spices?" I asked.

Her mouth fell open. "He makes his own and sells them?"

Harmony nodded. "He does."

Katie hooted. "What an easy moneymaker. I'll give that some thought. For these, I combined sage, cumin, pepper, and fennel, added in chopped garlic, and marinated them with a lemon–olive oil dressing."

"The cumin gives it a real kick," I said.

Harmony agreed.

"Glad you approve." Katie beamed. "I'll be back with more selections in a minute." She strode away.

A young woman with hard-edged features halted in front of Harmony and said, "She's mine. I saw her first. Miss Bold, I—"

"Cut it out, Deedee Doolittle," cried the amber-eyed blond woman who trailed her. "She's mine. I have her business card." She flaunted it. "Did she give you a business card at the expo? No, she did not! Remember me, Miss Bold?" She slapped a hand on her chest. "We met as you were leaving the expo yesterday."

"I need her more than you do," the cranky Miss Doolittle whined. "My wedding planner quit."

With good reason, I mused, *if that was how entitled she acted.*

"Ladies, please," Harmony said. "Let's take this outside." She leaned forward and whispered to me, "Bridezillas on the loose. I'll just be a minute." Rising, she said with the authority of a general in battle, "Follow me."

I watched them go, thinking how lucky I was that Harmony was in charge of my wedding. But that thought led to one about Rhett suffering in the hospital, and my heart snagged. How was he? I didn't want to go to Mercy and sit on pins and needles in the waiting room again. I couldn't. I didn't have the patience. I needed to keep busy until they contacted me and said he was alert.

One of the women outside with Harmony whooped so loudly the sound spilled into the café.

Through the glass door, I saw the blond woman hugging Harmony. If looks could kill, given the way her rival, Miss Doolittle, was glowering, the blond woman had better watch her back.

Something else caught my eye. Beyond them, standing beside a dark blue Mercedes, were Matias Lajoie and Sarita Strachline. He was dressed for work. Sarita was wearing a white jumpsuit and white heels. Was that what she'd worn when Cinnamon had interrogated her? Had she hoped the white-on-white getup would convey innocence? Yeah, right. She was guilty. I felt it in my bones. Sarita was grinning at Matias, but he appeared to be ticked off. His forehead was creased and his eyes were a smoldering black. He said something. She threw her head back and laughed, clearly mocking him. His nostrils flared with annoyance.

I recalled Todd Strachline asking Sarita about her finances at the expo and demanding to know how she'd managed to rent the boat. She'd said she'd gotten a loan from a friend. Was Matias the one who had loaned her the money? Had he asked for it back, and she'd said no? Or had he asked her out, and she'd turned him down? Rejection could sting.

Matias extended a hand. Sarita batted it away.

Oh, to be a fly on the windshield so I could hear their conversation.

"What are you staring at?" Harmony slipped into her chair at the table. "The show is over."

"Yours might be, but"—I hitched my head at the parking lot—"the next one is getting started."

Chapter 13

For the next few hours, edgy and needing something to occupy my mind so I wouldn't think nonstop about Rhett and the bomb and the what-ifs, I went through cash register receipts and upcoming orders. When my eyes were too blurry to read numbers, I shifted to the display table to neaten it. Customers had left books lying on their sides or with their covers facedown. At four p.m., when I still hadn't heard from Mercy Urgent Care, I decided that, no matter what, I would visit Rhett after work and stick around until they wakened him. I wanted him to know how much I cared.

"Jenna." Gran traipsed to me while redraping the beautiful scarf she'd slung around her neck.

"Nice accessory," I said. "The silver filigree sparkles in the shop's lighting."

"This old thing?" She grinned. I was pretty sure Gran didn't have any *old things*. She was quite the clothes horse and often donated her gently used clothing to women-in-need charities.

"How's your granddaughter feeling?" I asked.

"Right as rain. By the by, two young women came in while you were out. They asked about *The Complete Cooking for Two Cookbook*."

The full name of the book was a mouthful. *The Complete Cooking for Two Cookbook, Gift Edition: 650 Recipes for Everything You'll Ever Want to Make (The Complete ATK Cookbook Series)*. I enjoyed the ATK series. The chefs really did their homework when it came to getting recipes precise. I wasn't a seat-of-your-pants cook. I needed exact amounts so I wouldn't mess up the dish.

"We haven't ordered it lately," Gran said. "Can we? The brides left a contact number."

"Sure." Our supplier in San Francisco was amenable to last-minute requests. "If he has two copies in stock, I'll have them by tomorrow. If not, we'll put in a rush order. If the women aren't local, we'll send it to them with no shipping charge."

"Excellent."

I moved to the sales counter and sent off an email to our supplier. He responded instantly in the affirmative.

"Hello-o-o, everyone!" Tina Gump crooned as she breezed into the shop pushing Bailey's daughter Brianna in a stroller. Tina had secured her tawny hair in a messy bun. Her ripped jeans and tank top clung to her svelte frame. "Bailey, we're here!"

Bailey emerged from the storage room with an armful of books.

"I'm off to my cooking class," Tina continued. "We're learning to flambé today."

"Have fun," Gran said. "Like Mrs. O'Leary, I love a good fire."

"Oh, Gracie, you're such a tease."

"You know" — she strolled to Tina — "Katie is giving a flambé demonstration Saturday. You should come."

"I plan to." Tina was bubbling over with good vibes. "Can you believe it? Tomorrow is my last day of school. Ever. Then I graduate and it's like . . . Whee! Gotta go."

"Hold on a sec. How is your new beau?" Gran asked.

"New beau?" Tina's voice rose in a cagey way. "What new beau?"

Gran shook a finger at Tina's face. "You have that look in your eye, young lady."

"I do not."

"I'm seasoned in the game of love," Gran said. "I know the signs."

Tina giggled. "Oh, Gracie, stop! No beau. I'm single." She wriggled her ring finger. "I'm leaving now. Bye!" She bent to kiss Brianna on the nose and sailed out.

Bailey pushed her daughter and stroller into the storage room and returned with Brianna and a primary colors, sit-to-stand activity station. She opened the station, set Brianna in it, and cooed to her. Brianna responded in kind, as happy as a clam. Tigger padded to her and thwacked her gently with his tail. Brianna giggled.

Over her shoulder, Bailey said, "She'll love a new k-i-t-t-y, don't you think?"

"Why are you spelling?" I asked.

"She knows the word. We watch children's shows on TV, and anytime a k-i-t-t-y appears, she squeals and points."

"Then, yes, she'll love it. Did you stop at the fire station yet?"

"Later on today. What kinds are there?" she asked.

"Orange and gray. Two different fathers, I think."

"I bet she'd like a ginger one. She adores Tigger."

"I bet you're right." I roamed the shop to talk to customers and noticed Gunther Hildenbiddle among them. He was fanning through a number of fish-themed cookbooks, but surreptitiously he was scanning the crowd.

"Jenna." Wren Weatherly strode into the shop with her daughter Darinda, who was checking the lens on her digital camera. "I'm so sorry," Wren continued, hustling toward me while Darinda lingered by the vintage table. "For the outburst at the café. We've had such lovely meals there. The lack of decorum—"

"It's fine. Brides are often on edge." Emotions were always riding high during Bride's Dream Expo, my aunt had warned me. "I'm sorry your daughter didn't get the site she'd hoped for. Could she put off the wedding?"

"She can't." Wren sniffed. "That didn't come out right. Of course she can. She's not with child. But when she gets her heart set on something, it's all she can think about. And her delicious dentist is eager to start their new life together. Isn't that sweet?"

"Very."

Wren aimed a finger toward the exit. "I did convince her to go upstairs with me to Vines and see if it was available."

Vines was the lovely, intimate wine bar on the second floor of Fisherman's Village that had taken over the lease where the Grotto had been located. A surf shop and a theater that showed classic movies were also located upstairs.

"I told her if she did something low-key and less expensive," Wren continued, "I could give her and her husband a dowry to begin their new life."

"That's a great idea."

"But she didn't go for it. She wants all the bells and whistles."

I smiled. "Well, a wedding at Vines would be a completely different kind of event than what she has in mind. Indoors. No view. A much smaller guest list. You know, I could call Baldini Vineyards, if you're interested. Alan's a personal friend. It's a beautiful venue with a view of the ocean. They might have a date suitable for Darinda."

Wren grabbed my hand. "Oh, would you?"

"Sure." I felt the body heat of someone hovering behind me. I glanced over my shoulder to see Gunther listening in on our conversation.

"Hi, Gunther," I said, turning slightly. "What are you doing here? I thought you were attending a religious retreat."

"It doesn't start until tonight. Thirty-six hours of pure silence. I can't wait."

"Well, have fun," I said, hoping to dismiss him so I could wind up my chat with Wren.

But Gunther didn't budge. Instead he said to Wren, "I couldn't help overhearing, ma'am. Do you need a caterer for your daughter's wedding?"

"No, a venue."

"Vines won't be able to provide a full menu," Gunther said. "But California Catch could work with them." He pulled a business card from the pocket of his blue shirt.

Wren declined the card. "Thanks, but I'm afraid not. Fish is out of our price range." She said to me, "The cost of fish nowadays is exorbitant."

"Not if the restaurant catches its own," Gunther said smoothly. "We can be quite affordable and flexible. And I will cook whatever the happy bride-to-be desires. Ask Jenna about the quality of our food." He acknowledged me with a nod. "She tasted some of our appetizers at the expo. Weren't they top-notch?"

Put on the spot, I bobbed my head. What else could I say?

"Think about it." Gunther dropped the card into Wren's tote bag. "I'm at your service. You will not be disappointed." He exited the shop.

I watched him suspiciously as he made his way to his car. Was he tootling around town, going shop to shop, hoping to drum up business? Hadn't he secured enough new clients at the expo?

Wren's brow puckered. "Well, that was unusual. I mean, hawking one's services at the expo is the norm, but here?"

"I had no idea he would do that," I said, feeling sheepish.

She brushed my arm. "No worries. I understand. I'm doing everything I can to expand my business. Say, why don't you come by Home Décor soon? I'd love for you to see my place. I'll give you a ten percent discount on your entire order. In the meantime, call me if Baldini Vineyards is open to an event. I'd love to check it out. Thanks so much." She pivoted, collected her daughter, who was scrolling through photos on her camera, and passed Flora Fairchild on her way out.

Flora craned her neck to watch Wren leave. When she turned back, her mouth was pinched. She crossed to me and said, "What did she want?"

"Nothing."

"Pfft! Liar." Flora flicked my arm with a finger.

"You don't look pleased to have seen her. Why?"

"Why? Because. You don't have any business rivals in town, Jenna, so you wouldn't understand, but Wren is always after my clientele. She promised you a discount, didn't she?"

"Yes." I wouldn't lie.

She shrugged. "Competition is stiff these days. I guess I'll have to provide discounts, too." She primped the sleeves of her floral T-shirt. "I'm actually here to buy a salt and pepper shaker set for a friend. She collects them. And she likes cats."

"Follow me." I led her to where we had dozens of sets on display as well as colorful aprons on hooks, recipe boxes, stackable measuring cups, and uniquely shaped spatulas sprinkled here and there — all treasures for our patrons to discover while they searched for a cookbook. "One of my favorite sets is this one." I lifted a three-inch pair of cats, one blue-and-yellow-striped and the other pink-and-red-striped. They were facing each other and both were grinning.

She inspected them, turning them this way and that. "Between you and me, Wren has money issues."

Okay, here we go, I mused. *A bit of gossip.*

Flora lowered her voice. "I happen to know because we have the same accountant."

"And who might that be?"

"Todd Strachline."

"Todd works for both of you?"

"Don't look so shocked. Many of us use him."

"Isn't that a conflict of interest, seeing as you're both in the homewares business?"

"Many of us have the same insurance agent, too. We're a small community. There are only so many professionals one can trust."

I supposed that was true. The Cookbook Nook and Nook Café had the same insurance agent as Intime and the Pelican Brief.

"Todd did all the books for his wife's business until the divorce," Flora went on. "That was a steady gig and put money in his coffers, but after they divorced, he hung his shingle and took on clients. When she went to jail, what could he do? He couldn't save her. She was on her own. We didn't judge him by Sarita's reputation. Besides, he's a wiz with taxes. And I hate, hate, hate doing taxes."

"Don't we all?" I joked. Aunt Vera did ours.

"He helps lots of restaurants, a couple of dress shops, and the toy store, too. He's always on time. He never misses a deadline." She replaced the set I'd given her and lifted a pair of hand-painted Biko cartoon cats, one blue and one white. "Back to what I was saying. I know Wren is struggling financially because . . ." Flora hummed. "Okay, I'll tell the truth. Because I saw her file on Todd's desk the other day."

"Wren's file was open on his desk?" That didn't sound remotely ethical.

"Well, no." Flora traced a nervous finger along the neckline of her shirt. "No, it wasn't *open* open. It was in a stack with a dozen others, and I know I shouldn't have stolen a look, but I couldn't help myself. When he stepped out of his office to take a private call with one of his girls, I peeked. She's my rival!"

As if that's a good enough reason, I mused.

"She's underwater with . . ." Flora bit her lower lip. "No. I won't discuss this any further. It's not my business." She put the set of cats back on the shelf.

"But—"

"I need to finish my shopping. Alone." Flora flounced to the far end of the shop to check out another array of salt and pepper shakers.

Leaving me to wonder about Wren and her finances. Was Flora right? Was Wren underwater? Was that why she couldn't drum up enough money to secure the venue her daughter wanted? Then I thought of Gunther. Why had he pressed so hard for her business? Did he have money issues, too?

Chapter 14

I skirted the sales counter and caught a glimpse of my cell phone faceup. I swiped the screen. No messages from Mercy Urgent Care. Irritation roiled inside me. I was ready to dial the facility when Cinnamon Pritchett and her mother strode into the shop via the breezeway. They must have dined at the café.

"Hi, Pepper. Hi, Cinnamon." I slotted my cell phone into the pocket of my sundress so I would feel it vibrate if a message came in.

Cinnamon was in uniform. Pepper was wearing a silver knit dress cinched at the waist with a glittery belt of gemstones.

"Hello, Jenna." Pepper greeted me with a wave. "I'm on a mission."

"Pretty belt, Pepper." My aunt often advised me to compliment customers. It made them feel special. And Pepper, in particular, appreciated praise.

"Thank you. I made it myself." She was quite the crafter. "I've got to find that cookie cookbook you told me about, Jenna."

I knew the one she meant, *100 Cookies: The Baking Book for Every Kitchen, with Classic Cookies, Novel Treats, Brownies, Bars, and More*. It had been nominated on Goodreads as one of the best cookbooks of 2020. It was gorgeous and was packed with pictures. Plus, the recipes were easy to follow.

"Right over there." I pointed. "Second aisle." As she strolled away, I cleared my throat to get Cinnamon's attention. "Can we talk?" I jerked my head toward the entrance and didn't wait for a response.

Outside, I paused near the bottom of the stairs leading to the second floor.

Cinnamon joined me. "What's up?"

"Have you interrogated Sarita Strachline yet? I saw her a while ago. Right here. In the parking lot. As free as a bird. She was standing with—"

"Stop. Take a deep breath." Cinnamon held up a hand. "I'll tell you what I know so far, but that's it. You keep your nose out of this."

"My fiancé is hurt."

"I know he is, but he's alive, so inhale and exhale and let me continue."

I obeyed and drank in a huge gulp of air.

"We did interrogate Sarita at her place of residence. She claims she was on her boat at the time of the incident. Two sailors saw her. She—"

"Your guy said the bomb at Intime was detonated with a timer."

"Jenna..."

"Which means anyone could have set it off. So having an alibi means nothing," I concluded. "Did you look for the makings of a bomb on the boat?"

"We did and found squat. No timers. No switches. No ball bearings or wires or combustible solutions. Zip."

"She could have made it someplace else," I reasoned. "Maybe she rented a storage unit."

Cinnamon's mouth quirked up. "I'll give you credit. You do think like an investigator."

"Thanks." I appreciated a compliment, too, especially coming from someone as exacting as Cinnamon Pritchett.

"We're looking into storage units," she went on. "We're also looking into trucks or vans that Sarita might have rented."

"Did you check security cameras for the shops that neighbor Intime? Perhaps Sarita was seen lurking around the bistro recently. Rhett hasn't installed any yet, even though I've told him to do so." Last year when a murder occurred, I'd impressed upon him the fact that if Harmony Bold's parents had installed security cameras in or around their building, the crime might have been solved days earlier. In addition, it might have been preventable because cameras were a deterrent. Crime wasn't frequent in Crystal Cove, but we had endured a few horrible murders.

"The security cameras for the businesses near Intime have been down. Some kind of short."

"How about canvassing the shops across the street to see if any of their security devices might have caught something? Oh, and did you get my message about the air-conditioning person?" I ignored her peeved expression and pressed on. "The AC at Intime was on the fritz. Sarita could have slipped into the kitchen and planted the bomb while Rhett was busy with the technician, or she could have hired the air-conditioning person to—"

"Stop, Jenna." Cinnamon clasped my forearm. "Yes, I got the

message. The AC guy was the regular guy. He serviced it and left. He said he and Rhett were in the kitchen the whole time."

"Have you questioned the staff?"

"We're getting to them. One at a time. A lot of people worked there. I've conducted a few interviews. Appleby and Foster are taking care of the others."

"Can you share what you've learned?" I asked.

"Sure. This time, seeing as you and Rhett were victims." She offered a tolerant smile. "When a sous chef found out she would have the night off, she stepped outside to call her boyfriend and tell him. She hadn't seen him in *ages*." Cinnamon stressed the word, making fun of the sous chef's delivery.

"That was snarky," I chided.

"But honest."

"Did anyone overhear her on her phone?"

"She isn't certain. However, she said she was on the sidewalk and in full view of everyone in Crystal Cove who passed by."

So that established that someone other than the staff could have known that Rhett and I would be in the restaurant alone. Had Sarita or a person in communication with her heard the sous chef?

"Plus," Cinnamon continued, "the woman admitted that she hadn't kept her voice down because her boyfriend was taking that moment to pick a fight about how busy she always was."

I pictured Sarita facing off with Matias in the parking lot. "As I was saying a moment ago, earlier today I saw Sarita and Matias Lajoie arguing. Over there." I aimed a finger.

"Why is that relevant?"

"What if he was in love with her, but when he confessed to her, she rebuffed him? So to prove his love, he attacked Rhett?"

Cinnamon shook her head. "I can't see Matias or anyone planting a bomb to prove his love. That's too extreme."

I blew out a quick burst of frustrated air. "Isn't that what terrorists do to prove their devotion to their beliefs?"

Cinnamon scowled. I'd stumped her.

"Maybe whoever did set the bomb," I continued, "waited until the cleaning crew was leaving, and somehow prevented the door from closing completely. Then they stole inside, planted the bomb, and split."

Cinnamon hummed, considering that angle.

"What about Todd Strachline?" I asked.

"What about him?"

"I heard his and Sarita's divorce was less than amicable. He threatened to burn down her house if she won the kids in the settlement. And he didn't get any money from the insurance payout that she recouped after the arson."

"Why would he help her attack Intime, then?"

"I'm not saying he did it to help her. Just the opposite. What if he set the bomb to make the police think Sarita did it? To frame her?"

"If that was the case, then he would have planted evidence on her boat, don't you think?" Cinnamon folded her arms. "Look, Jenna, somebody must have seen someone slip into Intime. Someone will come forward."

Somebody. Someone. Who? When?

"You of all people know investigations take time," she went on. "Leave it to us. Focus on helping Rhett recover, okay?" She gave me a warm hug, poked her head into the shop to say goodbye to her mother, and drove away in her cruiser.

At the same time, my cell phone buzzed in my pocket.

Chapter 15

I pulled my cell phone from my pocket and scanned the screen. I'd received a text from someone at the hospital. Rhett was awake. "Hallelujah!" I cheered. Hopeful that he was out of the woods, I bid goodbye to everyone and raced to Mercy Urgent Care.

A somber nurse with paintbrush-straight hair was placing a prayer plant on a side table when I tiptoed into the room. There was a vase filled with lilies of the valley and another with a summer bouquet. Rhett was propped up with two pillows, his eyes closed. He was still having fluids pumped into his arm. The monitor to the right beeped his vital signs with regularity. Additional ointment had been applied to his facial wounds, and the black and blue bruises from where he'd made contact with the kitchen floor had formed.

"Hi, I'm his fiancée," I whispered to the nurse as I crossed to the flowers and read the accompanying notes.

"Good evening. Remember, he needs to stay calm. No loud conversations. No surprises."

"Yes, ma'am," I babbled, slightly daunted by the woman. "May I kiss him?"

She smiled, dispelling my fear. "Of course," she said, and left the room.

I ambled closer to the bed.

"Hi, sweetheart." I kissed a spot on his cheek that was free of bruising.

He opened his eyes and attempted to smile, but I could tell it hurt him to do so. "What . . . happened?"

My stomach lurched. Hadn't the doctor told him anything, or did he have amnesia? "There was a bomb," I began. "At Intime. In the kitchen. It was detonated by a timer."

"Timer," he repeated.

"I was in the dining room. You took the brunt of the explosion and landed on the floor. But don't worry, you'll be fine."

"Liar."

"I'm not lying, I—"

He winked, and hope soared through me. That one gesture was all I needed to know that he was, indeed, fine and his sense of humor was intact. Which meant his mind was sharp, too.

"I remember it all," he rasped. "I heard a click . . . right before."

I knew nothing about bombs. I could only reason a guess based on movies I'd seen. I caressed his shoulder. "Oh, Rhett, I'm so sorry."

"It wasn't . . . your fault." He coughed and reached for the cup of water on the bedside stand.

I handed it to him and helped him fit the straw into his mouth. He drank.

"Do they know who . . ." He hesitated. "Who set the bomb?"

"I think it was Sarita Strachline, but Cinnamon won't buy into that assumption. She interrogated her."

"And . . ."

"And Sarita has an alibi. She was seen on the boat she's renting. The police couldn't find any evidence on it, but—"

"She's living on a boat?"

"A sailboat. At the Pier."

He took another sip of water.

"On another note," I said, "the police will be questioning your staff."

"None of my staff did this."

"That's what I told Cinnamon, but the person responsible stole into Intime's kitchen. How did they know only you and I would be there at that time?"

He started to blink rapidly.

"Let's not discuss it." I stroked his head, remembering the nurse's admonition. "For now, let's concentrate on getting you better."

"Something else is bothering you." He wiggled a finger at my face.

"I was worried, but I'm so relieved you're alive and you don't have amnesia."

"No, whatever is bothering you isn't about this." He gestured to the gauze around his head. "And not about the bomb. What is it?"

I averted my gaze.

"C'mon, look at me," he said gently. "Out with it."

"I think we should postpone the wedding."

"No way."

"Sweetheart—"

"You said yourself that I'm fine." His mouth curved up on one side. "I'll be out of here in a day."

"Maybe longer."

"A day," he repeated.

"Don't be stubborn. They want to make sure you're stable."

"A day."

I screwed up my mouth.

"I don't want to postpone anything," he said, returning to our previous thread. "I love you and I want you to be my wife. We have a venue. We have people coming to town. We're not canceling. Do you hear me?"

"Yes, sir." I stood at attention and saluted.

He cracked a smile, and I couldn't express how relieved I was.

"The restaurant," he said. "When will the police be done with it?"

I hadn't asked Cinnamon, but I would imagine it would be a long while before the police had collected all its evidence. "Sweetheart . . ."

"I'll need to get in and spruce it up for the out-of-towners' dinner."

"About that. Intime isn't in good shape. It'll need a lot of repairs. Those will take longer than a couple of weeks, I think. We'll need to find a new venue for the dinner."

He winced, as if the notion pained him. "Why don't you talk to Lola? She'll close the Pelican Brief for you."

"For us."

"For us." He stroked my hand. "And I'm sure she can do the menu I had in mind."

"That's a great solution."

"Will you contact our insurance agent, Jim Daley?"

"Yes."

"And the investors?"

"They've touched base," I said. "I've alerted them to everything. They sent the lilies of the valley. I guess they're your mother's favorite flower?"

He nodded.

"Eddie Milsap sent the prayer plant, and Dad and Lola sent a summer bouquet. Everyone wishes you well. Why don't you rest—"

"The employees," he said. "I want to keep as many as I can during reconstruction."

I petted his arm. "Sure thing, but they could file for unemployment."

"If I let them go, other restaurateurs are bound to snatch them up."

"You're right."

"Maybe Lola will take one or two of them on in the meantime," he suggested.

"Good idea. We could use a few at the Nook, too."

He scrubbed his hair with his fingertips. "I've sure had bad luck with restaurants, haven't I? Do you think I should give up and go back to Bait and Switch?"

"No way. Eddie loves managing the store. He's in his element." When Rhett sold half of the business to Eddie, he'd promised to remain a silent partner. "And you? You've finally rediscovered your passion. You can't give it up. This is a minor setback."

"Minor." He tapped the gauze around his head. "This isn't minor."

"You seem to be thinking clearly. That's a great sign."

"Do the police suspect anyone else?"

"You know Cinnamon. She's keeping her cards close to her vest. I suggested Matias Lajoie. Do you know him?"

"Sure. He came into Bait and Switch a lot. We talked fishing and cooking."

"Fishing and cooking?" I raised an eyebrow.

"He was a fisherman before he owned Tradewinds and a chef before that."

"He was a chef?"

"Yep. He went to culinary school and worked at one of the restaurants in town. I can't remember which one. I hadn't relocated here yet. When he failed—he couldn't make a roux to save his life—he settled for being a fisherman. And then a boat repairman. According to him, his father dubbed him a master dabbler."

"A jack-of-all-trades."

"Yep." Rhett chuckled. "He was doing pretty well with the boat repair thing, until one day, he started to hang around with a bad bunch. The rumor was drugs were involved. Illegal marijuana. To hear former friends tell it, he grew erratic and surly. He was spiraling downward at a fast clip." Rhett squinted, as if trying to remember something. "He must be okay now, though, because Tradewinds is thriving. Why did you mention him to Cinnamon?"

"Because I saw Sarita and him arguing earlier today. Outside the shop. I don't know what they were arguing about. Also, at the expo, I saw them chatting. I got the feeling she and Matias had a past. Before she married Todd. I suggested to Cinnamon that Sarita might've talked him into planting the bomb at Intime. To win her heart. Cinnamon didn't buy that for a second."

"How would he have gotten in?" Rhett asked.

"I don't know, but someone did. Perhaps one of the staff forgot to lock up."

Rhett grunted. "My staff isn't involved."

"I'm not saying they are, but if one was careless . . ." I threw my arms wide. "Rhett, somebody broke in and planted the bomb!"

The somber nurse poked her head in. "Miss, please keep your voice down, and don't upset him."

"Sorry." My cheeks flamed with embarrassment. Sufficiently chastised, I kissed Rhett on the lips. "It's time for me to leave. You go back to sleep."

"If I sleep any more, I'll turn into Rip van Winkle."

I chuckled.

"Sit," he said. "Watch something on TV with me."

I switched on the television and tuned the channel to a rerun of *I Love Lucy*. Sitting in the chair beside Rhett's bed, I texted my aunt and asked if she would take Tigger home. She replied instantly that not only would she do that, but she would ask Deputy Appleby to check inside and around my house to make sure there were no intruders and no bricks hurled through any windows. The notion that someone might attack me again at any given moment made me jittery.

To rid my mind of apprehension, I focused on the TV show—it was the episode where Desi invited the actor William Holden to dinner and Lucy's fake nose caught on fire.

An hour later, when Rhett closed his eyes, I kissed him and left.

Outside, night had fallen and it was raining. Stupidly, though I'd known a rare summer storm was headed our way, I'd forgotten my umbrella. I jogged to my VW beetle, trying to avoid puddles. Lightning lit up the sky and the roads were slick as I drove home, but I navigated them well.

When I strolled into the house, Tigger meowed like I'd forgotten him. Rook barked in agreement. I apologized to both of them profusely and promised them an extra treat for dinner.

I didn't feel like eating, but knowing I needed fuel, I plated the fruit and cheese from the to-go box Lola had given me the night before and poured myself a glass of chardonnay. After feeding the animals, I set a place in the dining room and took a sip of wine. The first taste was bitter and unexciting, so I pushed it aside.

More lightning flared through the pane-glass windows. Thunder rumbled. Tigger darted under the dining table and took refuge by my feet. Rook dove into the chair Rhett preferred to read in and curled into a ball. I cooed to both of them and told them not to be scared, but they remained in place.

"I've got to change my clothes," I told them. "I'll be right back." I slogged to the bedroom to put on something more comfortable and less wet.

In passing, I caught sight of myself in the mirror that hung over the bureau and gasped. My skin was slack, my hair snarled. Was that how I'd looked when I'd entered Rhett's hospital room? I retreated to the bathroom, combed my hair, washed off the modicum of makeup I'd donned in the morning, and dabbed my face with a coconut cream that I was crazy about. The aroma of coconut always lifted my spirits. Then I shrugged into a pair of heather-gray sweatpants and an *I Love to Cook* T-shirt and returned to the kitchen as rain started to drum the roof.

Rook bounded to me and flopped to the ground. "Yes, okay, you can have some love." I bent and rubbed his belly.

Tigger wandered in next and did a figure eight around my ankles. He meowed, asking how I was doing.

"Don't worry, buddy. I'm fine. And you are, too."

But I wasn't. I fretted, wondering if Sarita would throw another brick through my window or try to hurt Rhett. Was the hospital staff on high alert?

I fetched a bag of Earl Grey tea from the cupboard and set a teakettle filled with water on the stove. I needed something soothing to calm my nerves. While waiting for the water to boil, I tapped the music app on my cell phone and selected the *Secret Garden* playlist. Next, I covered the glass of chardonnay with plastic wrap and put the glass in the refrigerator. I would savor it at another time. Not tonight.

At the same time the teakettle whistled, something outside went *boom*. Not thunder. Not an earthquake. In fact, not natural. The dog howled and scuttled to my side. Tigger yowled and sprang into my arms.

"*Shh*, you guys." I hugged Tigger tightly and rubbed Rook's snout. "*Shh*. It's okay."

But then there were two more *booms*. The windows rattled. I bounded from the chair. It had to have been an explosion. Where? Close by? I peeked out the window. Rain was coming down in sheets. I could barely make out my aunt's house or the cottage or the neighbor's house. Everything nearby appeared to be unharmed. Praying that a house in the neighborhood hadn't suffered a gas leak, I ordered the pets to stay inside, donned a pair of flip-flops, shrugged into a lemon-yellow slicker, pulled up the coat's hood, and raced out the front door.

Instantly I smelled the putrid odor of gunpowder and scanned the area for the source.

On the beach, people stood as if in a tableau. All were staring slack-jawed in the direction of the Pier. I followed their gaze. Despite the rain, flames glinted in the night sky, and smoke coiled into the air. Had another bomb gone off?

I started to follow the crowd, my arms chugging, my chest tightening with fear as it dawned on me that Bait and Switch might have been the target of the explosion. Had Eddie been hurt? Had anyone else?

"A boat burst," a shaggy-haired man yelled to the rest of us while waving his cell phone and displaying a text message.

"A sailboat!" hollered a woman who was also consulting her cell phone.

A sailboat. Not Bait and Switch.

"Any casualties?" a redheaded man yelled.

"Don't know," said the shaggy-haired guy. "The Pier is fine. Unscathed."

All boats were moored near the far end of the Pier, away from the shops and restaurants. Only a few were used as full-time housing.

A siren pierced the air. A fire truck, its lights whirling, whizzed along the highway to the left. A patrol car *whooped*, too.

I arrived at the Pier and sprinted along the boardwalk with the others. A pair of policemen were trying to manage the mob, but curiosity couldn't be contained.

When we arrived at the carny games, I spied nearly fifty people standing beside the boardwalk's railing, many shading their eyes to block the rain and get a better view of the wreckage.

"Look!" A person pointed. "There. A body. See it?"

Indeed, a woman was floating facedown in the ocean along with the debris. And not just any woman. I recognized the white jumpsuit and the ebony tresses fanning outward from her head. The victim was Sarita Strachline.

Chapter 16

An hour later, I was still standing on the boardwalk amid the throng, which was abuzz with speculation, including employees I recognized from Mum's the Word, Bait and Switch, and Seaside Bakery. No other explosions had occurred. Mercifully, the storm had passed through. The police had cordoned off the area stairs leading to the lower docking area. A huge spotlight that they'd set up on the Pier focused on the crime scene. Another spotlight on the wreckage recovery boat that was trolling the ocean, its crew taking photographs and collecting debris, provided more illumination. A rescue team had recovered Sarita's body and had ceded it to the coroner.

Many of my fellow onlookers were speculating about the incident. Reporters, including Tito, were roaming the Pier asking questions. An unsmiling blond female from KSBZ news stood in front of a camera speaking into a handheld microphone and reporting what she knew to date—not much more than we did, though she had provided a brief history of Sarita's incarceration and the arson at the Grotto.

Outside Mum's the Word, Cinnamon and Deputy Appleby had set up a tented area for questioning. Officer Foster was keeping the witnesses organized. The Seaside Bakery was providing hot coffee for those willing to bear the elements to watch the story unfold.

I moved away and stood off at a distance, still spellbound by the activity in the water as well as the number of people willing to offer their two cents. A couple of times, I saw Cinnamon frowning in my direction. She couldn't be upset that I was there, could she? I had every right to be interested in what had happened, especially considering that I believed Sarita had detonated the bomb at Intime that had nearly killed my fiancé.

Was this blast merely a result of an experiment that had gone sideways? Had Sarita been messing with explosives while planning another attack on me and Rhett? Had the police missed finding materials on her boat in its previous search because she'd stowed her stash in the hull or had hidden them in a carved-out section of the mast?

Cinnamon motioned with her hand. I thumbed my chest. *Me?* She jerked her head, annoyed. *Yes.*

I hustled to her, suddenly aware of the casual attire beneath my slicker. "Chief Pritchett. How can I help you?" I noticed a Fire Sale Kittens Adoption poster in the window of the diner. Bucky was definitely spreading the word.

"What are you doing here?" Cinnamon demanded.

"What everyone else is doing, trying to understand what happened. It was a bomb, right? Not a gas or propane tank explosion?"

"It was a bomb."

"Did Sarita make it? Was it like the one you found at Intime? Did she accidentally blow herself up?"

Cinnamon pursed her lips.

"Was it similar?" I asked.

"Different."

"Was it triggered with a timer?"

She cocked her head. "Where have you been for the last few hours?"

I gulped. "I'm sorry, what?"

"I'd like to account for your whereabouts," she said with clipped precision. "It wasn't a difficult question."

"You can't possibly think that I—"

"Answer the question."

"I was with Rhett. At the hospital. He woke up. He was alert. He remembered me. No amnesia. We watched television." I was blathering, my mind reeling. There was no way Cinnamon could think I had a hand in this. Me, kill Sarita? With a bomb? *I'd more likely have strangled her with my bare hands,* I mused, but banished the thought from my mind. Heaven forbid the wish-fulfillment image burst from my mouth. "It was an *I Love Lucy* rerun." I recapped the storyline.

"When did you get home? Telling by your outfit"—Cinnamon assessed my casual attire—"that's where you were when you heard the explosion."

"I got home an hour ago," I stated, and revised. "No, two hours ago. I've been here an hour. I fed the pets, cleaned up, changed clothes, and ate a snack. I was making tea when I heard the boom."

"Uh-huh." Cinnamon slipped a hand into her trouser pocket, assuming a casual pose meant to convey *Don't worry about me, I'm your friend.*

Yeah, right. My insides turned to jelly. "I didn't do this."

"I didn't say you did."

"But you're thinking it." I aimed a finger at her face and instantly curled the finger back toward myself so I didn't come across as hostile. "Someone must have seen me running with the crowd from my house to here. The nurse saw me at the hospital. And Rhett, of course. I'll bet my aunt saw me arrive home, too. You've got to ask all of them. You didn't answer my question before." I jutted my hand at the remains of Sarita's boat. "Was this bomb discharged using a timer? If so, you have to wonder whether the killer is standing somewhere close, holding on to the device."

"Are you?"

"What? No!" I wailed. "C'mon, Cinn—" I stopped mid-name. "Chief, I did not do this!"

She remained maddeningly stoic.

"If you had a K-9 dog, you might be able to track the bomber if he's here," I suggested. "Also, if this one was sparked by a device, it would suggest the killer might be the same one who set the bomb at Intime."

Cinnamon's brow furrowed. "Are you speculating now that Sarita *wasn't* the designer of the bomb that hurt your fiancé?"

"I'm willing to look beyond her as a suspect."

"Because she's dead," Cinnamon stated.

I shifted feet.

Cinnamon mirrored me. She wasn't mocking me. She looked as uncomfortable as I felt. "One of our witnesses tells us that you were seen admiring Sarita's boat the other day."

I inhaled and exhaled, wondering which person in the horde had ratted me out. "Yes, I was here looking at a lot of boats. For fun. I don't mean *fun* . . ." Words snagged in my throat. "I was looking for windsurfing equipment for Rhett. Not a sailboat. The sailboats were there, and they were colorful, and it was . . ." I pressed my lips together to prevent myself from uttering the word *fun* again. "I was with my aunt. I wanted her opinion. See, I want to get Rhett windsurfing equipment as a wedding gift."

"Pretty big gift."

"Pretty great guy." A chill swizzled up my spine. I folded my arms to ward it off, but instantly released them, afraid I'd look defensive.

"Did you buy anything?"

"Not yet. The Airush Freewing Air Wing is really cool, but it's on backorder. It comes complete with a backpack, leash swivel, rope-style bungee leash, which Rhett will really appreciate, and harness line." I ticked the items off on my fingertips.

"I don't need the particulars, Jenna," Cinnamon said.

The fact that she had used my first name helped me relax—a tad. When conducting interviews, she typically used formal names. Had she referred to me as Miss Hart, I would have been more worried than I already was.

"Chief," Appleby said as he joined us, "Jake Chapman wants a word."

"What about?"

"Wouldn't say." He eyed me. "How are you holding up, Jenna?"

"I didn't do this. I think she's starting to believe me." I regarded Cinnamon, who revealed nothing. Scrabbling to provide more proof of my innocence, I addressed Appleby. "Deputy, were you home with my aunt when the explosion occurred? Did you see me at my house?"

"Nope. I was checking out a theft at Bride's Dream Expo."

"What kind of theft?"

"Photography equipment went missing."

"Oh, no," I said. "That's terrible."

"Not as terrible as this."

"No, of course not. I didn't mean . . ." I willed myself to stop jabbering.

"The vendor was insured," Appleby said. "Every venue at the expo is. It's a requirement, but the vendor is concerned as to how someone got into the tent undetected."

"Aren't there security cameras?"

Appleby shoved his hands in his pockets. "They were disabled."

"On purpose?" I asked, flashing on the security cameras coincidentally being down around Intime.

"We don't know."

"If you're through shooting the breeze, Deputy," Cinnamon said curtly, "please bring Mr. Chapman over."

Appleby blanched. "Sure thing, Chief." He lumbered away.

"Someone savvy had to have disabled the security cameras at the expo," I theorized.

Cinnamon grumbled. "It doesn't concern you, Jenna."

Appleby brought Jake to Cinnamon and returned to address the line of witnesses.

Jake was dressed in a short-sleeved plaid shirt and cargo shorts and didn't look cold in the least. "Chief Pritchett." He bowed ever so slightly. "I heard Jenna is a person of interest."

Cinnamon narrowed her eyes. "Who told you that?"

"Gossips." He motioned to the crowd. "I can attest to having seen Jenna in her house for a full hour before the explosion." Jake lived down the street from me in a gorgeous two-story home, and he often walked at night. "She was pacing to and fro and talking to herself." He said to me, "You should close your drapes, young lady."

"You watched her the entire time?" Cinnamon asked.

"I wasn't stalking her, if that's what you're insinuating," Jake said. "I was cleaning up the neighborhood." He had a penchant for taking care of Crystal Cove. For years, at his own expense, before the sun rose he had driven a sandboni on the beach to gather garbage that beachgoers might have left behind. Though he was a wealthy man, thanks to investment advice that my grandfather had given him, he still felt the need to clean. "I gathered a full bag of trash. The wind carries it off the sand. If left alone, it would be an eyesore."

"Seeing Jenna pacing doesn't mean she couldn't have detonated the bomb," Cinnamon said.

I huffed, exasperated. "Check my house. Right now. I give you full permission to enter. You won't find anything but two very frightened pets awaiting my return." I drew in a deep breath and released it. "Look, you know I didn't do this. Sarita must have enemies. I told you she and Matias Lajoie argued. Well, it turns out he repaired boats before he went into the boat purveyor business, meaning he has a knowledge of how things work." *And possibly go boom.* "Have you questioned him?"

"He's on the list." Cinnamon surveyed the crowd.

"And Sarita's ex-husband isn't a fan, either."

"Okay, Jenna, that's enough." Her gaze flickered.

I pointed at her. "Aha! You're keeping something from me. What did you discover?"

"Mine to know."

"C'mon, Chief, please," I begged. "First Intime and now this. If you have a suspect, other than me —"

"You'll get no more from me." She shooed me away. "Go. You, too, Jake."

Anger churned inside me. Cinnamon had no right to dismiss me that way. Okay, sure, she had a right, but it wasn't, um, *right.* She knew I was reliable. Knew I could keep a secret. And, heck, I was good at brainstorming.

As I trudged with Jake toward the crowd, I said, "I've been meaning to ask, did you forget about your appointment with my aunt?"

"I did." He tapped his temple. "Too much on my mind, and I forgot to put it on my calendar. I'll call her tomorrow."

"I was surprised to hear about your engagement."

He fanned the air with a hand. "When Z.Z. proposed, how could I refuse?"

"She asked *you*?"

"Sure." He guffawed. "It is the twenty-first century, after all."

Someone tapped me on the shoulder. I wheeled around, fists raised.

Tito Martinez threw up his hands. "Friend, not foe!" he said, his cheeks puffing out in that blustery way he had. He lowered his arms and pulled on the tie string of his hoodie. "Hiya, Jake," he said, then addressed me. "You look ticked off to the max, Jenna."

"I'm irked alright."

"Why?"

"Cinnamon knows something and won't share."

"Well, I've got a scoop." Tito leaned in. "Sarita Strachline was seen loitering around the Velvet Box on Tuesday."

"Loitering?" Jake echoed.

"Yep." Tito bobbed his head.

I said, "That's the jewelry store across the street from Intime." The shop, which was next to Crystal Cove Bank, across the street from Intime, was filled with beautifully designed pieces made with gemstones and gold. I'd never been in but had window-shopped.

"My source, who shall remain anonymous," Tito went on, "said Sarita looked like she was casing the joint, but when asked, she said she was there to water the plants, claiming the owner was a friend."

A theory swirled in my mind. "What if she wasn't casing the jewelry store but, instead, scoping out Intime, trying to figure out when to plant the bomb? Do the police know about this?"

"My source contacted them earlier today."

"So much for remaining anonymous," I quipped and wondered if that was what Cinnamon had been keeping from me. "Did the police question Sarita?" I asked, and blanched, realizing that if they hadn't, that ship had sailed, so to speak, because they wouldn't be able to any longer.

"They did. Actually, Officer Foster did. I couldn't corroborate Sarita's story because the owner, Ilya Bakov—"

"Is on a cruise to the Mexican Riviera," I cut in.

"How did you know?" Tito pressed the recording app on his cell phone.

"Because yesterday at the expo I overheard Sarita's ex-husband, Todd, berating her. He'd demanded to know if Ilya or Matias had given her a loan to get her on her feet. Sarita wouldn't tell. Todd said he'd find out, but Sarita taunted, 'Good luck with that,' adding that Ilya was on a cruise. She seemed quite pleased with herself."

Tito studied the crowd at the far end of the Pier. "Do you think Todd set off this bomb?"

"Maybe. Maybe not," I said. "Sarita had to have other enemies."

"How could she not?" Jake said snidely. "I heard she was a wicked, miserable woman."

Tito said, "Her daughters loved her."

"Miss Hart." Officer Foster drew near. "Could my partner and I take a tour of your house?"

I glanced past her at Cinnamon, who was standing with one of her subordinates but glowering at me. "Sure, Officer. I'm ready right now."

Jake and Tito remained on the Pier, and I went with the officers to my house. On the way, for a fleeting moment, I worried that by leaving my house, Sarita's killer might have slinked into it and planted evidence that would convict me, but I pushed the fear aside, convinced that Sarita was the only one who'd had it in for me and Rhett. Nobody else.

Foster and her partner spent the better part of an hour scouring every closet in the house for the makings of a bomb or a detonator. To assure them that I wouldn't meddle in their investigation, I sat at the dining room table petting Rook and Tigger.

I didn't budge until, a few minutes shy of midnight, my aunt rapped on the front door and opened it.

"Jenna, dear, what is—"

"Don't come in." I held up a hand to thwart her. I didn't want the officers to think she would tamper with anything. From a distance, I explained what was going on. Sarita dead. The bomb. Cinnamon questioning my involvement.

"Oh, my." Aunt Vera started worrying the strings of her blue jogging suit hood.

"Go home," I coaxed.

"No. I'm staying."

"Fine," I said, "but don't come in. Please stay on the porch."

When the officers were assured that I was innocent, they radioed Cinnamon and departed.

"I thought they'd never leave." My aunt rose from the rattan chair and shuffled inside. "Are you all right?" She took me in her arms and stroked my hair.

"I will be. If I can sleep."

"At my house."

"Here," I said firmly.

"Are you sure?"

I wasn't, but I couldn't live in fear. "I have Rook and Tigger. They'll alert me to trouble."

Upon hearing their names, the two scampered to my side and sat dutifully by my feet.

My aunt sniffed her disapproval of my decision, but she knew she'd lost the battle. "What did you learn on the Pier?"

I told her everything.

"Ilya is a lovely lady," my aunt said. "I can't imagine her being friends with Sarita."

"Maybe before Sarita turned to the dark side and torched her restaurant, she was a nice woman."

Aunt Vera shook her head. "Poisonous toadstools don't change their spots."

I knew the reference. My aunt and I had read the entire collection of *Harry Potter* books at the same time and had discussed them. This particular quote was when Ron was talking to Hermione about not trusting Snape.

Had Sarita always been a vile person? How many people had hated her enough to kill her?

Chapter 17

I awoke Friday morning with bags under my eyes. A warm compress helped. So did a swipe of caffeine-infused cream, which a saleswoman had assured me promoted circulation and reduced swelling. After walking Rook and dressing in a bright pink-and-white-striped dress and white sandals, I fed the pets, downed a scrambled-egg-and-cheese sandwich, and headed to Mercy Urgent Care. After last night's ordeal, I desperately needed to see Rhett.

Because the temperatures had cooled—the weatherman had been right on that front—Tigger didn't mind staying in the car. I left the window open a few inches, and he snoozed on the passenger-side floor.

Rhett was asleep when I stepped into the room. The nurse, a different one from yesterday with a much friendlier demeanor, said I could sit in the room. I did and watched the television, which was on mute. After an hour and Rhett still hadn't wakened, I kissed his cheek, asked the nurse to tell him I'd stopped by, and left.

When Tigger and I arrived at Fisherman's Village, Bride's Dream Expo attendees were out in force. Some were filing into the café. Others were sauntering into the shop, taking what looked like a raffle ticket from Gran.

I squeezed past them and placed Tigger on his kitty condo so he wouldn't get tromped on. I glimpsed Tina at the sales counter, which was unusual. She hadn't worked for us in ages.

"What's going on?" I asked Bailey. "And where's your daughter?"

"With my mom. She wanted some bonding time."

"And Tina? Why is she here?"

"Because we're expecting a lot of sales. Did you miss seeing all the customers on your way in?"

"I'm not blind. Why are they here?"

She grinned. "Look what arrived."

She held up a copy of *Wedding Planner Book and Organizer for Brides with Gift Box | Engagement Gift for Couples | Hardcover Bridal Planning Journal Notebook | Wild Flowers.* One of my favorite features in the book were the checklists for everything from the seating plan to guests lists and budget planning. The pink-and-moss gift box it came in was another plus.

"We only have twenty copies on hand," Bailey said. "I put the word out that we would have a lottery. So everyone is here to pick up a lottery ticket." She motioned to the jar where women were dropping off the mirror image of tickets Gran was handing out by the entrance.

"Of course" — Bailey polished her fingernails on her aqua blue blouse — "the winners will be announced in an hour, so everyone will stick around and shop until then. Hence, the need for Tina until noon. Great idea?"

I patted her shoulder. "Brilliant." When I'd worked at Taylor & Squibb, I was always concentrating on top-line growth — what would increase our clients' gross sales and revenues. Now, I paid attention to the bottom line. So did my pal. "Did you stop by the fire station yesterday and take a peek at the kittens?" I asked.

"I did. I'm really partial to Sparks and Spitfire. Both are ginger cats. I can't decide which one. Bucky said he'd hold on to both for me so I could bring Tito and Brianna."

"Sounds like a plan."

"Jenna." My aunt rose from the puzzle table, where she'd been giving a tarot card reading for a young woman. She collected the cards and slid them into the pocket of her burgundy caftan. "Our supplier came in earlier with two copies of *The Complete Cooking for Two Cookbook*. Gran said you ordered them for a pair of young women. I've set them by the register with a note that they're on hold."

"Perfect."

"How are you feeling after last night's nightmare, dear?"

"Right! My bad." Bailey grimaced. "How are you? I'm sorry I didn't lead with that. My darling husband didn't tell me about it until breakfast."

"I'm okay. Innocent."

"Good to know." Bailey swatted my arm.

"I went to see Rhett this morning, and he looked much better than he did yesterday, but he was asleep, so I didn't stay long."

"Tell me about what you gleaned last night," Bailey said. "On the Pier."

My aunt nudged me. "Not here. Let's go in the back. Gracie and Tina have this crowd under control."

"First"—I ticked a fingertip—"I need to speak to the police about getting access to Intime. Then I need to talk to the bistro's insurance agent so we can get an adjuster out and start the ball rolling to repair it."

My aunt petted my shoulder. "Do what you need to do. You have a lot on your plate."

A half hour later, after receiving the release from the police for Intime and scheduling an appointment with the adjuster recommended by Jim Daley, I beckoned my aunt and Bailey to follow me. We passed through the drapes into the storage room, and I launched into a recap of last night's events.

"While we're here," Aunt Vera said, "why don't the two of you unpack those three boxes of merchandise? One's books. I think the other contains aprons."

On a near daily basis, we received shipments of cookbooks, cookware, and more. We never wanted the shop's shelves to look bare.

Bailey fetched a box cutter and sliced through the tape on the topmost box. She set the box cutter on one of the shelves and started handing me spiral-bound copies of *5-Ingredient Cooking for Two: 100 Recipes Portioned for Pairs.* I appreciated that all the recipes were small-batch portions, tailored for couples. The fact that they were all five-ingredient recipes helped, too. Not every new bride or groom was a wiz in the kitchen.

"I can't believe Cinnamon considered you a suspect," Bailey said.

"She was simply doing her job." The stack of books was clumsy because of the bindings, so I placed it on one of the lower shelves. When organizing books, even in a storage room, I liked the bigger or awkwardly shaped ones at the bottom and the lighter ones, like paperbacks, at the top. It wasn't purely for visual purposes. I didn't want the metal storage shelves to topple.

"Do you think whoever killed Sarita set off the bomb at Intime, too?" Bailey asked.

"I'm not sure. Unless whoever killed her used a bomb because he or she knew Sarita had used one at Intime."

"That suggests insider knowledge."

"Perhaps. Plus, I've got to wonder who might have had it in for Rhett and possibly me, as well as Sarita?"

I told them about Sarita and Matias Lajoie's argument. "We have no connection to Matias, of course, other than Rhett and he have talked about fishing and such. There's certainly no bad blood between us."

Tigger sauntered into the storage room and hopped onto the desk. He meowed.

My aunt lifted him and petted his head. "Matias was in love with Sarita, once upon a time. Back when he was a chef."

Oho! I'd guessed right about them having been involved.

"He was a chef?" Bailey asked.

"Yes," Aunt Vera replied.

"Rhett said he couldn't make a roux to save his life and quit," I added, and regarded my aunt. "Tell us more. I figured you'd know about him and Sarita. You know everything about Crystal Cove. Can you share their history?"

"She broke his heart when she ended it with him."

"Why did she end it?"

"As for that, I'm not sure."

"Rhett mentioned Matias might have gotten involved with drugs—illegal marijuana—after his career as a chef didn't pan out."

"*Pan* out." Bailey snorted. "He was a chef. Ha-ha. Bad pun."

"Unintentional," I muttered, not feeling in the least glib.

"If Sarita found out about the drugs, and that's why she ended it," Bailey went on, "maybe Matias decided to blow her up. *Boom!*" She clapped her hands.

Tigger startled. So did I. *Boom* was not our favorite go-to word.

"After all these years?" My aunt set Tigger on the floor. He scampered out of the storage room to calmer territory.

"You're right," Bailey said. "That's a long time to hold a grudge."

"On the other hand, seeing her again at the expo could have triggered feelings," I suggested.

"*Triggered.*" Bailey echoed. "Ha!"

I blanched. "Again pun not intended. Promise." I eyed my aunt.

She was rubbing her phoenix amulet, something she did

whenever she felt an imbalance in the universe. "Her ex-husband, Todd, was very angry with Sarita when they divorced."

"What do you know about him?" I asked. "He seems nice. Is there any reason he might lash out at Rhett and me?"

"Maybe he ate a bad dinner at Intime," Bailey joked.

"Stop it. This is no laughing matter." I planted my fists on my hips.

She lowered her head, chagrined.

"And for your information, I don't think Intime has received a terrible review in all the time it's been open." I lifted the box cutter off the shelf and opened the carton holding a variety of aprons featuring a Fourth of July theme. We planned to display them next week, even though it was still June. One of my favorite designs was the American flag made with grilling tools laid out in red and white stripes abutting a blue square with white stars.

Bailey removed a few aprons from the box and shook each to eliminate creases. "Okay, so figuring Sarita was the one who triggered the bomb at Intime, and she wasn't involved in her own death, who else might want her dead?" She hung the group of aprons on the utility hooks beyond the shelves and reached in for more. "Didn't you tell me that Gunther Hildenbiddle, the guy who owns California Catch, has a history with her, Jenna?"

"He does," Aunt Vera said.

"What is it?" I asked.

"The Grotto was so successful that it put his first restaurant, Open Waters, out of business. They had very similar menus. As a result, his wife left him."

"She left him?" I cut the packing tape on the remaining box. "I got the feeling she'd died. He referred to her as the *love of his life.*"

"He loved her alright, until she up and left him." My aunt *tsked.* "She wasn't a money-grubber, but she did expect a certain lifestyle, and when he couldn't provide, she relocated to Florida."

"Do you like Gunther?" I asked.

"I do," my aunt said. "He can be a bit of a hothead, but what chef doesn't have a bit of a temper?"

Rhett, I thought, but kept mum.

"Gunther's new restaurant, California Catch, has wonderful ambiance," Aunt Vera went on.

"You've been?" I asked.

"Marlon has taken me a few times." She folded her hands in front of her. "It's very much like Open Waters, and it's quite a success, on par with the Pelican Brief."

"Being a success doesn't always remove a bad taste from one's mouth," Bailey said. "Losing a wife . . ." She spread her arms. "That's tough to forgive and forget."

My aunt agreed.

"Okay, so Gunther had motive to kill Sarita, but why would he bomb Intime?" I asked.

Bailey screwed up her mouth. "To eliminate the competition."

Aunt Vera shook her head. "No, I can't see it. He's a spiritual man."

"That's right. And"—I snapped my fingers—"he couldn't have blown up Sarita's boat because he's at a retreat until tomorrow. I doubt he could trigger a bomb from as far away as Pasatiempo. What about Wren Weatherly?" I asked. "She was a partner in Sarita's first restaurant."

"Oh, my." My aunt fanned the air. "The rumors that swirled around the animosity between those two are legendary. They were the best of friends, but after the arson at the Grotto and Wren's husband . . ." She didn't finish.

"Rhett said he committed suicide."

Bailey gasped. "That's so sad."

"Mm hm," my aunt murmured. "The financial loss crushed him. He felt so stupid not to have seen the signs. That's what his suicide note said. He'd had an MBA, after all. Wren was bereft, of course, and in a public setting, vowed she would hunt Sarita to the ends of the earth and make her pay for ruining her family."

"But that was years ago." I splayed my hands. "So I'll ask the same question I posed about Matias Lajoie. Why would Wren wait this long to kill Sarita?"

"For one, Sarita was in jail," Aunt Vera stated.

"How about prior to being incarcerated?" I asked.

"Sarita split town in the wink of an eye. None of us knew where she'd wound up until you started the ball rolling. Also . . ." My aunt tapped her chin with a fingertip. "Also I suppose Wren pushed vengeance aside because she needed to turn all her focus on raising her child. Darinda had required serious therapy after the loss of her father."

I said, "What if seeing Sarita anew stirred a deep well of anger?"

Chapter 18

Bailey dusted off her hands. "All this speculating is making me hungry. Want to get a snack, Jenna?"

"Let's check on Tina and Gran first. Then, yes, I could use a boost."

Tina and Gran said we were free to leave. They were thoroughly enjoying managing the lottery and customers. Bailey and I didn't wait for them to change their minds. We headed to the Nook Café, but when we arrived, we saw it was packed to the gills.

Unwilling to wait for a table and loathe to impose on Katie in the kitchen—she had to be working double-time to serve everyone—we opted to go to Taste of Heaven across the street.

A few months ago, Keller Landry's mother, Eleanor, had decided to retire and had asked her son to run the place. Keller had jumped at the chance. He and Katie were doing their best to sock away money for their daughter's college fund—she wasn't two yet; they had plenty of time—but even so, he had grown weary of his entrepreneurial, bicycle-pedaling ice cream business.

Bailey and I sauntered into the shop and hailed Keller.

"Hey, hey, Jenna and Bailey, welcome!" he shouted. His unruly hair was captured beneath his cap, and his white uniform was spotless.

Keller had only altered a few things in the place. The décor was still royal-blue-and-white-checkered floors and white counters, and the same arty canvases of ice cream cones and sundaes hung on the walls. However, the music was no longer classic rock and roll tunes; it was bubblegum pop. And the little red coupe that had stood on the counter—for years Keller's mother had hinted that she'd had an affair with one of the Beach Boys—was no longer there. Change, Eleanor had confided the last time she'd come into the Cookbook Nook, was inevitable. She hadn't seemed miffed, simply resigned.

Keller could be quite a chatterbox. Given the chance, he would talk a customer's ear off, as he was doing to Todd Strachline, who was at the head of the line, paying for three cups of ice cream. I didn't see his daughters at any of the tables. I supposed they could be waiting for him outside or in a nearby shop.

Todd seemed quite genial chatting with Keller. Didn't he have a clue about what had gone down last night? Hadn't he heard about the explosion? Hadn't he listened to the morning news? He paid Keller and offered a parting remark.

"You bet I will, Todd," Keller said, offering a wave goodbye.

Todd pivoted without making eye contact with anyone and proceeded out of the shop.

When Bailey and I arrived at the front of the line, I said, "Keller, you seemed pretty chummy with Todd. What can you tell me about him?"

"He's the accountant for this place."

Who wasn't Todd the accountant for, other than us? I wondered.

"He's a nice guy. Mom trusts him. So do I. He sure loves that truck of his."

"What truck?" I asked.

"The silver Ford Ranger parked in front. The four-door with the extra-wide wheels."

I spied the truck on the street. Sunlight was gleaming off the metal.

"He buffs that beauty every day," Keller added.

"That's a lot of buffing."

"Yup. He was telling me I should buy one so I could join him at some rallies."

"Rallies?" I tilted my head.

"Yeah, he goes to truck rallies to check out all the gear. When he was a teenager, he wanted to race. Now, not so much, but he was telling me that he wants to drive the most treacherous road in the world someday. It's in Turkey, and, like, there are so many switchbacks, it's ridiculous." Keller hooted and slapped the counter. "Doesn't it sound like fun?"

It sounded crazy, I mused. *Switchbacks? In a truck? Not in my lifetime.* "Don't let Katie hear you talking this way."

"Heh-heh. As if."

Katie used to be a daredevil. She'd been passionate about jet skiing, but ever since she'd adopted Min-yi, she'd grown conservative. She drove under the speed limit and expected her husband to do the same.

"What can I get you two?" Keller asked.

I ordered a peach smoothie for me and a caramel sundae for

Bailey. It wasn't even close to lunchtime, but the two of us believed ice cream was good any hour of the day.

Keller put the fixings for my smoothie into a blender and pressed *whirr*, and then dished up Bailey's sundae.

On our way out of the shop, I saw Todd in his Ford Ranger. He was rolling down the windows. A single cup of ice cream rested on the dashboard, leading me to believe he'd found his daughters and had handed off the other two.

Bailey said, "He doesn't look like he's heard the news."

"He sure doesn't."

"Think we should tell him?"

I balked. "Us? No. I wonder why Cinnamon hasn't touched base with him yet."

"Maybe she has. She might not consider him a suspect. That could be why he looks so relaxed."

"Or she's up to her eyeballs questioning others." Already I could imagine her advising me, *Cool your heels, Jenna. Investigations take time.*

Bailey prodded me. "Go talk to him."

"Me, why me?"

"Because you're better at it than I am. Plus, you were there last night." She grabbed my drink and gave me a shove. "Go!"

I stumbled off the sidewalk directly in front of the truck. "You!" I snarled at my pal over my shoulder.

A *beep* from the truck startled me. Todd was staring at me through the windshield, his mouth agape.

"Oh, sorry," I said, and pretending I'd only now realized who he was, exclaimed, "Oh, it's you!"

Todd hopped out of the driver's seat and hurried to me. He clasped my arm and guided me to the sidewalk. "Jenna, you're lucky I hadn't put the truck in gear. I would've run into you."

"I'm sure glad you didn't," I said, meaning it. Bailey hadn't thought that shove thing through. "I suppose you heard about your ex-wife. I'm so sorry."

"Sorry for what? What did I miss? What happened?" His forehead creased.

"There was an explosion."

He gasped. "An explosion? What kind of explosion?"

"Last night. Her sailboat blew up. By the Pier."

"Blew up? What? I can't believe—" His voice cracked. "I didn't hear an explosion, and I was home with my girls."

"You didn't hear it?" I figured everyone in Crystal Cove had heard the *boom*.

"I suppose I would have had I not been wearing headphones to drown out the girls' video game madness. They were upstairs interacting with their girlfriends. What is it with kids and video games?"

I shook my head, commiserating. "You should touch base with the police."

"Why?"

My mouth went dry. As much as I'd wanted to share the news, suddenly I couldn't. If only I'd walked on by. "S-Sarita," I stammered.

"Is she okay?" he asked. "We're not close, but if she needs me to help her find a place to stay—"

"Todd, she was on the boat. She's dead."

"Dead! Oh, no!" He whipped his head to the right and groaned when he caught sight of his daughters heading our way. He motioned for them to halt, but they continued toward us, ice cream cups in hand, each with a shopping bag from Swim and Fins looped over an arm.

"Shay, Sela, get in the truck," he ordered. He whipped open the rear passenger door.

"What's wrong, Dad?" Shay squealed.

"Just do it, Shay! We're going home. Get in. You, too, Sela. On the double."

"Don't yell at us," Shay snapped, while hoisting herself inside and over the cup holder dividing the seat.

Her sister followed, crinkling her nose, loathe to put her feet on the dirty wet clothes that were lying in a heap on the floor.

Todd caught me staring into his truck and jutted a hand at the heap. "Radiator burst last night. On my way home from the pizza place. Got caught in the rainstorm. What a mess I was. Soaked through. Glad I had an old racing jumpsuit and tennis shoes to slip into. I was even gladder when Eddie Milsap came along with some radiator weld. What a savior he was. I was able to patch the thing and get home without it ex—" He went pale, realizing he was about to say *without it exploding*. "I didn't mean . . . I'm not heartless . . . It's just such a shock."

"What is, Dad?" Sela asked.

Todd glanced at his daughters and back at me. "What do I tell them?"

I offered a sympathetic sigh. "The truth."

Chapter 19

Summers were always busy in Crystal Cove, but this year's Bride's Dream Expo had really brought out the crowds. At the shop, Bailey, Gran, my aunt, and I—Tina left after she and Gran had announced the lottery winners—worked nonstop.

Luckily around noon, Katie brought in a sample tray of wedding appetizers for us to savor. Brie bites on crackers, topped with a variety of jams. Filet of beef with mushrooms *en croute*. Mini lobster or whitefish panini sandwiches.

I'd just popped a fennel-marinated feta-and-olive kebab, sans skewer, into my mouth when my father strode into the shop looking quite serious and official, his white shirt tucked neatly into his chinos, arms by his side.

"Daughter," he said.

"Father," I replied, which came out sounding more like *fodder*. I swallowed the rest of the appetizer. "Why so grim? Do you have news for me?" I looped my hand around his elbow and steered him toward the kitty condo. "Did you talk to your guy at the FBI?"

"I did, and I'm sad to say he has no information about your bomber. As you'd surmised, the materials used for the bomb at Intime are typical homemade bomb items. Ball bearings, nails, and even the odors you detected aren't a particular bomber's signature."

I groaned. "Anyone could have made it."

He nodded. "I'm sorry I don't have better news. I was glad to hear that Cinnamon didn't consider you a suspect in last night's explosion."

"Word travels fast."

He pecked my cheek. "Rhett's doing better I hear, as well. I'll stop in on him soon."

"Thanks for trying, Dad. And thanks for sending him flowers."

"Anything for my girl." He gave me a squeeze and left.

Around two, anticipating flashbacks, I unlocked the front door of Intime and tried to breathe normally. Before heading over there, I'd quickly run home and changed into clothes I didn't mind getting dirty—skinny jeans and a *Crystal Cove* sunrise-themed T-shirt. I'd also switched into canvas tennis shoes to protect my feet from loose debris. When I'd spoken to our insurance agent, he'd told me that the adjuster needed to see the site as it had been after the explosion with none of the mess cleaned up. There was a smattering of rubble by the hostess's stand. I didn't move beyond it. I couldn't.

When the adjuster, a sandy-haired man named Parker, arrived, I allowed him to enter the kitchen first. He stepped gingerly around the debris and pots and pans while making notes on a chart attached to a clipboard. The dinner Rhett and I had been making was on the floor and had coagulated. The flour that had billowed after the explosion had settled onto the floor, as well, and was now a hardened paste because of the water that had spewed from the broken faucet.

Seeing the chaos stirred memories of that night for me. The sound of the explosion. The smell. Rhett on the floor. The EMTs rushing him into their vehicle. I shivered and wrapped my arms around myself.

"Are you okay, Miss Hart?" Parker asked.

"Yes," I lied. I'd dreamed of the explosion each night. When would the nightmares stop?

"This looks like quite a project," he said, jotting more notes. "You'll need to get a couple of contractors' estimates, I imagine. Paint. Plaster. Flooring. Plus replacing the equipment."

In between notes, Parker snapped photographs of the area with his digital camera. He crouched to get close-ups. He stood back to get the wide-angle view.

"I'll need to pay the staff in order to keep them," I added. "Does our policy cover that?"

"I'm afraid not."

I groaned, worried about what that might mean for Rhett and me going forward. He'd recently hired a second executive chef so he could spend more time with me. I wouldn't be selfish. If he needed to go back full-time until he found new hires, so be it. I was just thankful that he was alive.

Parker and I surveyed the scene for a half hour more, and then he left, promising he'd send a report ASAP, and I returned to the shop.

When I arrived, I found Cinnamon sitting at the puzzle table searching for edge pieces, all of which were solid dark blue. She rose and left her hat on the chair. She hated wearing it but carried it with her.

"Why are you here?" I asked, a nervous twitch starting in my cheek. "Not to arrest me."

"I placed a to-go order at the café. Katie told me to wait here." She slipped her hands into her trouser pockets. "How's Rhett?"

"Better, but not out of the woods."

"And you?"

"I'm glad your officers didn't find anything at my place last night that would implicate me."

"Me, too, if I'm honest." She smiled supportively.

"How long were you at the crime scene last night?"

"Until well after four a.m."

"You must be beat."

"I'll manage."

"Say" — I beckoned her to follow me to the rear of the store, where there were no customers — "have you talked to Todd Strachline yet?"

"Why do you ask?"

"I ran into him and his daughters outside Taste of Heaven this morning, and he had no clue Sarita was dead."

"We spoke to him an hour ago. He came in."

"And . . ."

Her gaze flickered with impatience. "As you know, Jenna, it takes time to conduct an investigation."

I tamped down a smile, having anticipated what she would say. "Do you think he blew up his ex-wife and her boat?"

"He has an alibi."

"Right. He was at home with his daughters, but they were playing video games, and might not have — "

"How do you know where his daughters were?" She narrowed her gaze. "Tell me you didn't question him."

I folded my arms defensively. "I learned it in the course of normal conversation. I did not ask."

"Good. Because this is not your bailiwick, got me?" She twirled a finger in front of my nose.

"Got you." I flicked her finger away. "I know how much it bugs you if I figure out who committed a murder before you do."

"It doesn't bug me. It . . ." She scowled, but then her face softened.

"It worries me that you get involved. I'm your friend. I care about you. I don't want you to get hurt and miss your wedding."

"I won't. Did you question Matias Lajoie?"

"Jenna."

"Or Wren Weatherly? She was Sarita's business partner with an axe to grind."

Cinnamon forced a smile. "How are the preparations going for the wedding?"

"Swell." To be honest, I'd barely thought about any of it in light of recent events. I hoped Harmony was following through with her to-do list. Mine wasn't as long. Meet with the florist one more time. Do another taste testing with Katie, which would definitely include all the appetizers she'd prepared today. Have a final fitting for my dress. Go to the jeweler's to check on—

"Jewelers!" I blurted. My sharp tone must have frightened Tigger. He bolted off the kitty condo and galloped to me, his tail flicking nervously. I bent to scratch his neck.

"Don't tell me you forgot wedding rings." Cinnamon clapped a hand to her chest in mock horror. "That was the first thing Bucky and I did. It takes time."

"No." I stood back up. "We have our rings selected, but I thought of something that Tito said last night."

"Not about Sarita's murder?"

"No, it pertains to my case . . ." I revised. "*Rhett's* case. The explosion at Intime."

"It's your case, too. You were a victim. Go on."

"A source told Tito that she saw . . . I suppose the source could be a *he*. Tito didn't say. Anyway"—I flapped a hand—"the source saw Sarita Strachline loitering outside the Velvet Box on Tuesday. The jewelry store is across the street from Intime."

"I know the place."

"When the source asked Sarita what she was doing, she said she'd stopped by to water the plants for Ilya Bakov, claiming Ilya was a friend, but Ilya couldn't corroborate—"

"Because she's out of town. We know, Jenna. Tito's source spoke to Officer Foster, too."

"What if Sarita lied?" I asked. "What if she was really scoping out Intime at the time?"

"Look"—Cinnamon placed a hand on my shoulder—"don't think about this. I'm on top of things."

"I didn't say you weren't."

"Concentrate on your wedding. It's only a few weeks away. And focus on Rhett. Make sure he's one hundred percent healthy when he says 'I do.'"

"Did Ilya Bakov lend Sarita the money?" I asked.

"What money?" Cinnamon removed her hand.

"Enough cash to rent a sailboat and pay for the mooring. That doesn't come cheap. Sarita couldn't have saved enough in jail. Prisoners make less than five dollars a day."

"How do you know—"

Katie appeared through the breezeway with a to-go box for Cinnamon. The aroma was divine, a savory mixture of cheese and rosemary. "Here you go." She handed it to her.

Cinnamon pulled a wallet from her pocket. "How much do I owe you?"

"It's on the house." Katie winked at me and strode back through the breezeway.

Without skipping a beat, I resumed theorizing. "Sarita was in for five years. She couldn't have earned more than twelve thousand dollars." Numbers and figures had always come easily to me. "The insurance company demanded she give back the money she'd recouped for the loss of the restaurant, but she'd spent a lot of it. To make herself whole with the insurance company, she'd had to cash out all of the art that she'd stolen. Therefore, she was broke and going to jail.

"Where did Sarita get enough money to rent the boat?" I continued, patting my thigh trying to keep up with the thoughts whizzing inside my head. "At the expo, she told her ex-husband she'd gotten a loan, and he asked if Ilya or Matias had given it to her."

"Jenna—"

"I doubt a bank would lend to someone who'd torched her business and had no job and no assets to secure the loan. Todd got the house in the divorce."

"Enough."

"I guess Sarita could have lied about getting a loan to cover up some other illegal activity or . . . Hey!" I aimed a finger at Cinnamon. "What if she didn't spend all the insurance money? What if she stowed it somewhere?"

She exhaled exasperatedly through her nose. "You have a suspicious mind."

"Don't you?" I smirked.

"Yes, and it's my job to have one." She poked my chest with her finger. "Not yours."

Chapter 20

After touching base with Lola and getting her on board to host our out-of-towners' dinner as well as coaxing her to agree to hire at least one of Intime's sous chefs on a temporary basis, I spent an hour sprucing up the shelves in the shop. Customers had made a mess of the books. Many spines were upside down. The books that were supposed to be standing upright on the main displays were prone. In addition, aprons were twisted, and the fronts of cookie jars were facing the walls. I didn't mind the tedium of the job. It calmed me.

"Jenna." My aunt beckoned me to the sales counter and jiggled the telephone receiver. "Eddie Milsap from Bait and Switch is on the line about the windsurfing equipment."

I took the phone from her. "Hi, Eddie, it's Jenna."

"How're you doing, Jenna?" Eddie had been the assistant manager at the sports store for over two years. "I went to visit Rhett earlier. He looked pretty good for someone who'd lived through a blast."

With a loan from his folks, Eddie had been able to buy half of the business and had negotiated to take on all aspects so Rhett could be a silent partner. Eddie was a real people-person. He loved talking about sports and fishing. To everyone. He'd even discuss the weather, if that was the prevailing topic. "An Airush Freewing became available," he said. "A buyer backed out of the sale. Interested?"

"You bet I am."

"Can you come in today? Another customer is keen on buying it. But I promised you first dibs."

I eyed my aunt. "Will you cover if I go to the Pier to close the windsurfing deal?"

"Of course. I have two readings in a bit, but Gracie and Bailey are here, and the mad rush of this morning has died down."

I told Eddie I'd be right over and ended the call, then turned to my aunt. "Is Jake one of your readings?"

"No. Two regulars."

I wondered why he wasn't following through, but put it from my mind. Not my concern.

Aunt Vera whispered, "Is everything all right between you and Cinnamon, dear?"

"Yes. Same old, same old. She wants me to keep my nose out of her affairs, but how can I when my fiancé is in the hospital having been nearly blown to bits?"

My aunt hugged me.

"The one suspect I thought detonated the bomb at Intime is dead," I said, and revised. "Yes, she might have done it, but what if she didn't? That means whoever tried to hurt Rhett" — it still felt odd adding myself into the equation — "might be at large."

"Be careful. Please."

A short while later, I strolled into Bait and Switch Fishing Supply and Sport Store and felt instantly at home, even though the place was as gigantic as a warehouse and buzzing with activity. At least a dozen customers were exploring the variety of fishing poles, horseback riding equipment, surfing items, clothing, and more.

"Jenna." Eddie approached me, hands extended. When I'd first met him, he'd reminded me of a Hobbit with his curly hair, rosy cheeks, and engaging smile. He gave me a warm shake. "So glad you could make it on short notice."

"I can't believe the Airush became available."

"My father always says, 'When you want something badly enough, throw out a lure and hope for a miracle.'" His father was a minister and avid fisherman. His mother owned a horse farm at the edge of town. "I love making dreams come true. Follow me." He guided me to the sales counter, where we drew up the contract. "It might be hard for you to carry the board home in one of our totes." He chuckled at his own wit. "How do you want me to deliver it?"

"Could you store it for him? Do you have space?"

"Absolutely."

"Can you figure the storage fee into the price?"

"We can make it an automatic debit charge monthly. All right with you?"

"Sure."

"Say, did you hear about the explosion off the pier last night?" Eddie gave me a pen and a form for the auto-debit approval. While I filled it out, he keyed the transaction into the sales register and asked me to insert my credit card into the card reader.

"I saw it." I paused and rephrased. "No, I didn't actually see it. I heard it and came over."

"Pretty sick, right?" Eddie pulled on his ear. "What're the odds of two bombs going off in one week? Do you think the same person set both of them?"

"I'm not sure. The police are investigating."

His gaze drilled into mine. "How are you managing?"

"I'm okay. Shaken. But now that Rhett is out of the woods, I'm much better. What's the scuttlebutt around here about the incident?" I asked. The Pier, with its many shops and restaurants, was like its own little town. There was definitely a rumor mill.

"A female carny worker named Carla—"

"I know her. Cotton candy–pink hair, toothy grin."

"That's her. She saw someone standing by the third piling, the one that abuts the water, as if the person had been watching the explosion. And a fisherman, I'm not sure which one, claimed he saw a guy crawling out of the water." Eddie aimed a finger at me. "You know, Matias Lajoie was in this morning and mentioned he saw someone crawling out of the water, too."

Was Matias the killer, I wondered, offering an eyewitness account to corroborate his own whereabouts?

"Did any of them talk to the police?" I asked.

Eddie rubbed his chin. "Beats me. Want a gift receipt that you can wrap?"

"That would be excellent."

He clicked a button on his computer screen. A nearby printer started to whirr. "Hey, did you hear the joke about the minister and the sheep?"

I shook my head. Eddie's father shared a joke in each of his sermons.

"A shepherd lost his favorite Bible while he was out looking for one of his sheep. Three weeks later, a little lamb walks up to him carrying the book. The shepherd can't believe it. He takes the book from the lamb's mouth, looks to the heavens, and cries, 'It's a miracle.' The lamb says, 'Uh, not really. Your name is written inside the cover.'" Eddie howled with glee.

"Very cute."

"Come to church and you'll hear a slew of them. This Sunday

Dad's talking about how good deeds open the gates of heaven."

"Speaking of good deeds, I heard you were a knight in shining armor last night. Since when do you carry radiator weld in your car?"

"Ha! You must've run into Todd. Yeah, his truck went kaput when he was on his way home from the pizza parlor. I might have missed him on the side of the road if lightning hadn't lit up the sky." Eddie wagged his head. "There he was, soaked to the bone, trying to fix the danged thing. Gotta help a fellow Crystal Covian in distress, right?"

"Your father would be proud of you."

"Faith is all about good works." Eddie pulled the receipt from the printer, tucked it into a Bait and Switch envelope, and offered it to me.

I slid it into my purse. "How did you know about radiator weld? I'd never heard of it."

"Yeah, about that . . ." Eddie scratched his ear. "My radiator went kablooie last March when I was thirty miles from anywhere. The knight who helped *me* out had some on hand." He gestured to a new customer entering. "Gotta go. Be well."

On my way out of the store, I heard a woman call my name. Z.Z. was walking arm in arm with Jake. Both were in shorts and T-shirts. Their faces had been gently kissed by the sun.

"Hi, you two!" Typically I would chime *Sunblock*, but I kept my opinion to myself.

Z.Z. said, "Jake was showing me where the boat exploded. Horrible. Just horrible. He said you were here."

"Not at the time it blew," I countered.

"No, I wasn't implying . . ." Z.Z. sputtered. "I know you weren't. You wouldn't. Couldn't."

Jake said, "Word is the police didn't find a detonator or any bomb stuff at your place."

"No, they didn't." I brushed his arm fondly. "Thank you for corroborating my whereabouts."

"Always happy to be at your service, ma'am." He gave a modest salute.

"Have you two set a date for your wedding?" I asked.

Z.Z. beamed. "Not yet. We'll get to it. We have all the time in the world."

She squeezed Jake's hand, and he winced, making me wonder again whether he might be regretting having said yes.

My cell phone rang. I pulled it from my purse. Harmony was on the line. "I've got to answer this."

Z.Z. blew me a kiss, and she and Jake meandered away.

I stabbed Accept.

"Jenna, mini snafu," Harmony launched in without a hello. "The florist says her supplier for moss has gone bankrupt. She can't find another."

"But moss is supposed to be the primary source of soft green for the wedding palette."

"Don't fret. We can substitute ferns that are the same color. There are some lovely ones, and they'll add terrific texture."

I sighed. "Whatever you think is best. I trust you."

"How about we meet at the expo tomorrow morning to take a gander at other floral ideas?"

"Isn't it too late for that?"

Harmony *pshawed*. "It's never too late to change the whole darned thing. Not when you have me, Wedding Planner Extraordinaire."

"Ha-ha." I laughed. "Is your ego inflated because you made some Bridezilla very happy today?"

"Yup. I got her the venue of her dreams!" She told me to meet her at nine a.m. and ended the call with a cackle.

In the ensuing silence, I released the breath I'd been holding. Was this *mini* snafu yet another sign that Rhett and I should wait to get married?

Chapter 21

Without moving from my spot on the Pier, I dialed Cinnamon's cell phone to tell her about the carny woman named Carla. Possibly she'd already heard about her, but if she hadn't . . .

She didn't answer. I phoned the precinct. The clerk who took the call said Cinnamon was in the field following up on a break-in. I declined to leave a message.

Instead, I walked down the steps to the sand and strode to the third piling on the left side of the Pier. The area wasn't cordoned off by police tape and didn't look like the police had searched it at all. Footprints and shoeprints were everywhere. I saw rocks, bits of tar, and seaweed. There were discarded cigarette butts and candy wrappers, too, which made me grumble. I hated people who trashed nature. I stared harder at the area, not sure what I was looking for. Did I honestly expect the killer to have left a calling card?

Giving up, I texted Cinnamon about the carny woman's sighting—she'd have to follow up—and I hurried to Mercy Urgent Care, eager to see Rhett. The staff were in as much as a rush as I was. Doctors and nurses swept past me, a few nodding hellos, most studying their cell phones. I stepped into Rhett's room. He was sitting up in bed. The television was on mute. A news channel was providing a weather update. The crawl feed read *Sunny skies*. So why did I feel so gloomy?

"I want to get out of here," Rhett said after I kissed him. "I'm cranky."

"And I want you to get out of here. What does your doctor say?"

"Maybe tomorrow. That's Saturday." The tension in his voice was unmistakable. "Or Sunday, that's the day after Saturday."

"At least you know the days of the week," I joked.

"I'm one hundred percent A-OK. Ask me anything."

"What's two hundred and twenty-two times forty-three?" I checked my watch. "Ten seconds. Nine. Eight . . ."

"Not fair."

I squeezed his shoulder affectionately. "Be patient because patience is what you'll need going forward, considering the damage at Intime." I filled him in on the meeting with the adjuster. "I'll reach out to contractors next."

"Leave that to me."

"As for employees, their salaries aren't covered in the policy, as I'd expected."

He moaned.

"Lola has agreed to take on at least one of the sous chefs, and I could hire your executive chef, if he's willing." The moment I made the offer, I regretted it. These were decisions Aunt Vera, as the principal owner of the Nook Café, should handle. Katie should have a say in it, as well.

"I'll have a chat with him," Rhett said. "But I'm warning you, he doesn't like to share the limelight."

"What chef does?" I joshed. "There's one more thing. A little snafu. With the wedding."

"Don't tell me. The DJ wants double the asking price."

"Wrong. The florist for the wedding can't get the soft green moss."

Melodramatically Rhett pressed a hand to his heart. "Say it ain't so."

"Don't joke. Our palette was something you and I agreed on at the very start."

"So"—he opened his hands—"find something else that's soft green. We can adapt. It's not a game changer."

"I know, but is it one more sign that we shouldn't be getting married right now? I mean"—I couldn't keep the angst out of my voice—"perhaps we ought to postpone after all."

"Are you changing your mind altogether?" He raised an eyebrow.

"No. I can't wait to be your wife."

"Then stop saying we should put it off!" He was adamant. "I love you. I want to be married to you. C'mon, be flexible. This is both of our second marriages. We're not silly, heads-in-the-clouds kids. Snags are snags, not omens." He groaned in an eerie ghostlike way.

Lovingly, he slung his arm around my waist and pulled me closer. The bedrail came between us, but we managed a healthy kiss. When my back could no longer take the awkward position, I wriggled free, pecked him on the cheek, and told him to get a good sleep, adding that I'd spring him from hospital jail as soon as I could.

On the way back to the shop, I decided to make a quick run into Crystal Cove Florists. Before meeting Harmony tomorrow morning, I wanted to get a jump on looking at soft-green-colored plants.

As I was parking near the shop, I saw Wren Weatherly supervising the unloading of a truck parked in the alley beyond Home Décor. What I also noticed was Flora Fairchild lurking out of sight on the opposite side of the building. What was she up to? Retail espionage?

I weaved around a knot of people studying a poster for the Fire Sale Kitten Adoptions and entered Home Décor. It was not at all cozy like Home Sweet Home. Z.Z. had been right about the overall upscale feeling of the place. The walls were painted soft grays and blues. The wood shelving was dark and rich. Artful placement of gold and silver wall hangings were in abundance. Niches were fully furnished, each with a different flair. One recess to the left of the entrance that caught my eye had been outfitted with a huge piece of blue-and-gray modern art as well as a pair of white chairs with silver chrome frames, a chrome-and-glass table, chrome lamps, and the fluffiest white throw rug I'd ever seen.

"Help you?" Wren shuffled into the shop with her head down, occupied with dusting off her trousers. When she looked up, she startled. "Oh, Jenna, it's you. How lovely to see you. Sorry for my appearance. I just got a new shipment. The packaging can be quite filthy." She gestured with her hand. "This set you're admiring is one of my favorites. Perfect for a sitting room and quite reasonably priced. I have a great supply chain that helps me keep costs low. We all appreciate a bargain, right?"

"Absolutely." I thought of what Flora had said the other day about Wren being short of funds. If she was, how was she purchasing her costly inventory? On extended credit?

"Are you hoping to spruce up your house before your wedding?" she asked.

"No. I'm window-shopping today. Rhett and I redid our house a year ago. But this is really lovely. You have exquisite taste."

"Darinda!" Wren motioned to her daughter, who was chatting to a man by a denlike setting of leather chairs and brass lamps fitted with oilcloth shades. "Look who's here." Wren whispered to me, "That's the dentist. Don't they make a sweet couple?"

I bit back a smile. Would she always introduce him as the dentist? Would she ever use his name? He was reed-thin with a narrow jaw. Darinda did look madly in love with him and he with her as he stroked her hand with his index finger.

I spied Flora sauntering on the sidewalk by the plate glass window.

Wren saw her, too, and chuckled. "Oh, that Flora. She can't seem to help herself. She passes by at least once a week. We're not competitors in the least. My inventory is so much different than hers."

"You carry much more furniture," I said.

"And no trinkets or collectibles, but still she peeks in. Between you and me, I've often sent customers to her shop, especially if they want those homemade items she carries. Quilts and ornaments and such. And she has a wondrous array of baby gifts."

"That's nice of you to do. I have to say this business is so much different than what you were doing before, being a partner in a restaurant."

A pained look crossed her face. "I was never a partner."

"I heard you and your husband—"

"We invested. We provided seed money. We were never consulted on anything. Sarita . . ." Wren sighed. "No. I shouldn't speak ill of the dead. Shouldn't. Shouldn't." She blinked repeatedly as if transfixed. After a long moment, she made eye contact with me again and, with a forced smile, gestured to the shop. "Have a look around. If you need anything, let me know."

That was interesting. It was as if she'd forgotten I was there for a moment, her hatred of Sarita so acute. I moseyed to a collection of colorful ottomans and poufs thinking Rhett might appreciate one by his reading chair. Yes, I'd recently invested in sporting equipment for him, but I could afford an ottoman. As I studied the price tag for an ocean-themed pouf, I heard Darinda talking sotto voce with the dentist.

"It's too much," she said.

"I'll help out," he offered.

"No, mother wants to do it all. She's hoping . . ." The rest faded away. " . . . the expo prize. Wouldn't that be something? We could afford . . . If only that shrew hadn't . . ." She caught me craning an ear and steered her fiancé away.

I decided to pass on the pouf and headed for the exit and hailed Wren as I left. "Thank you. I'll be back for sure."

As I exited, Flora scooted up to me. I offered a wry grin. "I think you can stop spying, Flora. Your two shops are nothing alike."

"Did you see her offloading that truck?" she asked conspiratorially.

"Yes."

"What if it's stolen goods? What if she hasn't spent a penny on anything in her shop?"

"Oh, Flora, you need to stop reading suspense novels. They're filling your mind with conspiracy theories."

"You're one to talk You're always sticking your nose into murders."

"I do not."

"Not intentionally." She elbowed me fondly, and I realized she was teasing.

Back at the shop, the *Open* sign had been flipped over to *Closed*, and the lights were dim. Bailey was setting out items for the children's morning workshop. Tigger was happily snoozing at the top of his kitty condo. And my aunt was wrapping up what appeared to have been a rapturous tarot reading. Her customer, a woman in her thirties with a blunt haircut and huge brown eyes, was gushing about how the reading had made her day. No, her month. No, her year!

I tossed my purse by the register and moseyed to Bailey. "Gran left already?"

"She promised to take her granddaughters out for pizza. How's Rhett doing?"

"He feels like he's in jail."

"Ergo, cranky."

I aimed a finger at her. "You nailed it. Where's Brianna?"

"My mother wants more bonding time and asked if she could keep her overnight." Gleefully, Bailey drummed her fingertips together. Other than having Tina help out as a nanny and Lola lend a hand on occasion, she didn't have any other babysitters. "Of course, Tito is working overtime, covering the theft at the expo as well as last night's explosion, so I'm single tonight. Want to do something? Shake out all that tension? Grab a glass of pinot upstairs?"

"Hi, you two." Katie strode into the shop carrying a tray of what smelled like spinach quiche. The aroma of nutmeg was intoxicating.

"What are you doing here at this hour?" I asked.

About a month ago, she'd decided to oversee the morning and lunch shifts and had ceded the evening shift to Reynaldo, the head chef. It dawned on me that he might be the one I'd have to appease if I brought on Rhett's executive chef temporarily.

"I'm working on your wedding appetizers," Katie answered. "I won't let up until I get it right." She held the platter out to me. "Hungry?"

"Starved." I took a mini quiche and popped it into my mouth. "Heaven. What you can do with a crust astounds me."

"It's all about kneading in the right amount of butter." She set the appetizers on the sales counter. "You two look conspiratorial. What's up?"

"We're both single tonight, and we're thinking of having a glass of wine upstairs."

"Count me in! Keller's doing a Daddy and Me class with Min-yi." She hurried down the breezeway, calling over her shoulder, "Meet you there in ten."

Vines Wine Bistro was the perfect place for those who wanted a nice glass of wine and quiet conversation. The handcrafted tables were set to seat four patrons or fewer. Only a few stools stood beneath the curved bar. Classical music—Chopin, I was pretty sure—was playing softly through a speaker system. Strings of tiny white lights were the only decoration. The owner, Charley, a willowy woman in a *Lord of the Rings* elfin kind of way, had taken over the bistro when the last owner was sent to jail. Charley had kept it exactly the way it was.

"Bailey, Jenna, so nice to see you," Charley said as she approached us. "Table for two?"

"Three," Katie said, trailing us and holding up three fingers. "Girls night! At least for an hour."

Charley grinned. "Sounds good. This way." She seated us in a quiet nook, far from the bar. "Now, ladies, no hooting or hollering."

I laughed. "We'll keep the noise level down to a minimum." I glanced at my friends. "Pinot for everyone?"

They nodded.

"Bring us a bottle of the Dundee Hills pinot, please," I said. "It's one of Rhett's favorites."

A moment later, Charley returned with an uncorked bottle and three wineglasses. She poured a swallow into mine and let me do the honors.

"Delicious."

As she departed to tend to other customers, I filled our glasses halfway.

Bailey raised hers in a toast. "To Rhett. To his health. To your future together."

"Amen," Katie said. "And to great food and friendship and . . ." She made a face.

"What?" I asked, curious what had sparked the pained expression.

She snorted. "May your wedding weekend be nothing like my college girlfriend's fiasco. Have I ever told you the story?"

"No," Bailey and I chimed in unison.

"So . . ." Katie took a sip of wine and set it aside. "We were all invited to Austin, Texas, and we had reservations at a super nice hotel, but then the bride, my girlfriend, said she'd rather we all stay at this Airbnb so we could party the whole weekend."

"Sounds fun." I exchanged a look with Bailey, who concurred.

"Yeah, not if none of the guys know each other." Katie rolled her eyes.

We all laughed.

"There we were, twelve of us," Katie continued, "all stuck in the same place, and get this, there were only three bedrooms and an open loft. You do the math."

"Gack." I pulled a face.

"Of course, my girlfriend and her fiancé got the master bedroom. Then the rest of us flipped coins for the other two rooms. Keller and I ended up in the loft with two other couples. And there were only two bathrooms." She snorted.

Bailey and I howled with laughter.

Charley threw us the evil eye.

I held up an apologetic hand and lowered my voice. "Go on, Katie. What then?"

"We did okay, got through it, but then on the wedding day, they had this brunch wedding with nothing to drink. Nada! Not even mimosas! And after the ceremony, the happy couple holed up in a suite at the luxury hotel without telling us. She texted and reminded us not to forget to clean up the Airbnb."

"Clean up?" I gaped at her. "Maid service wasn't included?"

"Apparently not. Well, before you know it, all the other couples split, and Keller and I were left holding the bag. Literally!"

I groaned. "Your friend sounds like a —"

"My friend soon to be ex-friend."

"Ouch," Bailey said.

"What a nightmare scenario." I shook my head, commiserating. "I can't believe someone would do something like that. That is *not* happening at my wedding. For one, we're staying in town, and for two, everyone knows each other here, other than my brother and Rhett's sisters, so we'll have plenty of friendly times. And no cleaning up. I'll make sure of it."

"Speaking of schedule . . ." Bailey said, her transition clumsy. "Have you finalized everything, plan-wise, since, you know, Intime is in need of . . ."

"Repairs? Yes." I told them about the Pelican Brief taking over the out-of-towners' dinner on Friday. "On Saturday, we're having a brunch buffet at my aunt's place." I hadn't spoken to her about the menu. It was time to pin that down. "On Saturday night, we're having a wine tasting here at Vines."

"And on Sunday," Bailey said gleefully, "we're off to CC Vineyards for an exquisite and much-anticipated wedding."

"As long as nothing else goes wrong," I muttered.

"Stop that." Bailey batted my hand. "Do not be an Eeyore. The worst has passed. The best is yet to come."

Katie chortled. "You could always elope."

I scoffed. "And be drawn and quartered by my father, Lola, Rhett's parents, and so many more? Ha! Can you imagine what my sister would say?"

"Especially after what David did to you," Bailey said. "Denying you a proper wedding."

"I'd agreed with him."

"Only because he'd guilted you into it."

David. I exhaled softly. How had I missed so many signs about him? "Don't worry. I'm doing this by the book. Everyone wants a happy ending."

"Just saying." Katie raised her glass. "You could save a lot of money."

Her comment left me thinking about Wren Weatherly. If she was in financial trouble, why wouldn't she suggest her daughter elope?

Chapter 22

A short while later when I walked into the house with Tigger in tow, Rook bounded to us. I hooked a leash onto his collar, stowed Tigger in his cat backpack with the windows down, and the three of us walked on the beach. Of course, I couldn't help staring at the Pier and thinking about the bomb that had ended Sarita's life. Who had set it? Was it the same person who had sparked the one at Intime? Did that person intend to attack Rhett . . . or me . . . again? On the way home, I thought about the warning brick that someone had tossed through our window. Had the culprit been a teenaged prankster, as Appleby had proposed, or Sarita . . . or someone else?

Because my nerves were on edge—the glass of pinot noir at Vines hadn't settled them at all—I wasn't craving food. Nevertheless, I ate a light meal of Monterey Jack cheese and chopped avocado on an English muffin. If I didn't eat, I'd wake in the wee hours craving a snack. At ten, I crawled into bed and hoped Rook would be my alarm bell if anybody approached the house.

Saturday morning, I again awoke feeling anxious. I dressed in a cherry-red sundress that was sure to buoy my spirits, fed the pets, downed a protein shake that I'd made with fresh peaches, milk, yogurt, and non-GMO protein powder, and headed to the shop. A fire truck was stationed in the parking lot in front of Beaders of Paradise. Adults and children were huddling around the display of kittens in the wire crate. Bucky and Nico, both in uniform, were overseeing the Fire Sale event.

Only Bailey and her sweet Brianna were in the shop. I set Tigger on his kitty condo, but he instantly hurtled to the floor to sniff Brianna in her sit-to-stand seat. She stretched her arms, her hands wiggling for him.

"I see your mother finally gave you your baby back," I joked.

"Bright and early, but she wants her to visit soon. She adores her."

"What's not to adore?" I peered out at the parking lot. "Did you get the k-i-t-t-y?" I asked.

"Yes! Tito approved of a ginger cat, so I took Brianna over before we opened and showed her the two. She chose Spitfire. We'll take her home at the end of the day and get her settled."

"Spitfire is a she?"

She bobbed her head. "Bucky gave them all gender-neutral names."

I spotted Todd Strachline and his daughters among the kitten-hunting crowd. I wondered how his girls had received the news. Would a new kitten console their broken hearts? I noticed Z.Z. and Jake in the throng, as well. "Hey, has Jake come by to consult with my aunt yet?"

"Not that I know of."

I studied him again. He didn't look fretful. His arm was comfortably around Z.Z.'s shoulders, so I decided to let it go. He was a grown adult. He could manage his appointments and certainly had the option to change his mind about having a tarot card reading.

"Heads up. I'm only here for a short while," I stated. "I'm supposed to meet Harmony at nine at the Expo." I told Bailey about the flower snafu.

"Flowers, shmowers," she teased. "All you should care about is the food being delicious and the *I dos* going off without a hitch. Talking about food . . . I'm hungry. Would you go ask Katie to make me a snack?"

"Now?"

"Yes, now. Pretty please. For me? I skipped breakfast. You've been wanting to talk to her about taste testing more appetizers for the wedding anyway. Oh, and make sure she's on target for the flambé demo this afternoon. We have lots of people coming."

"Yes, ma'am." I saluted and strolled to the café's kitchen.

Katie was bustling from the prep station to the ovens. Her staff skirted one another with ease.

"Morning, Jenna. Sit." Katie flourished a spoon at the chef's table in the corner. "What brings you in?"

I slid onto the banquette. "Bailey is hungry and wants whatever morsel you can throw her way. She also wants to know if you're on target for this afternoon's flambé demonstration."

"Absolutely. I thought I'd show them how to do bananas Foster and flaming Spanish coffee, though I will warn you, I don't want any of our customers to even attempt making the drink. It's dangerous!" She chortled. "We'll serve it as an after-dinner drink here. Reynaldo has mastered it."

"Sounds decadent."

"What else is on your mind?" She cocked a hip.

"I was hoping to taste a few more appetizers."

Katie harrumphed. "I haven't made enough for you to choose from? I have ten that you've approved."

"You know me." I offered a coy smile. "I could make an entire meal of appetizers."

"But you don't want your guests to get so stuffed that they don't enjoy the entrées and the cake, do you?"

"True. Even so, I'd love to taste test at least two more appetizers. Thus far we have ten . . ." I rattled off the names while ticking my fingertips. "I'm forgetting one."

"Smoked salmon and avocado roll," she said.

Sheesh! How had I forgotten that? It was one of my all-time favorite appetizers. "How about adding two more to make an even dozen?"

Katie's gaze traveled to the prep table. "What do you think of crab cakes? I happen to be serving them this morning."

"Great. And what about something with potatoes, like potato poppers? I had some the other day that were terrific."

Katie's nose flared with mock disapproval. "You ate someone else's food?"

"You know I did. At the expo. Remember? I was with Harmony, and California Catch was serving them. You should come with me to the expo. See what everyone else is serving."

"Perhaps I will." Katie did like to keep up with the competition. "I'll send you back with the crab cakes, and Bailey can decide."

"Excellent."

She put together a box of crab cakes, and I started to return to the shop, but paused near the hostess station when I caught sight of Flora Fairchild waiting for a table with a blond woman in apricot-colored linen slacks and an ecru sleeveless blouse. She was slightly hunched and blubbering her eyes out. Flora was patting the woman's back, trying to calm her. Customers were looking.

I hurried to them and said, "Flora, can I help you with—"

The woman lifted her chin, and I recognized her as Sarita's friend Ilya Bakov, the fortyish owner of the Velvet Box jewelry store. Tears streaked her cheeks. Cool-girl tendrils hung down the sides of her face, the rest of it pulled into a messy bun.

Flora offered a weak smile. "Ilya recently learned about Sarita's . . . demise."

Ilya burst into more sobs. "I . . . I . . ." She flapped a hand.

Flora finished for her. "When she debarked from her cruise in San Francisco."

"At s-six a.m.," Ilya sputtered. "Six!"

"Yes, they like to boot us off early, don't they?" Flora said sympathetically. She and her twin sister were avid cruise lovers. "They have to get the ship ready to launch by three p.m. They figure you've had enough R&R and won't mind. You got enough R&R, didn't you, Ilya?"

Ilya slurped back tears. "Until . . . Until . . . Until you told me about poor Sarita." She inhaled sharply and started to weep again.

The hostess caught my eye and spread her arms in a what-should-I-do gesture. I grabbed two menus and bid Ilya and Flora to follow me to the most remote table, away from the majority of guests.

"Ilya, I'm sorry for your loss," I said over my shoulder.

"Thank you," she simpered.

As the women sat down, a waitress approached to take their beverage order.

Flora requested tea for both of them and said, "Sit, Jenna. Join us."

"Jenna," Ilya said, taking me in with a head-to-toe gaze. "You're Jenna Hart?"

"Yes."

"The woman who sent the police to New Orleans to arrest Sarita."

"I didn't exactly send them. Rhett came up with the theory, and—"

"You should know that Sarita didn't hold a grudge," Ilya said. "In fact, she told me she was glad that the truth had come out, and she no longer had to be on the run."

That didn't jibe with Sarita's tongue-lashing at the expo when she'd told me to back off, but I let it slide. "How well did you know Sarita?"

"We'd been friends since kindergarten."

Flora said, "Ilya and Sarita saw each other through many hard times. Ilya losing her husband. Sarita losing her business."

Torching it, I mused.

"I know she had her faults," Ilya said, as if sensing my thought, "but . . ." He voice drifted off.

"After Ilya's husband died," Flora continued, speaking on behalf of the woman, "Sarita helped Ilya put her business plan together and open the jewelry store. Her husband was a dollars-and-cents guy. Ilya has always been the creative one."

"I've never been in your store, Ilya," I admitted, "but I've certainly admired the items in the display window. You have excellent taste."

"They're one of a kind," Flora said. "Ilya makes everything herself."

"She does?"

"Mm-hm."

"Being an amateur artist," I said, "I admire anyone who can turn her art into a thriving business." I painted landscapes and the occasional ballet dancer, but I had never sold any of my works.

The waitress brought the tea and asked if I wanted anything. I declined. Flora added honey to hers and stirred it with a spoon. Ilya simply cupped hers, as if to warm her hands.

"You should see Ilya's workshop at the rear of the Velvet Box," Flora said, with true admiration. "It's a mess of metal and loose stones, wire nippers, and more. She even has a rock tumbler."

"Yipes. Those are noisy. My brother had one in junior high." I remembered how he'd gone through a phase when he'd wanted to become a gemologist. He'd visit the various mines around California and bring back unrefined rubies and sapphires. After his repeated bouts of begging, our parents caved and bought him the rock tumbler for Christmas.

"Did he keep it up?" Ilya asked.

"No. For six months all we heard were the grinding gears as he polished stones. My sister Whitney, who ruled the roost, finally told him she'd had enough assaults on her eardrums. As it turned out, so had he." Fondly, I recalled a trip to a cavern near Lake Tahoe, the two of us panning for gemstones and rubbing the soil through our fingers. Whatever we found, we got to keep. Our sister had no interest in getting her fingers dirty. I still had the ruby stud earrings that he'd made me.

Flora said, "I don't know where you find the time to do it all, Ilya."

"I don't sleep," Ilya said, offering a modest smile. "Sarita used to say I was an insomniac for my art. It's why I needed to take a vacation. I'm a workaholic. Sarita said . . ." A single tear slipped down her cheek. She swiped it away.

"You were a good friend to her," I said. "Giving her a loan when she needed it."

"It was the least I could do. She was there for me when . . ." She faltered. "When I lost my son."

Oh, my. She'd lost her husband and son? The poor woman.

"Stillbirth," Flora confided.

"She kept telling me I'd get pregnant again, but I never did." Ilya finally sipped her tea. "How she loved her girls. They must be devastated."

"Todd will take good care of them," Flora said.

"Todd." Ilya sniffed. "Don't get me started. He was a mooch throughout their marriage. She did all the heavy lifting."

"He's built a good business for himself," Flora countered. "And he adores his daughters."

"Yes, I suppose he does. Luckily, they got their looks from Sarita's side of the family."

The elder did, I mused. *Not the younger.* "Ilya, do you mind if I ask how much you lent—"

"What do you think, Jenna?" she asked, cutting me off. "Have you met the girls?"

Accepting that she planned to dodge my question forever, I replied, "Yes, briefly."

"Don't they look like Sarita?"

"They're very pretty." I rose to my feet. "Ladies, breakfast is on me."

"That's very sweet of you, Jenna. Thank you." Flora smiled. "We came in for Katie's famous scones."

"Whatever you want."

I informed the hostess to comp their meal and returned to the shop with Bailey's snack.

"Bless you." She peered into the box and hummed her appreciation.

"Where is everybody?" I asked. She was still the only one there. And Brianna, of course.

"Your aunt texted that she's running late. She had a hair dryer snafu. Gracie is on her way in."

I checked my watch. I needed to meet Harmony.

"I know you have to leave," she said. "It's okay. Customers for us are scarce because there was another robbery at the expo. Isn't it amazing how people love to be in the know? They can't help themselves. It's like car drivers who stop to stare at a crash." She shooed me with a hand. "Go. I'll head over to get the scoop once Gracie gets here."

The Aquarium by the Sea parking lot was teeming with cars, including a handful of police vehicles, their lights flashing. Deputy Appleby was standing outside the expo's entrance, studying the people filing into the tent.

I sidled up to him. "What was stolen?"

"A video camera from That's Amore Photography."

"Oh, my. Are the expo's security cameras still disabled?"

"Yep."

"Do you think the crook is still here?" I asked, searching the area myself.

"Doubtful, and if it's one of the brides, how would I know? They all look the same to me. Dewy-eyed and innocent. And they're all carrying bags big enough to hold it."

Chapter 23

Officer Foster strode from the event through the archway and said hello to me. Then she pulled Appleby aside. I heard her mention something about spot-checking tote bags. Appleby agreed that it was a good idea, and the two of them went in the direction of the exit.

I spotted Tito among the multitude, talking to a woman, his cell phone out as if he was recording her answer.

Beyond him I caught sight of Harmony striding toward me. "Jenna!" She'd dressed in a red power suit and red patent leather heels. "I see you got the color memo." She motioned to my cherry-red sundress.

"Except I look ready for summer, and you look prepared to head up a board meeting."

"Dress for success," she said. Based on how other wedding experts were presenting themselves at the expo, she had her work cut out for her. They all looked primed and ready to dazzle.

"Did you hear about the theft?" she asked.

"How could I not?"

"My bet is a rival videographer swiped it."

"That would be brash."

"Competition is fierce." I thought of Flora and Wren's supposed rivalry. "On the other hand, one video camera wouldn't make a business hum along. A videographer would need a lot more equipment, don't you think?"

"True." She hooked her hand around my elbow. "Before we get started, I need coffee."

The food court was hopping. Today, in addition to snacks and coffees, caterers and restaurateurs were featuring items that were perfect for bridal rehearsal brunches.

"Ooh, the Pelican Brief is offering *sous vide* egg bites." I pointed to its foodie booth. Breakfast was not the typical fare at Lola's restaurant, but she did serve brunches on the weekends. "Have you ever eaten one?"

Harmony shook her head.

"They're creamy bites of eggs, cheese, and whatnot." I was already mentally savoring one. "To cook them, you steam them in a water bath. However, you can't do it on the stove using a double boiler. They require special equipment." I'd tried making them, but they'd overcooked. The next time I attempted them, I'd do it at Intime in its sous vide cooker.

"Are you okay?" Harmony brushed my arm. "You sighed."

"I was thinking about the theft and the security cameras that were disabled, and that made me think of Rhett and Intime, and . . ." I swatted the air. "Everything is going to be fine, and he'll rally, but the whole thing is disturbing. Needless to say, I'm not sleeping well."

"I'll bet you aren't."

I purchased two gruyere-bacon sous vides, and we went to the Latte Luck cart for our coffees. The owner, brimming with good cheer, was manning it. A chalkboard sign listed the selections. After Harmony ordered our lattes, I heard a man call her name. Gunther Hildenbiddle was approaching. The brown leather messenger bag he'd slung across his chest had pinned down the collar of his plaid shirt. He was struggling to free it.

Harmony helped him arrange his shirt and kissed him on both cheeks. "I thought you were at Mindful Nourishment."

"The retreat is over already."

"Wow, that was fast. Did you enjoy it?"

"Indeed. As promised, thirty-six hours of pure silence. No contact with the outside world. I found my inner peace." He patted his heart.

"That's why you look rested." Harmony aimed a finger at Latte Luck's menu. "Would you like a coffee? My treat."

"No, thank you. I only imbibe water for seven days following one of these getaways." He smiled at me.

"Did you hear about Sarita Strachline?" Harmony asked.

Gunther's face grew properly somber. "I did. Her daughters must be devastated."

Again I wondered whether he should be considered a suspect, given his bad history with her, but ruled him out because of the retreat.

"Jenna, how is your fiancé doing?" he asked.

"He's out of the woods and clamoring to leave Mercy Urgent Care, thanks for asking."

"Let me know if there's anything you'd like me to do to help with your wedding, though I imagine Katie Keller has everything well in hand."

"She does." She'd texted me that she was taking my suggestion and coming to the expo with my aunt and Bailey.

"Good. Good." Gunther hooked his thumb. "Who knew the expo would be so busy at this hour? Where's the fire?"

"It's not a fire," Harmony said. "There was a robbery."

"Crime often brings out lookie-loos." I told him what had been stolen.

His forehead puckered with concern. "What is Crystal Cove coming to? Bombs? Robberies? It's not safe. Our police force needs to do a better job."

"They're very good," I said, believing it. "Chief Pritchett is top-notch."

"If you say so." He bid us goodbye and hustled to his venue, where his son Ulrich was already in attendance. They chatted amiably as Gunther removed his bag and donned an apron.

Harmony paid for our drinks, and we sat at an unoccupied bistro table.

Wren Weatherly, who was seated with her daughter at the next table, acknowledged me with a nod, and I reciprocated. Both had a to-go cup in front of them.

Darinda's shoulders were slumped, making her smock dress pooch in an unflattering way. "Mother, stop worrying," she said, as if in the middle of a heated conversation. "California Catch will do a great job."

Wren smoothed the skirt of her peacock blue dress with deliberation.

"Ulrich is giving us a huge discount, too," Darinda continued. "Two-thirds of what everyone else is quoting."

Harmony whispered to me, "Uh-oh. Sounds like Gunther's son made a deal while Gunther was at the retreat. That's a steep discount."

I told her about Gunther approaching Wren at the Cookbook Nook on Thursday. "Maybe Gunther approved the deal before he went to the retreat. Perhaps he needs the business."

"How could you?" Wren's sharp tone drew me back to their

conversation. "How could you make that kind of decision without me?"

"Look who's talking about making good choices," Darinda said snidely. "I'll bet it was wet camping under the stars."

"Don't. Start. Darinda." Wren pried off the lid of her drink, blew on the contents, and cut a look in my direction.

Loathe to be caught listening, I took a bite of my sous vide. Yum. Just the right amount of bacon.

"Guess you should have taken a look at the weather channel before you left," Darinda continued, not heeding her mother's warning.

"Don't get sassy with me, young lady. If your father was here—"

"But he's not, Mom. It's just us. You and me." Darinda wagged a finger between the two of them. "That means I get to make fifty percent of the decisions. Fifty. I'm sticking to my guns on this one."

"Why didn't you mention this to me yesterday when you came to the shop?"

"I didn't feel like it."

"Ladies." Matias Lajoie drew near to their table, his Tradewinds-emblazoned work shirt tucked neatly into jeans. "Might I join you?" Without waiting for their reply, he swiveled a chair and straddled it. "You don't know me . . ."

What was he up to? I didn't get the feeling he was there to hawk his services as a boat purveyor.

"I couldn't help overhearing you," he said. "You do not want to have California Catch cater your wedding."

I gulped. Why was he panning Gunther's restaurant? Harmony must have heard him, too. She'd turned ash white.

"There's a reason the restaurant is desperate for your business," Matias went on. "Its food is subpar at best."

"Are you a restaurateur?" Wren asked. "I don't recognize you."

"No, ma'am. I'm owner of Tradewinds." He traced a finger under the logo on his shirt. "I rent and sell boats on the Pier. I also do sunset cruises and the like."

"I don't want a cruise," Darinda said.

"No, miss, my interest in chatting with you is solely for your benefit. I don't want you to be disappointed on your wedding day."

"But California Catch is giving me a huge discount," Darinda protested.

"So I heard." Matias attempted a smile, his lips pulling nastily across his teeth. "However, I warn you, if you stick with your plan, your guests will not be pleased with the food. The fish will be old. People could get sick. If I were you, I'd ask for my deposit back and find someone else. The Pelican Brief or Mum's Diner. Anybody but—"

"I've heard enough." Darinda fluttered her fingers at him. "Leave."

"Yes, indeed." He spanked his thighs, rose to his feet, and strutted away. Was he whistling?

Harmony gripped my arm. "How dare that vile man poison the well. I have to warn Gunther."

But before either of us made it to our feet, Darinda and Wren were out of their chairs and storming toward the California Catch venue.

"Mr. Hildenbiddle, I want my deposit back," Darinda demanded at full volume.

The cluster of brides-to-be near the venue gasped.

Gunther's eyes widened. "What are you talking about?"

Ulrich said, "That's the wedding that I was telling you about, Dad. The one I arranged after you left for the retreat."

Gunther held up a hand, silencing him, and rounded his counter to address Darinda and her mother. "Ladies, what seems to be the problem?"

"I hear your food is subpar," Darinda said.

"S-subpar?" Gunther stammered.

"And I want my deposit back."

"You were pleased at the taste testing, Miss Weatherly," Ulrich said, skirting the counter while wiping his hands on his apron. "What changed your mind? Are you reneging because your mother's out of money after paying off a hit man?"

"What?" Wren's voice skyrocketed. "A hit—"

"I heard you on your cell phone, Mrs. Weatherly," Ulrich said. "In the parking lot. Trying to hire someone to knock off Sarita Strachline."

"Knock off . . . Don't be preposterous. I had no such conversation. Liar! Why, I ought to sue you for defamation." Wren's eyes sparked with indignation. "Why are you making this up? Why?"

"My mother is not a killer!" Darinda yelled.

Wren aimed a finger. "Maybe you're the one who had the conversation with a hit man, Mr. Hildenbiddle." She sneered at Ulrich. "On behalf of your father. He certainly had reason to want Sarita dead."

Ulrich said, "Now wait a minute! My father — "

"Ulrich, enough!" Gunther bellowed, and addressed Darinda. "Miss Weatherly, we will return your deposit. I only want satisfied customers."

"But Dad — "

"Hush!" Gunther ordered.

"C'mon, Dad, you said Wren Weatherly was furious that Sarita Strachline made her lose so much money. Plus, you said her husband committed suicide because of it. That's a huge motive to want Sarita — "

"Son!" Gunther growled. "I did not share that information with you so it would become public knowledge."

"Mom?" Darinda's eyes pooled with tears. "Is that true? Dad committed suicide?"

Holy moly. Had Wren lied to her daughter all these years about what had happened? Darinda would have been a teenager — old enough to hear the truth.

Harmony looked mystified as to what to do. I didn't know what to do, either. I couldn't imagine Wren Weatherly having a conversation with a hit man anywhere that another person, in this case Ulrich Hildenbiddle, might have been able to listen in. I studied him. His mouth was twitching maliciously. Was he deliberately stirring up trouble so the police wouldn't look more closely at his father?

I caught sight of Matias Lajoie, who had mixed in with the onlookers. He appeared to be gloating about the chaos he'd created.

"Son, leave the expo now," Gunther said between gritted teeth. So much for having found his inner peace at the retreat. "I apologize, Mrs. Weatherly, for my son's hurtful words. I want you to know that I am an honorable man. Please stop by the restaurant tomorrow, and I will refund your deposit." Head hanging, he pivoted and trudged off to close his venue.

Harmony nudged me in that direction. "Gunther, wait up!"

He pivoted, his eyes awash with embarrassment.

"I'm so sorry," she gushed.

Gunther opened his hands. "I don't understand where she heard such despicable things about my restaurant. All of our Yelp reviews are four and five stars. Reviews in the *Crystal Cove Courier* have been stellar, too."

"I'm afraid Matias Lajoie fed her the information," Harmony said.

"Aah." Gunther heaved a sigh. "Well, that explains it. Matias still holds a grudge against me."

"Why?" Harmony asked.

"He and I used to be friends."

I glanced toward where Matias had been, but he'd disappeared.

"Tell me more," Harmony coaxed.

"He supplied the fish for my restaurant." Gunther heaved a sigh. "At one time, he had a healthy business, but when things went south for him, he started selling drugs to balance the budget."

"Illegal marijuana," I said.

Gunther sniffed. "Sadly, he couldn't get his act together if his life depended on it. I couldn't save him. Or wouldn't, I should say. I made it worse when I informed Sarita about the marijuana thing."

"They dated before she married Todd, isn't that right?" I asked.

"Yes. They were in love, but she dumped him after my warning. Matias has hated me ever since."

Chapter 24

I said, "Why would your son lie about Wren hiring a hit man? I'm presuming it's a lie."

"I don't know. He and I will have to talk." Gunther gave Harmony a rueful look and proceeded to close up his booth.

Harmony faced me, her gaze filled with misery. "People can be so spiteful."

"Sadly, my friend, that's what keeps therapists and our police department in business."

"I'm afraid you're right. But enough with the drama! Gunther will rally." She dumped her coffee and sous vide into a garbage can and forced a smile. "On to the florist. That's what you and I came to tackle. I want my favorite bride-to-be to remain cool, calm, and collected."

"Favorite?" I cocked my head.

"All-time favorite." She linked her hand around my elbow. "C'mon."

"Jenna and Harmony," Posey said as we strolled into the Crystal Cove Florists stall. Dressed in a floral-patterned apron over an olive-green dress, she looked like a flower herself and fit right into the environment. "I'm so sorry about the lack of moss. I can't believe there's a shortage. I know you had your heart set on it, but climate change is real." She opened her hands. "I've put together a selection of ferns for you and Harmony to choose from."

For the next half hour, we vacillated between the choices before settling on asparagus fern as the replacement. Mission accomplished, Harmony bussed my cheek and went to meet up with another bride, the fracas between the Hildenbiddles and Weatherlys all but forgotten.

I headed for the exit but stopped when I spotted my aunt, Katie, and Bailey strolling toward me. Each was wearing a badge and carrying a tote bag.

"Jenna, dear, there you are," Aunt Vera said, arms open for a hug. Her tote bag rapped my back. "Sorry."

"No worries. I'm durable." I grinned.

"Gracie is minding the store," she said.

"I'll relieve her. I was just leaving. Where's Brianna?" I asked Bailey. "Is Gracie minding her, too?"

"No. Mom wanted even more bonding time, so she's taking her to a Mommy and Me class."

"Oho." I snickered. "Better watch out, or before you know it, she'll want to adopt."

"Whewie!" Katie exclaimed, her gaze tracking left and right. "I'm sure glad I didn't have a clue about all this before Keller and I got married. It's overwhelming."

I agreed. "You have to know what you're looking for, for sure."

"I saw Marlon at the entrance with Officer Foster," my aunt said. "Checking tote bags like TSA personnel."

"Yeah." Bailey elbowed me. "Do they think the thief could still be here?"

"It's a possibility," I said.

"Yoo-hoo!" a high-pitched voice trilled. "Jenna, Bailey!" Tina, in denim shorts, white roll-cuff top, and leather sandals hurried to us, her ponytail bouncing blithely. "Isn't this expo fabulous?"

"What are you doing here?" I asked.

"I'm thinking about getting married."

"Thinking about it?" My aunt gawped. She believed she could always tell when someone was in love. That kind of intuition paired nicely with her ESP. "You've got a boyfriend, and I didn't know?"

I'd heard Gran tease Tina about having a beau but hadn't thought anything about it at the time. She hadn't been wearing an engagement ring of any kind, then or now. "Who's the lucky young man?" I asked.

"Mine to know." Tina twisted flirtatiously in place.

Aunt Vera exchanged a concerned look with me. "Is he married?"

"Ha! As if! I would never date a married man," Tina declared. "Not even an almost-married man. Not after what happened with you-know-who." A couple of years ago, she fell head over heels for a guy who had come to town to help manage the Wild West Extravaganza. Not only hadn't the cad let on to Tina that he was dating a slew of women, but he'd kept secret the fact that his fiancé was pregnant. "I'm older and wiser now."

"Good girl!" Bailey raised a celebratory finger into the air. She'd had her own bad luck with married men.

"Who wants to come with me to check out brides' dresses?" Tina waved a hand.

"I'll go," Katie said. "I need to put some swag in this tote bag. I particularly want one of those fans. Min-yi will love it."

"I'll come, too," Aunt Vera said, and whispered to me, "I'll find out who Tina's new guy is. Don't you worry."

"Been here, done this." Bailey flailed a hand at the displays. "No need for me to pine over wedding ideas. I'll go back with Jenna. To be honest, I simply came because I wanted to find out if they'd apprehended the thief."

At the exit, people had lined up single file to pass by Officer Foster and Deputy Appleby. Foster was using her cell phone flashlight to inspect occasional tote bags and purses. Appleby was surveying faces. Was that how TSA personnel determined guilt, too? Appleby let two people pass and stopped the next one. Then one more passed and he stopped another.

Darinda and Wren were at the tail end of the line. Darinda was rifling through her Bride's Dream Expo tote bag. She removed a fistful of receipts as if she needed to present a proof of purchase to exit.

A woman at the front of the line yelped for no apparent reason. The sound startled the woman in front of Darinda, who reeled into Darinda, causing Darinda to lose hold of the receipts. They fluttered to the ground. Everyone nearby helped her retrieve them.

One landed by my feet. I picked it up and handed it to her. "Here you go."

She flushed with embarrassment. "Thanks. My tote bag is like a garbage pail of brochures and stuff I'll never use."

"But stuff that we have to review," Wren reminded her. "Jenna, whatever you heard earlier at the food court, I hope you didn't believe a word of it. I did no such thing." She pressed a hand to her chest. "Utter nonsense."

"Nonsense," her daughter echoed.

Bailey elbowed me and rasped under her breath, "What are they talking about?"

"I'll tell you later," I replied softly.

"Sarita Strachline and I definitely had our differences after the fiasco at the Grotto," Wren said, "but I never would have murdered her."

"Or hired someone to kill her," Darinda added.

"Hired someone?" Bailey gasped.

"I don't know where Ulrich Hildenbiddle got such an idea," Wren went on. "I think he made it up in the heat of the moment to protect his father. At least Gunther was a gentleman about the whole affair."

"He was," I said. "By the way, did I hear correctly? You went camping the night Sarita died?"

"Yes." Her eyelids fluttered. "Can you believe how stupid I was? That rainstorm came out of nowhere."

Her daughter snorted.

Wren threw her a fearsome look. "I did check the weather channel, Darinda, despite what you may think. The weather girl thought the storm would miss us."

"My mother is a diehard camper."

"It's a way for me to find my center, rain or shine," Wren said.

"Me?" Darinda continued, talking over her mother's comment. "I prefer hot chocolate and popcorn and a good old wedding-themed rom-com."

"While making bad business deals," Wren carped.

"The taste testing *was* good," Darinda countered.

Wren progressed in line and squinted at me over her shoulder. "Jenna, did you ever hear from Baldini Vineyards?"

"I'm so sorry. I forgot to call." I whipped my cell phone from my pocket.

"Not now." She fluttered her fingers. "When you have time."

I sent myself a text reminder.

Bailey said, "Darinda, I loved having my wedding there. I hope you can arrange it."

Darinda smiled, but the smile didn't meet her eyes. How often did she face off with her mother? I wondered. My mother and I had been best friends. Cancer took her from this world way too soon.

"Also"—Wren touched my arm—"do you think the Nook Café might consider doing the catering? I have your chef's card, but I haven't touched base with her yet."

"Mo-om," Darinda cautioned.

After witnessing the set-to between them and California Catch, I wasn't sure I wanted to do business with them, but I said graciously, "Give Katie a jingle. She's very accommodating."

Appleby started to stop Wren, but when he saw me, he said, "You four can go on through. Next." He held up the woman behind Bailey, who obliged and opened her tote.

"No luck?" I asked him as I passed by.

"Nope. If only the item was as big as a bread box instead of the size of my palm."

Chapter 25

Over thirty people showed up for the flambé demonstration at the Cookbook Nook. We'd only put out twenty chairs, so ten-plus people were standing behind and to the sides of the seating. Bailey and I hung back with them to observe.

For the presentation, we'd stocked the store with a number of dessert cookbooks, including one written by Katie and published by an indie publisher named *Flambé: You Light Up My Life*. Katie had included twenty recipes with photos that Keller had taken. Five were beverage recipes. One entire chapter was dedicated to how to flambé safely.

"Are we ready?" Katie, dressed in her chef's coat and apron with her curls tucked beneath her toque, wheeled her demonstration cart into the shop from the breezeway. She set it in front of the chairs and locked the wheels. "Hello, everyone! Nice to see some regular faces among the crowd."

Crystal Cove had plenty of cooks, providing us with a steady clientele, but I spotted new faces among the attendees, too, thanks to the expo being in town.

"Why are we focusing on flambé today?" She scanned the audience. "Because it's elegant and will impress your party guests . . . or your new in-laws." She winked conspiratorially.

That elicited laughter.

Tina entered the shop and tiptoed to Bailey and me. "What did I miss?"

"Not a thing. Katie just started," I said. "Did you have a good time at the expo?"

"You bet!" She patted her tote bag, which was filled to the brim with swag.

"How many of you have ever tried to flambé?" Katie asked.

A few hands went up.

"How many of you own a kitchen torch?" She held one up. "This is fueled by butane. It has a safety lock and adjustable flame. If any of you are feeling daring after today's demonstration, you'll find kitchen torches on the wall over there."

We'd ordered ten, as well as boxes of long matches and extra kitchen mitts. Some early birds had scored theirs before sitting.

"You must always be careful when working with heat," Katie said. "Safety first. No children or pets in the kitchen when you're using a kitchen torch. Don't wear flammable clothing. Secure your hair." She chuckled and widened her eyes. "No lie. I nearly lit myself on fire when one of my corkscrew curls escaped my toque. Big oops. Now, let's get started. Today, I'm making bananas Foster."

Tina leaned in to me. "That's what we made in my class at school. It's delish!"

"The dish is made with bananas, brown sugar, and rum. Hooboy!" Katie shimmied her whole body. "The liquor-based sauce is caramelized using the flambé technique." As she set a sauté pan on the cart stove to heat and added a huge dollop of butter using a long-handled wooden spoon, she said, "Many think this recipe originated in New Orleans at a restaurant named Brennan's, but it was actually created at Owen Brennan's Vieux Carré restaurant and named for Richard Foster, a friend of Brennan's who was the chairman of the New Orleans Crime Commission."

I enjoyed when Katie added a dash of history to her chats.

She brandished her spoon. "Don't go reading anything into that last tidbit. Brennan was on the up and up as far as I can tell. He was not a criminal."

The audience laughed.

For the next few minutes, she chatted amiably as she walked the audience through the steps.

Bailey leaned in to me. "I've been meaning to ask, what was up with Wren Weatherly and her daughter at the expo? Sparks were flying between them."

I told her about the upset with Gunther Hildenbiddle and their demand for a refund.

"*Oof,*" she said. "That had to hurt."

"When his son accused Wren of hiring a hit man to kill Sarita, she went ballistic."

"Is there any truth to it?" Bailey asked.

"You heard Wren when we were leaving the expo. She said it was utter nonsense. And she certainly didn't do it herself. She has an alibi for that night."

"She was camping and got soaked," Bailey said. "That much I heard."

The audience applauded, signaling Katie had completed the dish.

Katie said, "You can find recipe cards for this dish at the checkout counter. Now, who would like to see me make a flaming Spanish coffee?"

More applause.

Katie shook a finger. "I do not recommend that you try this at home. It's really dangerous. However, yes, this is a sales pitch. The Nook Café will be serving this drink after dinner from now on." She held up a bottle of Sunset rum. "Here's the liquor I'll be using. If I could get my hands on a bottle of 151 rum, that is what I would use for this recipe, but they stopped producing it a few years ago." For effect, she lowered her tone as if imparting a secret. "Why use that one? Because it had a walloping seventy-five-point-five percent alcohol by volume. Heart be still." She fanned herself. "Even so, this version will be tantalizing and provide quite a flame. If . . . *if* . . . you decide to try this at home, you will need flame-resistant stemmed glassware."

Katie went through the steps, edging the glass with sugar and preparing the coffee concoction. When she was ready, she poured liquor into the glass, tipped the glass at a forty-five-degree angle, fired up the torch, and lit it. When the fire ebbed, she sprinkled the drink with cinnamon and nutmeg, then added a liqueur and the coffee. The audience could see every move she made in the cart's slanted overhead mirror.

"Voilà!" Katie held up the drink and the audience hooted its approval. "Thank you all for coming. I'll be around to answer questions." When the flame extinguished, Katie took a sip and grinned. "Perfection, if I do say so myself."

I elbowed Tina. "She's such a natural for this. She's a born ham."

Tina giggled. "She does love to entertain."

Enthusiastically the attendees got to their feet and roamed the shop. Within minutes, all of the kitchen torches, matches, and mitts were sold, as were all the copies of Katie's cookbook.

Tina cornered me by the display table as I was neatening the disarray. "Jenna, I need to tell you something."

"Sure." Was she ready to reveal the name of the man she was in love with? I'd been speculating. "What's up?"

"I heard you and Bailey talking about Wren Weatherly and the dustup at the expo."

"It was quite something. Matias Lajoie stuck his nose in to badmouth California Catch, then Ulrich Hildenbiddle got bent out of shape and—"

"Wren wasn't camping that night."

"What?" My mouth dropped open. "How do you know?"

"Because she was with me. Not *me*, in particular"—Tina hoisted her tote higher on her shoulder—"but me and a group of people. We're in a survivors' therapy group." Tina's aunt was murdered a couple of years ago. "It's very private, and we don't tell anyone about it."

"Why not?"

"Because most people think we're okay. That we've gotten *over* the shock. But we haven't. We dwell. And it's embarrassing."

Could that be why Wren had lied to her daughter as to her whereabouts?

"Tina, you should never be ashamed about dwelling on the past. It's natural." I still struggled with David's death.

"That's what our therapist says, but it's hard not to." She shrugged. "The session goes from six until eleven p.m. every Thursday night, and there's a lot of meditation, and sometimes hypnosis."

That could explain what had happened to Wren when I'd seen her at Home Décor. Momentarily she'd fallen into a trance when trying to control her angry outburst.

"So there's no way Wren could've had a hand in Sarita's murder," Tina went on. "Not personally."

Not personally, which still left the possibility that she'd hired someone. Had Ulrich truly overheard her talking on the phone to someone?

"Do you think she'll be mad that I told you?" Tina asked.

I put a reassuring hand on her shoulder. "She should be ecstatic that you've come forward. Your testimony confirms that she had an alibi. A verifiable one. I'd already been doubting that anyone had gone camping in that rainstorm."

"What about her daughter?" Tina asked innocently. "Would she lash out at Sarita on behalf of her mother? She was alone, right?"

"She was, but . . ." I flashed on the receipt I'd picked up for Darinda while standing in line at the expo exit. "I think she has an alibi, too." I hadn't thought much about it at the time, but the receipt was for Genie's Gold, a pawn shop. Was it possible Darinda had stolen the photographic equipment from the vendor at the expo so she could pawn it for cash? If her mother was straining to make ends meet and could barely provide a modest wedding, maybe Darinda thought pawning a big-ticket item was a way for her to help fund the wedding.

Chapter 26

As I was leaving to see Rhett—I would return to the shop later to pick up Tigger—I saw Bucky and Nico by the fire truck, which was still parked in the lot. They were knuckling each other on the arm and hooting.

I drew near. "Why the celebration?"

"We did it," Bucky cheered. "All ten kittens have new homes." He motioned to the wire crate.

I grinned. "I still count four."

"Because we agreed to keep them until the owners are ready to take them home."

"Well, congratulations."

"It's all thanks to you, Jenna," he said. "The posters we hung around town were what pulled people in."

Nico started to gather up trash that people had carelessly left at the site.

I helped and tossed what I collected in a garbage pail. "It didn't hurt that the kittens were cute."

"Super cute," Bucky said.

"Did you keep one for yourself?"

"Nah. With both of our busy careers, tending to a cat is the last thing Cinnamon and I need."

I didn't mention that a cat would have been a lot less trouble than a baby. Why pour salt on the wound? I was pretty sure they'd given up trying to get pregnant and had moved on with their lives.

"Help!" Pepper exited Beaders of Paradise, Phoenix in her arms. The kitten's claws were not ensnared in her pale blue sweater, so what was wrong? "Help! I've got to figure out what to do with him when I'm tending to customers." She held him out, his feet dangling and squirming. "I can't cradle him for twelve hours a day. What am I going to do?"

Bucky looked worried that she would renege on keeping the kitten.

I gestured to the wire crate. "Bucky, where did you get that?"

"The pet shop donated it, but I can give it to you, Pepper."

She beamed. "Really? You'd do that?"

"Sure. I'll pick up another to house these little guys. Nico, get the box we were holding them in."

After Nico had transferred the kittens into the box with holes, Bucky hoisted the empty crate. "Here you go, Pepper. Phoenix will be able to see everything that's going on but stay out of trouble."

She caressed his cheek. "You are the brightest boy."

Okay, I was the one who'd made the suggestion, but I didn't need the kudos. I waved goodbye to them and climbed into my VW.

At Mercy Urgent Care, I wended my way to Rhett's room.

He was sitting up in bed eating something from a bowl. "Soup," he said. "Want some?"

I wrinkled my nose when I got a whiff of it. "I'll pass. I've got my heart set on French onion soup and want to leave room."

He shook the spoon at me. "It's not nice to tease your fiancé."

I kissed his cheek.

"Good news," he said. "They're releasing me tomorrow midmorning."

"Hooray." Spirits boosted, I filled him in on the day's events.

"Have you told Cinnamon everything you know?" He studied my face.

"Like she'll want to hear from me."

"It's your citizenly duty." He chucked my arm with his knuckles. "Be brave. She doesn't bite."

"I'll think about it."

I spent the next hour simply holding his hand and watching the news. No rare storms were headed our way. The state was happily enjoying good economic growth. All was nearly right with the world.

When I was ready to head home, Rhett said, "Cinnamon. Don't forget."

I decided to call her. From the car. I didn't want to see her in person.

For once, our illustrious chief of police sounded happy to hear from me. She hummed as I replayed everything I knew, and it sounded like she was taking notes. Then she told me she'd handle it and to have a good night.

"Wait!" I said. "Anything new on—"

She hung up.

Grumpy about the way she'd snubbed me, I went to the Nook Café, picked up a to-go container of French onion soup, went to the shop, gathered Tigger, and drove home with my teeth clenched.

When Tigger and I walked in the front door of the house, Rook woofed with pleasure as if he, too, knew tomorrow would be a better day. After feeding them, I poured myself a glass of chardonnay and puttered around the house doing chores. A short while later, I warmed the onion soup.

I brought *The Diva Cooks Up a Storm*, a mystery that I'd started last week, to the kitchen table and read as I ate. I loved the feeling of paper in my hands. Loved turning pages. Loved the characters and trying to solve the puzzle. As I was reaching the climactic scene where the killer would be revealed, something went *pop!*

Pop-pop!

Rook barked. Tigger squalled. Heart hammering my chest, I bolted to my feet. Was somebody deliberately trying to give me a heart attack by lighting firecrackers outside? I peeked through the drapes but didn't see anything. Grabbing the baseball bat we kept by the front door, I whipped the door open and stepped onto the porch.

A truck was lurching down the road in fits and starts and backfiring. *Pop, pop, pop.*

I laughed and ordered myself to get a grip.

But then a dark figure materialized from beyond the cottage where I used to live. I raised the bat, my arms vibrating with tension.

"Jenna?" The figure drew near and I recognized him. It was Jake.

Rook peeked out from behind my legs. He didn't growl. He knew Jake was my friend.

"You okay?" Jake asked.

"I'm on edge. The truck. The noise."

He noted the baseball bat. "Did you worry someone had returned with another brick?"

"Yes . . . No . . ." It irked me that the police hadn't taken that incident more seriously, but with a murder to solve, I supposed they didn't have the manpower. "No," I repeated, to convince myself.

"I'll be glad to sit on your porch all night if that'll make you feel better," Jake said.

"I'm okay. Really. What are you doing out so late anyway?"

"Walking. Thinking about sleeping on the beach. You know me." Though Jake had a perfectly grand king-sized bed to sleep in, sometimes he preferred to snooze beneath the stars. He'd been a vagabond in his teens.

"Want to come in for some tea?"

"Sure."

He stepped into the house and turned in a circle. "It's homey," he said. "I like it."

"Thanks." I led the way to the kitchen.

He took a seat on a stool by the island.

"Honey or sugar?"

"Neither."

I made us each a cup of Earl Grey tea and set his mug in front of him, the tag of the teabag looped around the handle. "Tell me more about your engagement." Chatting about something mundane would help me forget about the *pop-pop* sounds. "Where did Z.Z. ask you? Are you excited?"

"Excited? That's a good question." He rubbed his jaw. "I guess I'm nervous, having never been married."

Jake had fallen in love decades ago, but Amelia, the woman he'd cared for, had split town, so he'd resigned himself to bachelorhood. A year and a half ago, he'd discovered that she'd been pregnant with his child. She was dead now, but he had a relationship with his fifty-something son and his granddaughter.

"Where will you live? Have you decided?"

"We'll keep both of our residences and live à la Hepburn and Tracy."

Not exactly like them, I mused. True, the famous acting couple had never moved in together because he'd been married to someone else, but Katherine Hepburn had sworn that living separately had helped their love survive. Given how independent Z.Z. and Jake both were, that might be the best idea.

"You wanted to see my aunt for a tarot reading," I said. "Was it to find out about your future with Z.Z.?"

He averted his gaze and sipped his tea. When he looked up, he smiled forlornly. "Yes. I'm afraid Z.Z. will realize it's not a good idea, and she'll . . ."

I sat on the stool next to him and put a hand on his shoulder. "I think Z.Z. knows what she wants, and when she decides that, nothing will change her mind. She's the little engine that could."

He chuckled. "Yes, that's what I love about her."

Chapter 27

The next morning, after a long walk with Rook and Tigger and eating a breakfast that included a power bar and a glass of juice, I dressed in a blue-and-white floral skirt, white peasant blouse, and sandals and headed to work. The sound of church bells carried on the wind as I drove.

My aunt and Gran were already at the shop. Tigger leaped from my arms and launched himself onto the kitty condo. A few customers were browsing the front display table. After yesterday's demonstration, I'd set out more of Katie's cookbooks as well as *The Couple's Cookbook: Recipes for Newlyweds*. It was a basic book with tips on how to stock a pantry and outfit a kitchen. One of the recipes in it, grilled green tomatoes with burrata toast, had caught my eye, so I'd Xeroxed it with the plan to make it for Rhett on a Sunday after we were married.

"Morning, Jenna," my aunt trilled. "How are you, dear?"

"Ecstatic. Rhett will be released in a few hours."

"That's wonderful news." She whooshed to me, her purple caftan wafting, and clasped me in a hug. She bussed my forehead and released me. "Harmony Bold is on her way in. She's been trying to call you."

"Uh-oh."

Aunt Vera *tsked*. "Don't worry. She merely wants to finalize something. She left you a message or two on your cell phone."

I scanned the phone's readout and saw that I'd missed two messages from her. I listened to them as I stowed my purse in the storage room and breathed a sigh of relief. Harmony wanted to review CC Vineyards' protocol. I also noticed my own text message reminding me to contact Baldini Vineyards. I didn't owe Wren Weatherly anything, but I'd made a promise to reach out. So I called there first.

Alan answered on the first ring, his voice bubbling with quirky energy. "Hiya, Jenna, what's up?" He always awakened early to tend to his vines so he could spend the remainder of the day doing tricks with his quasi bird of prey Crow—quasi because Crow was indeed a crow.

I explained the reason for my call.

"Sorry, we're off the wedding circuit for a year," he said. "The terrace needs a complete resurfacing, and we're tearing out some walls in the dining room to open it up. It'll become a much better event space."

"How about Hannah's place?" I asked him. Hannah Storm was Alan's wife and owned the neighboring Hurricane Vineyards.

"She's booked out for two years."

I thanked him and dialed Wren to give her the bad news. "I'm sorry to tell you that I couldn't get Baldini Vineyards or Hurricane Vineyards. They're fully booked. But—"

"Save your breath, Jenna," she said curtly. "There won't be a wedding. Darinda's fiancé the dentist ended their engagement when he discovered she was a thief. Are you the person I have to thank for her arrest?"

I gulped. "Wren, I can explain."

"Stuff it!" she hissed, and ended the call.

I saw Harmony pull into the parking lot in her BMW and told my aunt and Gran that I was going outside to chat with her. What I really needed was fresh air. I had no idea Cinnamon and her people would work so fast. Clearly, they had found enough evidence to book Darinda. I hoped they'd go lightly on a sentence. I didn't think she was a hardened criminal.

Harmony exited her car and closed the door. I noted the sensible shoes she was wearing and bet the spiky heels she'd worn yesterday at the expo had done a number on her calves. "I told your aunt today's meeting was run-of-the-mill. Why the frown?"

"Because I just got off the phone with an angry customer."

"Oh. Sorry to hear that."

"Want to grab coffee at the Nook?"

"No, thanks. I'm coffee'd out. Let's go over everything right here."

For the next ten minutes, she and I reviewed CC Vineyards' agenda for the day of the wedding, starting with the makeup and hair location. Bailey and her mother would join me for that. Next, where the pastor as well as the photographer were supposed to go when they arrived. Also where Katie and her crew would set up. Last but not least, where I'd position myself to throw the bouquet and where we'd cut the cake.

"I'll be on hand for every facet of this," Harmony said, "so you shouldn't worry about a thing. Not. A. Thing. We'll have no surprises. No bomb—" She blanched and pressed her lips together, trapping the word inside.

"Bombshells," I finished for her. "Got it. Don't worry." I touched her arm fondly. "Words don't scare me anymore. Rhett is coming home today."

"That's great news."

A truck rumbled. Todd Strachline pulled into the lot in his silver Ford Ranger, parked, and climbed out. Shay and Sela scrambled out, too. Both were dressed in drab colors. Neither wore a smile.

Shay said, "After this, Dad, we get to go to Hobby Fun, right? I want that science kit."

"Yeah, sure," he said.

The girls hurried into Beaders of Paradise.

Todd spotted Harmony and me as he was locking up and strode to us. "Morning, ladies."

"Your daughters looked sad," I said. "How are they doing?"

"Not well. They're broken up about their mother. Sela isn't talking at all. Shay cries a lot. I think they'll both need therapy."

"Did you adopt one of the kittens at the fire sale?"

"We decided to pass. For now, I've brought them here to buy some happiness. Then we're off to Hobby Fun. Sela loves crafts, but Shay is a scientist. Like I was at her age."

"Crafts are good for boosting spirits." Pepper Pritchett enjoyed telling me how adept she was at steering a customer to the perfect craft for his or her sensibility. "Science kits are good, too."

Todd eyed Harmony and me with concern. "I heard about yesterday. The outburst at the expo. The owner of Shredding restaurant is a client. You know that place, with all the chopped salads? Anyway, she touched base and told me all about it."

"Who don't you do the books for?" I joked.

He smiled modestly. "She said the Weatherlys really went after Gunther Hildenbiddle. Demanding a refund. Making a scene. I know he's a family friend, Harmony. He didn't deserve a public assault."

"But then his son retaliated," Harmony said.

"Oh, yeah, I heard that, too, about Ulrich claiming Wren killed Sarita." Todd shook his head. "He wasn't far wrong thinking she had motive. Wren has been upset with Sarita for years. Furious, in fact."

"Wren has an alibi," I stated.

Harmony raised an eyebrow. "Really?"

I nodded. "It's verifiable."

"Good to know." Todd lowered his voice. "If you ask me, Gunther had as much reason to kill Sarita as anyone. Of course, he shouldn't have blamed her. I've told him so many times. I mean, after all, it was Wren and her husband who fronted Sarita the money. Without that, Sarita never could have gotten the Grotto up and running." Todd ran his palm along his hair and down his neck. "We sure didn't have the funds for that kind of venture."

"Forgive me, Todd"—I cut in, unable to contain my curiosity— "why have you spoken to Gunther about this? Don't tell me he's one of your clients, too?"

Todd nodded.

"Didn't he blame you for your part in the Grotto?" I asked.

"Nah. Not after Sarita and I divorced. He knew she'd raked me over the coals." He rubbed his jaw. "I should've never helped her open that place. I should've stuck with my previous job. To be honest? I never should've dated her in the first place. But if I hadn't, I wouldn't have my girls." He nodded to us dejectedly and tramped to Beaders of Paradise.

Harmony gripped my elbow. "Jenna, I need to see Gunther. Will you come with me?"

I hooked my thumb. "I just arrived for—"

"Please. If Todd is spreading that kind of rumor, it won't be long before the police focus on Gunther as the killer. And I know he didn't do it. He couldn't have. Please?"

How could I say no? I poked my head into the shop and alerted my aunt. She told me she had everything under control.

California Catch was an upscale fish restaurant, designed with marble and glass and soothing ocean tones. It wasn't located on Buena Vista Boulevard with a view of the ocean, but the twenty-foot-long aquarium filled with blue- and aqua-colored fish made up for the lack of view. Brunch was being served. The aroma of butter and bacon permeated the air. I asked the fresh-faced hostess what smelled so good.

"Scallops benedict," she said, her eyes twinkling with delight. "It's my favorite dish on the menu. Take a recipe card." She pointed to a Plexiglas holder filled with cards. Nearby was an array of for-purchase California Catch spice bottles. There were mild, medium, and zesty blends as well as a number of dry rub choices. "Gunther loves sharing recipes."

I pocketed one, and Harmony asked if Gunther was available to talk.

A minute later, he emerged from the kitchen, a thin layer of perspiration coating his face. He removed the apron covering his blue-checked shirt and chinos and handed it to the hostess. "Ditch this, will you? Thanks." He bussed Harmony on the cheek. "To what do I owe the pleasure, ladies?"

"Can we sit somewhere?" Harmony asked.

Gunther scanned the restaurant, which was packed with contented customers, and opted for an empty table in the stylish bar that he'd fitted with tall round tables and tall stools. Harmony perched on a stool and folded her hands on the table. I did the same, ready to follow her lead.

"Have the police questioned you, Gunther?" she asked, no preamble.

"About?"

"Sarita Strachline's murder."

He brandished a hand. "They have no reason to. I was at Mindful Nourishment."

She stabbed the table with a fingertip. "You said yourself that once you arrived you had no contact with the outside world."

"That's right."

"Did any of the monks check in on you?"

He shook his head.

"Who served you food?" she asked.

"I didn't eat."

"For thirty-six hours?" Harmony frowned in disbelief.

I couldn't imagine going without food on purpose for thirty-six hours, either.

"Yes," Gunther said. "Why are you asking? Is somebody saying I'm a liar? It was a cleansing retreat. Only water was provided, which was already in the room."

"Gunther," Harmony said, "I think the police will be questioning you soon."

"Why?"

"It doesn't look good. Especially after the set-to with Wren Weatherly at the expo yesterday, and Ulrich accusing her of hiring a hit man."

"I told you, my son is a hothead." Gunther folded his arms. "He had no right to attack Wren like that. He told me afterward that the words just burst out of him because he'd seen a documentary about that very thing the week before. He didn't hear her on her cell phone."

I jutted a hand at him. "In her defense, Wren intimated that one of you might have murdered Sarita."

"No way. Neither of us did." A stream of air escape Gunther's mouth. "As you know, I was at the retreat, and I know for a fact that Ulrich was home with his family. He never works nights during the week. His wife is adamant that they have dinner with their kids. Afterward, he helps the children with homework and reads them stories. He's a model father."

"He made a deal with Darina Weatherly that night," Harmony argued. "He said she taste tested foods."

"Before he left for home. *Before.*"

Harmony worked her lip between her teeth.

"What do you want me to do?" Gunther leaped to his feet. "Go to the police and swear on a stack of Bibles that I was where I was and Ulrich was where he was?"

"That would be a start."

"Forget it," he hissed. "We're innocent. We don't have to prove ourselves to you or to anyone." He pivoted and stormed back to the kitchen.

Chapter 28

"He can't be guilty," Harmony said as she veered her BMW left onto Buena Vista. "Someone must have seen him. Heard him pacing. Heard him chanting."

I swiveled in the passenger seat. "He said it was thirty-six hours of quiet."

"That doesn't mean he was quiet. It simply means he wasn't disturbed. He had to have moved around. Maybe in the cell . . ." She cut a glance at me. "Is that what they call rooms at a retreat? A cell? Like in a prison?"

"A cell, like in a monastery," I clarified. "Don't make more of this—"

"Jenna, I like Gunther. I always have. My parents say he's salt of the earth." She was near tears.

"And he probably is," I said, "but he would do himself a great service if he'd go to the police and tell them everything he knows."

"You're right. 'You can lead a horse to water' . . ." She swerved into the parking lot, rolled into a spot, parked, and idled, drumming the steering wheel.

"Harmony," I began and hesitated. My mouth tasted like metal.

"What?" Sadness flooded her face.

"I don't feel comfortable leaving it up to Gunther to decide whether he'll chat with the police, knowing what I know. I need to be forthright with Cinnamon if I want to preserve our friendship."

She bobbed her head. "I understand. Say hi to Rhett when you see him."

I slipped out of the car and caught sight of Jake Chapman leaving the shop with a spring in his step.

I went inside and said to my aunt, who was rising from a chair beside the vintage kitchen table, "Did Jake finally get his tarot reading?"

"He did."

"And?"

"He's happy as a clam." She pressed the tarot deck to her chest. "Sometimes the stars align."

And sometimes you help them align, I mused.

"Bailey texted me. She's on her way in," Gran said from the sales counter.

Knowing that the shop was well staffed, I informed my aunt and Gran what I'd learned about Gunther and told them I felt obligated to convey the news.

"After you go to the precinct," Aunt Vera said, "continue on to Mercy. Stay with Rhett until you take him home. We have this covered."

"We sure do," Gran said. "I've set up a few three-book bridal packages with dinner-for-two cookbooks and the like. They'll be a big hit." She held up *The New Newlywed Cookbook: 100 Recipes for Every Couple to Cook Together* as an example. "Not every kitchen has one cook. As the author says, this book helps two work as one."

"Excellent," I said. "And might I say, you look like a bride yourself in that elegant white lace blouse and white skirt."

Gran blushed. "Hardly a bride. More like grandmother of the bride. I'm too old to think about marriage again."

"Don't sell yourself short, Gracie Goldsmith." I shook a finger at her. "If Z.Z. and Jake can get hitched, you can, too."

Gran squeezed my aunt's arm. "I'm excited for Z.Z. She deserves happiness. That Jake is such a good guy. A knight in shining armor."

I spruced up in the restroom at the back of the shop before heading off to see Cinnamon. The precinct wasn't too busy. Sunday mornings rarely were. One team was dealing with a car crash. Another pair of officers had been dispatched to deal with a pickpocket at the expo.

I asked for Cinnamon. The clerk reached out via the intercom, told her I was there in person, and after receiving Cinnamon's blessing, buzzed me through the secure door. I strode to Cinnamon's office. She spied me through her inner window and beckoned me to enter. I stepped in. Sunlight streaked through the opened blinds and made me squint.

"Jenna, it's Sunday. My catch-up day. Why are you bothering me?" She folded her hands on the brown blotter. A stack of files on the desk stood to her right. More files were piled on the round table to my left, a table where I'd seen her interrogate suspects, in particular Tito Martinez. "Don't tell me you were threatened again."

"No." I stood in front of the desk, arms at my side. "This concerns Sarita Strachline's murder."

Cinnamon smoothed the front of her short-sleeved shirt. "What more could you possibly know that I don't already know?"

"Gunther Hildenbiddle, owner of California Catch, held a grudge against Sarita for putting his first restaurant out of business."

"Businesses fail all the time. People don't usually commit murder because of that." She held up a hand. "I heard about the fracas and the accusations at the expo. Ulrich Hildenbiddle—"

"Has an alibi for that night," I cut in. "He was with his wife and family."

"Did you question him?" Cinnamon sat taller and nailed me with a reproachful look.

"No, but I spoke with Gunther, and he said—"

"Why were you speaking with him?"

"Harmony Bold, my wedding planner . . ." I drew in a deep calming breath and let it out. "Her family, the Boldines, are friends with the Hildenbiddles. She got upset while we were talking to Todd Strachline—"

"Hold it!" Cinnamon barked. "Why were you speaking with him?"

"He was in the parking lot outside the Cookbook Nook, taking his daughters to Beaders of Paradise. We ran into each other. Apparently Gunther is Todd's client, and he expressed concern about Gunther after hearing about the set-to between him and the Weatherlys. He implied that Gunther had motive to want Sarita dead. That alarmed Harmony so much that she wanted to speak to Gunther right away, and she pleaded with me to go with her to his restaurant for support."

"Support," Cinnamon muttered.

"She questioned him about his alibi. If you didn't know, he was at—"

"Mindful Nourishment on a retreat. Yes, Jenna, I do my due diligence." Her voice dripped with sarcasm. She signaled for me to continue.

"Did you know that he was alone for the entire thirty-six hours?"

"Yes."

"None of the monks checked on him."

"They never do. It's one of the perks."

"He swears he didn't kill Sarita, but Harmony was worried that you might have him in your sites because his motive is clear-cut."

She drummed her desk, deliberating. After a long moment, she said, "Do you think he had anything to do with blowing up Intime?"

"What? No!" The notion hadn't even entered my mind. "I think they're two separate incidents."

"I concur."

The way she said that, however, led me to think she didn't concur. She had a theory that she didn't plan to share. Why would they be related? Why would someone want to harm Sarita as well as Rhett and me?

Cinnamon rose to her feet. "If you believe they're separate, why are you still pursuing this? Spit it out." She planted her hands on her desk. "Why? You have no skin in the game. Sarita is dead."

Boy, she could be harsh when she wanted to be. Almost as harsh as my boss at Taylor & Squibb. I'd had to stand up to him on more than one occasion.

"Because I care about Crystal Cove." I spanked one hand against the other. "I care about justice. Sure, I didn't like Sarita Strachline, but I don't like seeing any murderer run free. You should hope all citizens like me would come forward."

She barked out a laugh. "Go. Thank you for doing your citizenly duty."

"Did you question the carny woman named Carla? She saw someone running away from the pier. I left a message about her."

"We did."

"She thought the person might have been standing by the third piling, the one that abuts the water."

"We investigated, but we couldn't find any specific evidence."

"I noticed the area wasn't cordoned off."

"You went down there?" she hissed, her gaze sizzling with fury.

"I was curious."

"Curious. Dang it, Jenna—"

"What evidence do you have, if not the carny woman's statement? Is there anything that ties Sarita's killing to the explosion at Intime? Have you found a detonator? Or timer?" I ticked off the list on my fingertips. "I don't know how bombs are made. Is that how it works? Is there a limit to how far away the bomber could be? Was there anything left of Sarita's boat to—"

"Jenna, listen to me!" Cinnamon moved to the front of the desk and nudged the files away from the corner. She perched beside them, then drew in and let out a deep breath. "I love you. I appreciate your dedication to our fair town and to your friends and family. But I've got this. *We*"—she brandished a hand toward her team—"have got this."

"You still haven't figured out who set the bomb at Intime. You—"

She pushed away from the desk and grabbed me in a bear hug. "Breathe."

"I would if you weren't squeezing the life out of me," I squeaked.

She pressed apart and held me at arms' length. "Please, please, please focus on your wedding."

"I was. That's why I was with Harmony."

Cinnamon gave me a rueful look. "You know what I mean. Rhett is being released today. Focus on him. His recovery. I will follow up with the monks at the retreat and everything else. Promise."

Chapter 29

When I stepped into Rhett's hospital room carrying the travel case I'd packed for him, I was surprised to see my father and Lola there. Rhett was still in bed and in a hospital gown, but his bandages and the gauze had been removed, thank heaven. I crossed to him and pecked his cheek. I noticed some bruising on his nose and around his ear, but for the most part, he appeared to be healthy.

"Ready to go?" I asked.

"You bet I am."

"What are you two doing here?" I asked Dad and Lola. Both were wearing jogging outfits, as if they'd been out for a run, but neither was perspiring. In fact, Lola's makeup was perfection, as was her spiky hair.

"We had a little matter to discuss with your intended," Lola said, her eyes gleaming with mischief.

"What kind of matter?"

"A none-of-your-business matter," my father said.

Rhett guffawed. "Don't let them pull your leg. They came to talk to me about hotel rooms for my family."

"I thought Harmony had taken care of all that," I said.

"She did," Lola nodded, "but it turns out we need a few more rooms than we thought."

Dad continued. "Your sister has decided she wants privacy and doesn't want to stay with us, so we went to Crystal Cove Inn to arrange for rooms. It will require moving Rhett's family to larger suites, at our cost of course."

"My parents will love it," Rhett said, "but you don't have to suffer the expense."

"It's our pleasure." Lola grinned. "I can't wait to meet them."

I'd visited his family in Napa a couple of times, but they had yet to travel south.

"Why are you late?" my father asked me. "Rhett's been ready to go for a half hour."

"Cary, give it a rest." Rhett plucked at his gown. "Don't give my fiancée a guilt complex. She has a life. I can wait."

Not cowed by my fiancé, my father pressed on. "You weren't at the shop, daughter. I checked." He lasered me with a look that used to make my knees buckle.

Used to. I cocked a hip. "Keeping tabs on me, Dad?"

"Possibly." He smirked. "So . . . where were you?"

"I was at the precinct if you must know. Chatting with Cinnamon."

"Doing your citizenly duty?" Rhett asked.

"You bet."

He held up a hand to high-five me. I obliged and then filled them in on the last few conversations with the chief. About Wren and her daughter Darinda. About the carny woman and the other witnesses' sightings. About Gunther having a clear-cut motive.

"Gunther's a decent guy," Dad said.

"Harmony feels the same way about him, but—"

"You don't think he put the bomb at Intime, do you, Jenna?" Rhett cut in.

"I can't for the life of me figure why he would."

"Do you know who else hated her?" Lola lowered her voice. "Matias Lajoie. Your father and I were chatting with the concierge Ginny at the inn—"

"Lola," my father cautioned.

"What?" She batted her eyelashes like a coquette, which was as far from her true nature as one could get. She was toying with him. "We didn't pry the information out of Ginny. She wanted to share." She faced me, once again somber. "Anyway, Ginny told us that Matias and Sarita came to the inn for dinner on Wednesday night."

After Sarita and he had run into each other at the expo, I noted, and after Sarita had handed off her children to their father.

"Ginny was taking a walk in the gardens," Lola continued, "and she overheard the two of them arguing after their meal."

"Ginny is a gossip," my father said.

But gossips glean pertinent information, I mused. "I saw them arguing, too. Outside the Nook Café on Thursday, but I couldn't hear a word. Did Ginny say what they were arguing about?"

"Drugs." Lola *tsked.* "Sarita said she knew Matias was selling drugs and warned him to stop. Maybe he killed her to keep his secret."

"It's not a secret," Rhett said. "I knew he was into drugs."

"You did?" My father raised an eyebrow.

"Illegal marijuana."

Lola gawked. "And you didn't turn him in?"

"It was years ago. He wasn't hurting me or my business, and honestly I thought he'd stopped. Plus, marijuana has since become legal in California." Rhett splayed his hands.

"Gunther knew, too," I said. "That's what broke up their friendship."

"But drugs . . ." Lola shook her head, visibly upset.

My father leveled a look at her. "Darling, he's not the only person in our fair town who's doing something outside the lines of the law."

She scowled at him. "I'm not naïve, Cary." She pointed at Rhett. "You should tell Cinnamon or at the very least Z.Z."

"Noted." Rhett exchanged a look with me. "Gunther and Matias used to be friends?"

"It was years ago." I rested a hand on his forearm. "At the time, Matias was supplying fish for Gunther's restaurant. When Gunther learned about the drugs, he ended their relationship. Gunther said that he even warned Sarita because she and Matias were dating then. I guess she believed him because she dumped Matias and started seeing Todd."

"Matias owns a boat company," my father said. "What if he's dealing in harder drugs than marijuana now, and he's transporting them on his vessels?"

Lola clapped her hands once. "Now that's a secret worth killing for."

A doctor entered the room and asked us all to step outside while he performed a few final tests on Rhett.

In the hall, I stopped Lola and my father from leaving. "I still can't figure out who blew up Intime."

Dad snapped his fingers. "What if Sarita found out about your private dinner date at Intime and decided to crash the party? What if she told Matias she was going there to confront Rhett and you?"

Lola's eyes glinted with understanding. "What if he plotted down to the minute how he would kill her so it wouldn't look like she was the target?"

My father jumped in. "But then Sarita never showed up, and Rhett took the brunt of it."

Chapter 30

After being released from the hospital, Rhett wasn't in the mood to sit home. In fact, he had his heart set on chicken potpie at Mum's the Word Diner. He was fed up with urgent care food. How could I deny his one request?

The sky was bright blue with puffs of white clouds, and the temperature was mild for June. Lots of people who were in town for the expo were strolling along the boardwalk. Some carried totes. Others were wearing the wedding-themed T-shirts that a bridal gown vendor had handed out. Many were waving swag fans. Two women in mini veils were sitting at one of the bistro tables—there were always tables along the Pier—sorting through a bridal emergency kit. Another group of women were flipping through complimentary copies of *Brides Around the World* magazines. Dozens of folks, dressed in beachwear, were merely there to enjoy the sunshine and the ocean breeze.

Rhett slung his arm around my shoulders. "Are you getting excited about our wedding?"

"I'm excited but nervous and worried that another shoe will drop."

"Shoes I can handle," he said. "No more bombs. We've had enough big surprises."

Mum's, a fifties-themed diner with turquoise-checkered tablecloths, yellow stools, and jukeboxes on every table as well as on the arced counter, was jam-packed with customers. Rhett and I were willing to wait. We knew turnover usually went quickly. People ate in a rush so they could return outside to enjoy the sunshine. I browsed the photographs of the construction of the Pier that hung on the wall while Rhett studied the menu. Why he was doing so was beyond me.

After the hostess suggested we take the two vacant stools at the counter, Rosie, a vibrant African-American waitress with asymmetric purple-tinged hair, set two water glasses in front of us along with silverware wrapped in turquoise cloth napkins. "Two chicken potpies," she said, pulling a pencil from behind one ear and writing our order on her pad.

Rhett laughed. "How well you know us."

"Habits are called habits for a reason," she retorted.

A man a few stools down clacked a glass on the counter. "Another beer!" he demanded.

Rosie flinched but forced a jaunty smile. "Coming, sir."

I peered past the diners at the rude customer, who was none other than Matias Lajoie. An empty beer glass sat in front of him. His usually tanned face was as gray as his T-shirt. Rosie set a bottle of Heineken next to the empty glass, filled his water glass, and slipped our order check into the queue for the cook.

"Look who it is." I elbowed Rhett. "Do you think he's drowning his guilt because he murdered Sarita?"

Rhett peeked in that direction. "Drowning is a bit of a stretch."

"He doesn't have food in front of him. He must've recently sat down, too."

"Forget him. Focus on me." Rhett slung an arm around my waist and gave me a squeeze.

For the next few minutes, we talked about Intime and what contractors he would need to meet tomorrow.

When Rosie brought our meals, she said, *"Bon appétit.* That's French, if you didn't know."

Rhett chuckled. He was fluent in French. I could manage the language, but I was much better with Spanish.

Rosie set our check on the counter and moseyed to another customer.

Rhett and I poked holes in the crusts of the potpies with our forks to let the steam rise and ate in companionable silence.

When our appetites were sated, we opted to take a walk on the boardwalk to digest our food. I didn't press Rhett to take it easy. He knew his limits. We were standing on the steps of the diner, deciding which direction to walk, when the door opened and Matias Lajoie lurched out. He bumped into Rhett.

"Sorry, fella. Oh, it's you." His bloodshot eyes widened. "How're you feeling, man?" He knuckled Rhett on the arm.

"I'm healing. You don't look so hot, though."

"Yeah, well, life sucks and death bites." Matias grimaced. "I apologize for my foul mouth. I shouldn't drink. Not even beer. Booze makes me ornery. But the past couple of days, I've been . . . Let's say I've been out of sorts."

"Did something set you off?" Rhett asked.

"You had to have heard. Sarita Strachline was—" He gestured to the ocean. "Her boat. *Boom.*" He flicked the fingers on both hands. "Oh, man, sorry. You, too . . . *boom.*" He swallowed hard. "But you survived. You're okay."

"I'm okay enough. I'm still having a bit of a headache and my ear throbs."

"I know you weren't a fan of Sarita's, Rhett, but nobody deserves—" Matias stopped and eyed me. "I saw you yesterday. At the expo. You're—"

"Jenna Hart."

"Yeah."

"I saw you, too, when you were throwing Gunther Hildenbiddle under the bus by badmouthing his food to the Weatherlys."

"I didn't badmouth—"

"Yes, you did, because, way back when, he was the one who told Sarita you were selling illegal marijuana. You wanted to hurt his business."

"Aw, that. He'll weather it. California Catch has great word of mouth. I was just messing with him."

"At the expense of his reputation." I'd seen the rest of what had gone down. He'd watched on with glee.

He scrubbed the back of his neck. "Do you think Wren Weatherly killed Sarita, Jenna?"

At a loss, I said, "Mr. Lajoie—"

"Do you?" he demanded. "I gotta know who did." He smacked one hand against the other as tears pooled in his eyes. "I need answers. See, I loved Sarita. She shouldn't have died like that. Not boom!" He juddered.

She shouldn't have died at all, I thought, *no matter how vile she might have been.*

"Who do you think did it? Do you have a clue?" His voice crackled with tension.

I cocked my head, having a hard time believing him. Had he had a couple of beers so he could put on a pity-me show for someone who'd dined at Mum's, namely Rhett and me? Did he hope we'd back up his emotional tale, should Cinnamon train her sites on him?

"I was there that night," Matias said.

"Where?" Rhett asked.

"On Sarita's boat. On Thursday . . ." His voice trailed off.

I gulped. Was he confessing to murder? "What time?"

"Around nine fifteen or so."

Way before the explosion, I concluded.

Matias motioned to the left side of the Pier, where other boats were moored. "I paddled out in a skiff and climbed aboard without permission so I could tell her how I felt. Lights were on. She was awake. But she wanted no part of me. See, I'd been drinking then, too, and she hated that. She called me weak. Told me that unless I cleaned up my act—no drugs and no booze—I'd never have a chance with her. But that's what I'd been trying to tell her all along. I've cleaned up my act. I stopped dealing drugs of any kind. And I was planning to stop all booze and go cold turkey if . . ." He held up both hands. "She didn't believe me. She started yelling at me."

"You two argued a lot," I stated.

"What do you mean?"

"You argued Thursday morning at Fisherman's Village. I saw you."

"You also went at it at the Crystal Cove Inn on Wednesday night," Rhett added.

"Yeah." Matias hitched a shoulder. "We both had tempers. But I didn't mind. I was nuts about her. Her passion. That fire in her belly. All these years, I couldn't get her out of my mind. I didn't care what she'd done. The arson. The art thefts. I had to win her back."

"But she turned you down on three separate occasions"—I trained my gaze on him—"so you retaliated."

"No!" His voice escalated upward. "No. Uh-uh. Thursday night, on the boat, I got down on one knee. I had a ring. I proposed. I begged her to accept. But like I said, she wanted nothing to do with me and pushed me over the side. Ring and all. I lost it—the ring—and her."

"What happened to the skiff?" Rhett asked.

"It probably blew up with—" His voice snagged.

I regarded him skeptically. "You told Eddie Milsap you saw someone crawling out of the water."

"That's not what I said. I said I was the one who crawled out of the water. I was so angry for believing Sarita might love me again."

"Angry enough to blow her up?" I asked.

"No. What aren't you getting?" He smacked one hand against the other. "I loved her! I was furious that she'd rejected me, so I started picking up discarded beer bottles and smashing them against the pilings. I stopped when I saw someone leaning against a piling. I told Eddie about that, too. About the person I saw."

"That would've been around ten o'clock?" Rhett asked.

"Uh-huh."

Seeing a figure by the piling concurred with Carla the carny worker's testimony.

"Thinking it was a cop," Matias went on, "and not wanting to be arrested for disorderly conduct, I hustled back to my place and drank myself silly until I passed out on the bed."

"Did you tell the police any of this?" I asked.

He shifted feet. "Not everything. I said that I was at home when the explosion occurred. I didn't even hear it." Tears leaked down his cheeks.

"That's a pretty flimsy alibi," Rhett said. "Being home. Would the person by the piling recognize you?"

"I don't know." Matias's shoulders sagged. "And even if I could describe him, I couldn't prove I did unless that person comes forward and—" He spun to his right. "Wait a sec! What if someone who works here on the Pier saw Sarita push me off the boat? What if—"

He tore off, jogging along the Pier, and stopped the first guy he saw. He gesticulated wildly with his hands. The guy shook his head. Matias moved on to a woman with red frizzy hair and repeated the motions. The woman shrugged.

Rhett said, "Think we should believe him?"

"Believe who, old man?" Eddie Milsap, in crisp white shirt, paisley tie, and black trousers, patted Rhett on the back. "Good to see you're out and on your feet. What're the odds I'd run into you before I started my shift?" He eyeballed me. "I thought I might catch you in church this morning, Jenna."

I smiled. "Not a chance. I was breaking Rhett out of Mercy Urgent Care."

"Breaking him out." Eddie chortled. "So, you were saying, Rhett, is *who* to be believed?"

"Matias Lajoie."

I said, "Eddie, do you remember what Matias said to you the day after Sarita's boat blew up? He saw something."

"Sure do." He reiterated what he'd told me.

I said, "Hmm. He revised that a moment ago by claiming he was the one crawling out of the water around half past nine."

"Huh." Eddie rubbed the back of his neck. "You know, my folks and I did hear glass breaking."

"You were here?" I asked. He hadn't mentioned that in our previous conversation.

"Yeah, it was Dad's birthday and he wanted to come to the diner to celebrate." He pointed at Mum's the Word. "There was a hefty crowd, so we didn't finish dinner until after nine. We were just leaving when we heard the sound of breaking glass. We didn't think much about it. We have a small homeless population. Finding shelter under the Pier when it's raining is typical for them, and breaking bottles is the norm." Eddie slipped his hands into his pockets. "I suppose it could have been Matias. I said good night to my folks and went to Bait and Switch to do a little bookkeeping. When the explosion happened, I hustled outside to check it out and see if I had to hightail it to safety."

"The timing jibes," Rhett said to me. "What do you think, Jenna?"

"Let's tell Cinnamon. She should question Matias and ask what color bottles he broke. Maybe she can corroborate his story if there are remnants in the sand."

Chapter 31

Rhett and I headed to the precinct. It was as quiet as it had been earlier. Cinnamon, still at her desk, accepted our request to chat with her. The stack of documents on the right of her desk appeared to be taller.

She grunted as we entered. "Both of you? Let me guess, Jenna. You have something else to tell me. You really don't trust me to do my job."

"That's not fair." I hated the whine in my voice, but it was there. She unnerved me at times.

"You're right. Maybe this is purely a social call." She set her pen down on her blotter and forced a smile. "How are you, Rhett?"

"Out of the woods."

"Good to know." She flashed me a phony smile. "And you, Jenna? How are you?"

I glowered at her.

She snickered. "Yeah, that's what I thought. Now spill whatever it is you came to say."

"C'mon, Cinnamon," I said. "The law of the land nowadays is if you see something, say something. Well, what if we heard something? Do you want us to keep mum?"

She said to Rhett, "Your fiancée is getting snarky with me."

"And rightly so," he replied, sticking up for me. "We did hear something."

Cinnamon sat back in her chair and crossed her arms across her chest. "Proceed."

In tandem, Rhett and I tried to explain how the conversation with Matias as well as Eddie had come about, adding that we hadn't actively searched for answers. We'd gone to the Pier for lunch.

After hearing us out, Cinnamon's interest was piqued. "I'll question Matias, but in the meantime, I want you both to steer clear. Rhett, you need to get in bed no matter what your adrenaline is telling you. I've suffered a concussion. It's not fun. Rest and be ready to say 'I do' in a couple of weeks. Do you hear me?"

Joking, he cupped a hand around his bad ear and said, "Eh?"

Rising to her feet, she aimed a finger at her door. "Go. Get out. Let me do my job."

Taking Cinnamon's advice, we didn't join the family for dinner as we normally would on a Sunday evening. We went home, and I made Rhett a simple meal, after which he went straight to bed.

Monday morning was a flurry of activity at the shop. Gran's three-book sale package had been such a hit yesterday that Bailey had decided to compile another one that featured apple-themed instead of bridal-themed books, combining *The Apple Cookbooks: Best Recipes Celebrating the Sweet, Sour, and Spicy Flavor of Apples* with Liane Moriarty's bestseller *Apples Never Fall* and the adorable children's book *One Red Apple*. She'd thrown in an apple-themed apron, to boot.

I joined Bailey at the display table.

"Why are we hyper focused on apples, you ask?" She motioned to the selection of books. "Because Adam and Eve were the first couple. And you know what happened when Eve bit the apple." Giggling, she added, "Blushing brides-to-be whose hormones are raging will love the imagery, don't you think?"

I laughed and whacked her on the shoulder, and then I paused, sensing something was missing. I scanned the shop. "Where's Brianna?"

"With my mother."

"Again?"

"They're touring the expo. It closes tomorrow. Mom wants some swag." Bailey snapped her fingers. "Oh, I almost forgot. Rhett phoned while you were driving over. He wants you to meet him at Intime to meet the demolition contractor stat."

"Stat?" I didn't like the sound of that.

"He set up some morning appointments already and wants your input."

"Phew. I was beginning to worry."

Last night, Rhett had changed his mind about meeting contractors alone, saying he wasn't sure how he'd react entering Intime so soon after the explosion. I'd figured I had at least until noon before he'd need me. I switched into the canvas shoes I'd worn the other day and jog-walked to the restaurant, my cross-body purse bouncing on my hip.

Rhett was feeding a parking meter as I arrived. Prepared to get dirty, he'd dressed in a T-shirt and sweats. Luckily, I'd donned a cute

T-shirt and denim skirt that would wash easily.

"Hey, beauty," he said, and kissed me on the lips. "After you." He unlocked the front door and held it open for me.

A lanky man with a soul patch and bony cheeks arrived from our right. "Mr. Baxter, I'm from Ace Demolition." He offered his business card to Rhett.

"Thanks for having the time," Rhett said. "Let's get started."

We hadn't moved five feet into the restaurant when Rhett stiffened. I could see he was holding his breath.

"Sweetheart?" I put a hand at the small of his back. "Are you okay?"

"Yeah, it's just . . . What a mess." He ran a palm down the side of his neck, probably wondering, as I had the first time I'd walked in, how he had survived the blast.

Less than a half hour later, we had figured out the first step for restoring Intime. Fifteen minutes after the guy from Ace Demolition left, we met with the painting contractor. Fifteen minutes after he left, the flooring guy arrived.

"How'd you get all these people to meet so soon?" I asked Rhett when we had a break.

"Good business relationships, and Jim Daley might have had some pull. He's very respected."

A woman showed up next to discuss the appliance replacements. The plumber followed her.

Inside of two hours, we'd scheduled every aspect of the renovation.

"What do you think?" I asked Rhett as he was locking up.

"As long as there are no snags or permit issues, it should take about a month."

"That's not too bad."

"As long as . . ." he repeated. "But there will be, and we're getting married, so I can't oversee everything."

"My father can. He knows all the ins and outs of reconstruction, especially with all his volunteer work for Habitat for Humanity. Do you mind if I ask him to consult with you?"

"What would I do without you?"

I walked him to his truck and lingered by the door. "Rest for the remainder of the day, please."

"Yes, ma'am."

"If you're good, I'll make you my specialty spaghetti and meatballs for dinner."

"With extra basil?"

"It's the only way I know." I caressed his shoulder. "Drive carefully."

As he was pulling away from the curb, I saw Ilya Bakov entering the Velvet Box across the street. She spotted me and waved. Having told her that I would visit the jewelry shop one day soon, I decided now was the time.

I cut across Buena Vista, dodging traffic, and paused to take in the shop's display window, an underwater paradise with seashells, sand, and silk seaweed. In the center there was a gigantic open clam shell, within which nested a gorgeous blue pearl.

A middle-aged woman sauntered into the shop. I followed her in and was struck by the numerous display cases, each containing one-of-a-kind designs. The walls were a restful pale blue. Behind the register, glass shelving held a variety of blue velvet boxes, opened to exhibit rings. In addition, there was a wealth of indoor plants: fiddle leaf figs, parlor palms, cascading pothos, and birds-of-paradise, all planted in deep-blue-glazed pots. I recalled Tito saying his source had asked Sarita Strachline why she'd been lingering outside the Velvet Box the day before the explosion at Intime. She'd claimed she was there to water Ilya's plants. Now her story rang true.

Ilya spotted me. "Welcome, Jenna. I'll be right with you." She was clad in an ocean-blue sleeveless sheath and bejeweled sandals. Had she dressed to match her store's décor? She pushed her blond curls over her shoulders as she tended to the customer who had entered before me. The woman appeared to be picking up something she'd ordered. Ilya was showing the woman the final product in its box.

"My sister will love it," the woman cooed. "You are so talented."

Ilya closed the box and inserted it into an aqua blue gift bag.

When the satisfied customer exited, Ilya met me by a display of ornamental bracelets. "Do you see something you like?" she asked.

"They're all beautiful," I replied. "The one adorned with rubies and sapphires is exquisite."

"Thank you."

"Do you polish all the gems yourself?"

"Yes. I remember you saying that your brother had a rock tumbler. Do you want to see mine?"

"I'm sure yours is much grander than his was."

"Come with me." She locked the front door and turned over a sign that read *Back in a Few.* "But I warn you, the workroom is a mess. I haven't been inside since I returned." She swept a hand through the air. "Too much paperwork and dusting."

"Flora said Sarita was the reason you opened the shop." I ogled the gorgeous necklaces on display in a glass-enclosed case as we passed.

"Yes. She inspired me to reach for the stars." She pressed a hand to her chest. "I still can't believe she's gone." She opened the workroom door and flipped the switch.

Bright spotlights flooded the room. A sturdy rectangular table sat in the middle of the room. Upon it sat a bright green tumbler three times the size of my brother's machine. There were also jewelry-making tools like pliers, saws, and wire, and numerous tubs of loose stones. Shelving to the right held clear boxes marked with their contents. The far wall was packed with boxes, suitcases, plastic containers, each labeled by a black Sharpie. There was also a silver overnight-sized suitcase with a combination lock and no label.

"What's that pungent smell?" I asked.

"Tar. They paved the alley last Monday, when I was out of town."

I was surprised my father hadn't mentioned that. He hated the smell of tar. His hardware store was a few doors down from the jewelry shop.

I stepped deeper into the room. "Many of the boxes have Sarita's name on them. Why are they here?"

"After the arson, she wanted to get out of town fast. She needed someplace to store her clothes and jewelry. She didn't dare leave anything of hers at the house she'd given Todd. She was afraid he'd junk it." Ilya mimed a tossing action. "Their divorce was bitter, to say the least. Sarita didn't want to move everything lock, stock, and barrel to New Orleans, of course. She always hoped to settle back here in Crystal Cove. Alas, jail came first."

"Did you know about her part in the arson?" I asked.

"No. In hindsight . . ." She braced her chest with one arm and sighed. "I think jail taught her a lot. She was remorseful."

Yet spiteful toward Rhett and me, I thought.

"You were a good friend to her, letting her stow her stuff and giving her a loan to help her get back on her feet."

"All I gave her was a couple thousand dollars," she said, not dodging the topic this time. "Enough for a hotel room and dinner with her girls. Big deal."

A couple of thousand wasn't enough to rent a sailboat, I noted. So where had Sarita gotten the money? Matias hadn't mentioned anything to Rhett and me about giving her a loan.

I tried out a theory. "Do you know if she stashed any of the insurance money? Rumor was that she'd run through it, but, gee, she had enough to rent that sailboat."

Her gaze tracked to the silver suitcase and quickly back to me.

"Is that suitcase hers?" I asked.

"Wh-what?" Ilya sputtered. "No. No, it's mine." Her eyelids fluttered. She was lying.

"What's in it?" I stepped toward it.

Ilya blocked me. "Don't."

"Ilya, what're you hiding?"

"Nothing. It's my private stash of gems. They're one-of-a-kind."

I didn't believe her and cut around her. I made it to the suitcase in three strides.

"Jenna. Stop. It's . . . please don't."

"I'm intrigued. May I see the gems, please? Maybe you could make trinkets for my bridal party. I've been thinking of getting some special bridesmaids' gifts." It was a lie. I'd already bought luxury gift boxes for Bailey, Katie, and Harmony, filled with heart necklaces, bottles of CC Vineyards sparkling wine, champagne glasses, and personalized floral robes. "What's the combination?"

"Stop."

"Don't you remember it?"

She drew up short, her hands clenching and unclenching.

"Ilya," I cooed, in a tone I might use on a toddler, "you won't hurt me. Tell me what's in the box. If it's illegal —"

"It's not . . . I don't think it is . . . I'm not sure." She wheezed. Her face blanched. "Fine. I admit it. It's not mine. It's . . . it *was*

Sarita's. She bought jewels at cost before she left for New Orleans."

"Through you?"

"With my help. She said it was her safety net. They're sewn into the lining of a jacket." She whimpered. "Am I going to jail?"

"I don't know." If Sarita had paid back everything to the insurance company by selling the recovered art, could they come after her for whatever she'd managed to salvage? Why sew gems into the lining of a coat? To keep them from her ex-husband? Had she used one of the gems to pay the rent on her boat? I turned to Ilya. "What're you looking at?"

She had eased to the exit door and was staring at something on the floor. "What's that?" She pointed at a black smudge and bent to touch it. She wrinkled her nose. "Eww. Tar. How did it—" She rose to a full stand and whirled around. "That!" she blurted and guardedly inched toward the boxes marked with Sarita's name, as if they might attack her. "That box doesn't belong here."

I joined her. "Which one?"

"That one."

She indicated the square brown box abutted by two similar boxes. Ilya reached for it.

"Don't touch it." I gripped her arm. "Are you sure it's not Sarita's?"

"Positive. I've never seen it before. She marked all her boxes in cursive. Her name on that one is in bold block letters."

I glimpsed between the box and its neighbors and spied a plastic sealed shipping label on the side of the unknown box. Carefully, I removed the nearest box to expose the entire label. It had been sent by the online retailer *Super Ship*.

Chapter 32

Like other e-tailers, Super Ship had a massive website, which offered virtually every product a person could need. Books, movies, toys, clothing, household products, and more.

"Perhaps Sarita put this here while you were away when she came to water your plants," I theorized.

"That might explain the tar on the floor," Ilya said, "but not why her name is written in block letters."

I opened both hands. "I change up my handwriting depending on my mood."

"Sarita didn't. She valued the look of cursive." She blew out a stream of air. "I'm going to open the box now. Make sure it's really hers." Intent on her mission, Ilya fetched a blade from the table holding her tools and returned.

"Wait!" I yelped, my nerves tingling. What if a bomb was inside? What if opening the box would detonate it? "Who else would have put it here?"

"I don't know. Not any of my staff." She sliced open the tape and folded back the top.

It didn't explode. I breathed easier.

She peered inside and shook her head. "Huh. Cleaning supplies."

I eased nearer to take a peek and spied a bottle of bleach, ammonia, and vinegar, as well as a box of baking soda.

She removed the items one by one and set them on the floor.

"Maybe she bought those things for when she found a place to rent," I suggested.

Ilya froze.

"What else did you find?" I asked.

She didn't respond and moved away, one hand cupping her chin with worry.

I peered in and gasped. At the bottom of the box were a box of ball bearings, wire, and switches. "Those are—" I swallowed hard. "These are bomb supplies."

"No way."

"I have to call the police."

"No, no, no." Ilya's voice vibrated with tension. "Sarita did not blow herself up."

"Maybe not, but she might have detonated the bomb at Intime. Ball bearings were found at the crime scene."

"No. Sarita didn't do it. She couldn't have. She wasn't like that."

"Grow up, Ilya. She torched her restaurant. She spent a lot of years in jail contemplating her next move. Getting back at Rhett and me for siccing the authorities on her had to have been central to her plan. She verbally assaulted me at the Bride's Dream Expo on Wednesday. Others heard her."

"No," she mewled. Her shoulders were quivering.

I kept my gaze on her as I pulled my cell phone from my purse, dialed the precinct, and asked for Cinnamon. When she came on the line, despite the exasperation I heard in her tone, I told her what I'd found.

She and Appleby arrived within minutes. I let them in the front door.

"This way," I said over my shoulder as I made a beeline for the workroom.

"Why were you back here, Jenna?" Cinnamon asked.

I told her about my brother's obsession as a teenager with gems and how I'd mentioned his rock tumbler to Ilya the other day. "While she was showing me hers, she spotted the errant box I mentioned on the phone. She noticed the block letters didn't match the cursive writing on the other boxes that belonged to Sarita." I added, "Ilya allowed Sarita to store things here when she relocated to New Orleans."

Cinnamon walked into the workroom first. Ilya was standing by her worktable, hands folded in front of her. Her gaze was downcast. Was she working through all the possibilities of how this discovery might affect her business? Her life? Was she guilty of aiding and abetting?

Appleby donned plastic gloves.

"Chief," I said, "in complete disclosure, Ilya . . . Mrs. Bakov and I touched the box. She put the items you see on the floor. Neither of us touched the items that are still in the box."

Using his cell phone, Appleby took photos of the items on the floor before casting his attention to those in the box.

"Chief, that's a toe print." I pointed to the tar on the floor. "I think somebody broke into this area while Ilya was on the cruise. There might be a complete footprint in the alley. It was recently repaved with tar. If it was Sarita Strachline—"

"That looks too large and wide to be a toe print from a woman's shoe," she remarked.

"How about a man's shoe?" Appleby asked, holding up a see-through envelope that he'd retrieved from the box. "In particular, Gunther Hildenbiddle's." He shook an envelope he'd freed from the exterior label. "This is a shipping label to Gunther at his restaurant."

I gawped.

"That explains it!" Ilya shot out her hand. "Gunther must have put the box there, not Sarita, and he wrote Sarita's name on the box to frame her."

"How would he have known this is where she was keeping her things?" Cinnamon asked.

"Maybe he followed her," Ilya said, "and saw her watering the plants for me. Or maybe he watched her from afar with binoculars and through the store window saw her enter the workroom. Maybe he spied her pawing through her boxes."

"That's a whole lot of maybes," Cinnamon said.

"But it makes sense," Ilya countered.

I wilted. Gunther looked guilty. Was his motive for bombing Intime simply to eliminate the competition, as Bailey had theorized? Had he then doubled down and blown up Sarita, a woman he'd resented for so many years? He'd seemed like such a gentle man.

Cinnamon called in the forensics team before leaving to track down Gunther Hildenbiddle, adding that she would question Ilya further and advised her not to leave town.

Chapter 33

Appleby stayed on-site with Ilya and me. "Is there anyone I can call to be with you, Mrs. Bakov?"

"My mother." She heaved a sigh. "She lives at the north end of town."

I placed a hand on her shoulder and said, "I'll stay with you until she arrives."

Ilya finally broke down and wept.

A half hour later, her mother drove up in her Chevy Tahoe. The woman, similar in appearance to her daughter with honey-blond hair and a trim figure, rushed out of her SUV. She hugged Ilya and with a gentle nudge prodded her into the car.

I wished Ilya well and headed back to the Cookbook Nook.

Bailey was at the sales counter ringing up the last of her specialty apple packages. "Success!" she exclaimed. "We had triple sales today. On a Monday of all days. I think it's because the expo-goers are sick and tired of seeing so many bridal things. In a few minutes, kiddies will be coming in to make bride- or groom-shaped cookies." She gestured to the children's table, which held an array of cookie sprinkles, icings, and gels. "Gran will supervise. Oh, and Harmony phoned, asking for you. She said you aren't answering your cell phone."

I'd seen messages from her as I'd driven back to the shop but had decided to wait to call her until I'd figured out what to say. Perhaps she already knew about Gunther's predicament. "Did she explain why she was calling?"

"There's a little snag with the wedding."

"Oka-a-ay." Last night with Rhett lying beside me in bed, too worried to fall asleep in case he needed me, I'd mulled over every last detail of the wedding and had decided that no hiccup would throw me for a loop. But now? Faced with another snag? *Oof.* I lifted Tigger from his kitty condo, held him close to my chest, and stroked his ears. I willed his steady purr to settle me down, but it didn't. The snag had to be the DJ. We'd have to find another.

"Don't worry," Bailey said, picking up on my unease. "Everything will be fine."

"Sure it will."

She rounded the counter. "Fess up. What's wrong?"

"Nothing."

"Liar."

My aunt exited the storage room and nearly bumped into me. "What's going on? Why are you two in a huddle?"

"No reason," Bailey replied.

"We're good," I said.

Aunt Vera huffed and jammed her hands onto her hips. "Have you girls forgotten how long I've known—"

"Jenna," Bailey cut in. "I forgot to add that Harmony said to tell you she's at the café having coffee with—"

A siren whooped. A police cruiser pulled into the parking lot and screeched to a halt. I jolted. Tigger wriggled to be set free. I returned him to the condo and rushed to the front door. Cinnamon was climbing out of the cruiser. She set her hat on her head and strode with a determined gait toward the Nook Café. *Uh-oh.*

I tore down the breezeway and met her as she entered. "Hi. What're you doing here? I thought you were heading to California Catch to talk to Gunther. Did you talk to him? Did he confess?"

"Out of my way, Jenna." She pushed past me and marched toward Gunther Hildenbiddle, who was sitting with Harmony at a table by the window.

Noise in the café lessened as Cinnamon approached the pair. I trailed her.

"Mr. Hildenbiddle," Cinnamon said. "A word."

Gunther's face turned ashen. So did Harmony's.

Cinnamon whisked a hand at me. "Leave, Jenna. This doesn't concern you." She pulled out a chair and sat. "You may leave, too, Miss Bold."

Gunther said, "I'd like her to stay."

Harmony raised her chin.

"Fine." Cinnamon folded her hands on the table. "Now then . . ."

I headed outside instead of going back to the Cookbook Nook. I needed air. My cell phone pinged in my purse. I pulled it out. Harmony was texting me.

She wrote: *The police searched Gunther's office at California Catch. They found a map.*

I responded: *What kind of map?*

She replied: *A map planning out his attack on Sarita's boat.*

Criminently, as my mother would say. How had Cinnamon gained access to Gunther's office without him being there? Had she gotten a warrant that fast? And how had she found the map so quickly? Had it been sitting on Gunther's desk for all to see? Or had he stupidly tucked it into a folder marked with Sarita's name?

I typed in a message, revealing something I probably shouldn't, but felt Harmony ought to know. *They also found a carton at the Velvet Box filled with things that could make a bomb. With a shipping label to Gunther at his restaurant.*

Harmony wrote: [sad-faced emoji] *The chief started with that. Gunther said he didn't order the items.*

Was it possible Ilya, not Sarita, had ordered the items from Super Ship and sent them to Gunther, and then filched them from California Catch and transported them to her shop to frame him? No. That wouldn't explain the map Cinnamon had found in Gunther's office. How about Gunther's son? Had he masterminded the plot?

I typed another text: *There's a man-sized shoeprint at the Velvet Box.*

Harmony wrote back: *She didn't mention that.* [frightened emoji] *Does Gunther need a lawyer?*

I responded quickly: *Yes.*

I spotted Todd Strachline exiting Beaders of Paradise with his daughters, both dressed in blue cutoffs and colorful T-shirts; both were smiling. The younger one was carrying a Beaders of Paradise tote bag as well as a two-foot-long macramé hanging of a moon with tassels.

Todd looked from the police cruiser to the café. "What's going on?"

I drew near. "Chief Pritchett is talking to Gunther in the café."

"Not because of what I said to you, I hope." He placed a hand to his chest. "Gunther doesn't have a mean bone in his body."

"They found some evidence."

"What kind of evidence?" He tilted his head.

"I can't say."

"What's going on, Daddy?" Sela asked.

With a nod I acknowledged the macramé that she was carrying. "That's very pretty. Did you make it?"

She nodded.

"You're quite talented."

"Get in the truck, girls," Todd ordered. When they were out of earshot, he said to me, "You know what I think? Matias Lajoie killed Sarita. He was fixated on her. She rejected him. He's mechanically inclined. He knows how to fix boats. I'll bet he figured out how to rig a bomb. Should I go inside and tell the chief? Yeah." He nodded, not waiting for my response. "I'm putting in my two cents. Girls! Stay in the truck." Todd started for the café.

At the same time, my cell phone rang. I withdrew it from my purse. Ilya was on the line. I answered.

"I have to show you something right now," she said. "It's urgent. I need your advice."

"What's this about?"

"I can't explain on the phone. Please come to my mother's house." She gave me the address. "Please." She ended the call.

I rushed into the shop and told Bailey where I was headed. As I drove at a clip to the area north of the community college, I pondered whether Ilya was luring me into a trap but dismissed the notion. She was Sarita's lifelong friend. She'd been on a cruise when her friend was killed.

Ilya's mother's lived in a set of white townhomes with red rooves that climbed the hill. Each had views of the ocean. Two large white fuchsia in red-glazed pots adorned the woman's front porch. When she opened the door and smiled broadly, I breathed easier.

"Come in," she said. The timber of her voice reminded me of my mother's, warm and caring. After I stepped inside, she closed the door and called, "Ilya! Your guest is here."

Ilya appeared, her face tearstained and drawn. She bussed her mother's cheek. "We're going to the patio."

"Okay, dear," her mother responded. "Would you like some tea?"

"No, Mom, thanks." Ilya guided me through the all-white furnishings to the patio, which, like my father's house, had a clear glass railing with white metal posts. The sound of surf hitting the shore reached us. So did the aroma of the ocean. The sun was halfway to the horizon.

"I've never been inside one of these townhomes." I glanced at the patio furnishings, equally as nice as those inside. "They're lovely."

"My husband bought it for my mother after my father died."

"He sounds like he was a very generous man."

"He was. He was the love of my—" She bit back a sob and motioned for me to sit in one of the webbed chairs. "Look, there's no easy way to say this." She fisted a hand and rested it beneath her chin. "I took Sarita's silver suitcase with me."

Aha! No wonder she'd struck me as anxious when I'd guided the police into the workroom. Where had she stashed it? The bathroom? Her office? No, she must have put it in the alley and retrieved it when her mother came to fetch her, after I left but before the police investigated the area. I swallowed hard. Was it evidence? Sure, it was, if the jacket with jewels sewn into the lining was in it and that factored into Sarita's deal with the insurance company.

I ran a hand along my neck to work the knots out of it. "Go on."

"In addition to the jacket I told you about, Sarita had stowed all of her important papers in the suitcase. She . . . She had a life insurance policy naming her daughters and Todd as beneficiaries. I didn't know about it." She produced a document and handed it to me. "If I tell the police about it now, they'll realize I removed the suitcase from the workroom."

"Not necessarily. Considering your friendship with Sarita, they might assume she gave you papers to keep in a safe place, other than in the workroom."

"You mean I should lie to them?"

"No!" I shook my head emphatically. "Don't lie. About anything."

"Just, um, omit details?"

"Unless pressed, yes. Is the insurance policy paid up?"

"I don't know. We never talked about her finances. Only mine. My business. My future." New tears pressed at the corners of Ilya's eyes. "She was a good friend."

To some, I reflected. *Not to all.*

"I was thinking, what if . . ." Ilya gnawed on the tip of her index finger.

"Go on."

"What if Sarita is the one who put that brown box in the

workroom? What if she ordered the supplies in Gunther's name?"

"There'd be a paper trail of the transaction."

"Not if she used a Super Ship gift card. What if she sent it to him at the restaurant, and then went there and intercepted the delivery and put it in my workroom to frame him?"

Interesting. That was exactly the scenario I'd imagined either with Ilya or Gunther's son as the perpetrator.

"What if Sarita thought she'd never work again because she'd been a felon?" Ilya went on. "What if she thought her life was worthless? What if she planted the bomb on her boat and killed herself so her daughters would get the payout?"

The notion made me shudder. "Was she unhinged?" I asked, knowing Sarita would have been fragile, at the very least, after serving time in jail.

"No, but—"

"Killing yourself that way is pretty extreme, not to mention if the insured person is found to have committed suicide, the life insurance policy is null and void."

"What if the police can't prove she did it?" Ilya asked. "What if the case goes unsolved?"

I thought of Cinnamon's comment earlier about *a whole lot of maybes*. This was a slew of what-ifs. And I didn't think her not solving the case was likely. Our intrepid chief of police was all over this investigation now, particularly after finding the makings for a bomb and a map of a plan.

"Let's call Sarita's insurance agent." Ilya hopped to her feet. "He can tell us more about the insurance policy."

I doubted Sarita would have told him she'd planned on killing herself, but I couldn't get the words out before Ilya was stabbing numbers on her cell phone. Someone answered. Ilya said, "Mr. Daley? It's Ilya Bakov."

I mouthed *Jim Daley?*

Ilya nodded. "Yes, hi. No, nothing's wrong at the Velvet Box. Everything's f-fine." She stumbled over the word. She must have realized that everything wasn't *fine*. "I'm calling about Sarita Strachline, on behalf of her daughters. I'm the executor of her will."

Was she, or was she lying? She didn't make eye contact with me.

Quickly, she recapped what she'd said to me about finding the insurance policy. "Are the premiums paid up?" She waited for an answer. "They are? Okay, so what's the next step? How does the policy get enforced?" She listened some more. "Uh-huh. Uh-huh. Yes, okay. Thank you." She ended the call and gazed at me.

"Jim Daley is our agent," I said. "Intime's, too."

"I think he covers most of the businesses in town. So here's what he said. Sarita bought the policy when the girls were born. Because they were a two-income household, she encouraged Todd to get one, too. If something happened to either one of them, they would be able to keep taking care of their daughters."

"I presume most couples would do that." Rhett and I each had policies in place so that our businesses and business partners wouldn't flounder if one of us died. If we were to have children, we'd have to discuss getting broader-scoped policies.

"She and Todd were so in love at first." Ilya stood at the railing and peered out. "I wish they'd been able to make it work."

"You called him a mooch when we chatted at the Nook Café, which means your opinion of him changed. Why?"

"When they met, Todd had recently moved back to Crystal Cove to help his sick mother and was commuting to San Jose for his dream job at Beyond Science. He was its accountant. According to him, management was simply the greatest. Good benefits. Hefty bonuses. But after a while, the commuting put a strain on his and Sarita's relationship. So Sarita suggested he give up his job and join her in her *dream* restaurant." She stressed the word. "He loved her, so he did what she asked, but the life didn't suit him. Restaurant hours were a real grind. Not for him but for Sarita. She worked twenty-four-seven."

Ilya turned from the railing to face me. "After the girls were born, Todd started to resent Sarita. He grew surly, wishing he'd kept his old job. He felt he was always giving and Sarita was taking. The bickering took its toll on them. Sarita decided to end the marriage amicably."

"You said the divorce was bitter."

"Well, it became bitter." Ilya tucked a hair behind her ear. "She offered him the house. She said it was a win-win. An even split. And the girls wouldn't have to move. He countered. She countered. How do you manage it all with your fiancé?" Ilya asked. " I mean, isn't he at the bistro all the time? Your hours are so different."

"He hired extra chefs and a co-manager. It's made his hours much more manageable."

Ilya's face screwed into a knot. "I would never open a restaurant. Ever."

Considering what had happened this week, I wondered if Rhett was feeling the same way.

Before I left, I made Ilya promise to come clean and call Cinnamon with the news.

Chapter 34

I returned to the shop. My aunt was manning the sales counter. Bailey had left to tend to Brianna, who had fallen and scraped her knee.

For the remainder of the afternoon, I balanced the books, readied orders for the coming weeks, and tidied the shop, starting with the children's table, which was still covered in cookie-decorating paraphernalia.

When I walked into the house with Tigger at six thirty, Rhett was asleep on the couch with Rook curled against him and the television on. Rook lifted his head. I told him to go back to sleep, set Tigger on the floor, and carried the groceries I'd picked up on the way home into the kitchen. As quietly as I could, I emptied the contents of the bags onto the granite counter and put on a big pot of water to boil. Then I moved to the massive island and diced Roma tomatoes, sweet Maui onions, and basil for my pasta sauce.

Next, I heated olive oil in a sauté pan on the stove, added the vegetables, and started in on the meatballs. Katie had given me a recipe that included panko, eggs, fresh chopped parsley, and spices. She generally guesstimated the ingredients, but for me, she had been specific. A quarter cup of this. A tablespoon of that. Soon, the kitchen was smelling as fragrant as an authentic Italian kitchen.

When everything was simmering, I fetched two plates from the cupboard, filled two water goblets, poured myself a glass of chianti, and took a well-deserved sip.

Rhett shuffled into the kitchen, smoothing his hair with his palm. Rook trailed him, his nostrils twitching. He whimpered and eyeballed me, begging to be fed.

"Yes, it's your turn for dinner in a sec, pal," I cooed to the sweet mutt.

"Sorry I was asleep." Rhett kissed my neck.

A shiver swizzled down to my toes. I pecked him on the mouth. "Sit down. You need to rest."

"I'm done resting." He grabbed a wineglass for himself, thought twice about it, and put it back in the cabinet.

"I'm s-sorry," I stammered. "I wouldn't have poured one—"

"Stop. You go right ahead. I'll wait another day." He perched on a stool by the island.

"How's your head?" I asked, stroking the back of his neck gently.

"Still intact." He offered a lopsided grin.

"And your ear?"

"The throbbing has subsided."

"That's great news."

"How was the rest of your day?"

"Where do I begin?" I recapped my visit to the Velvet Box, finding the bomb items, Cinnamon questioning Gunther at the café about the shipping label as well as the map she'd found in his office, and Ilya showing me the insurance policy.

Rhett listened attentively throughout, then whistled.

"Yeah." I echoed his whistle. "It was quite an afternoon."

"Do you think Gunther set both bombs?"

"Harmony doesn't think so, but she might be too—" I hesitated.

"Too what?"

"Harmony!" I blurted. "I need to speak to her. She told Bailey there was a snag with the wedding plans. I was on my way to see her—she was eating in the café—but Cinnamon showed up to talk to Gunther and banished me. Moments later, Ilya contacted me, so I dealt with that. Then orders at the shop needed my attention . . . " I fetched my cell phone and selected Harmony's contact.

She answered after one ring. "Hi, Jenna." She sounded exhausted. "What's up?"

"How's Gunther doing?"

"Thanks to his lawyer, he's free to go pending further investigation. They'll discuss strategy first thing in the morning. He wants me to be there. His son, too." She sighed. "I think the police are way off base, but the evidence is so . . ." Her voice trailed off.

So damning, I thought. I murmured that I was sorry and proceeded. "You were looking for me earlier. Bailey said there's a hiccup with our wedding plans."

"Oh, right. It's no biggie. Dancing Deejay can't make it."

I knew it! Was I psychic? *DJ,* I mouthed to Rhett, who frowned.

"But don't worry," she said hurriedly. "He arranged for his buddy to do the gig, and he says the guy—who happened to be his mentor—is eons better. He's the one who taught him how to crossfade and mix. He goes by the moniker Mobile DJ. He's sending me a reel tape as well as some YouTube links so we can approve."

"Okay." I let out the breath I was holding. "As long as he'll play oldies and my one walk-down-the-aisle song, 'Canon in D,' we're good."

"Are you looking forward to your bridal shower this Friday?" she asked.

With all the hoopla, I'd forgotten about it. "Sure am."

"Katie and Bailey have some fun surprises planned."

"Swell." Just what I needed. More surprises. *Not.* "Let me know what happens with Gunther."

I ended the call and put the pasta into the pot of boiling water. When dinner was ready, I plated it, set the dishes and water on a tray, and carried the tray to the rear patio.

Rhett propped the door open and inhaled deeply. "Nice night."

"It's lovely, and it's so good to have you home."

I adored our yard. It wasn't huge, but it offered four beautiful seasons of flowers. In the summer, honeysuckle was rampant and the fragrance divine.

Rook and Tigger scampered out and started a game of tag. Per usual, Tigger was in the lead. He had the ability to hop up and over things. Rook was always navigating chairs, table legs, and planters.

"Warm enough?" I asked Rhett as he settled into the chair next to mine. "I can get you a blanket."

"Stop." He clasped my hand. "Don't baby me. I'm fine. The doctor gave me a good bill of health. Besides, simply looking at your beautiful face warms the cockles of my soul."

I furrowed my brow. "What is a cockle, anyway?"

"A bivalve mollusk or a small shallow boat." He held up a finger. "Crossword clue with six letters." He enjoyed challenging his brain by doing crossword and sudoku puzzles.

I swatted his arm. "Showoff."

Rook yipped. Tigger growled playfully.

"Wish I had their energy," Rhett said.

"You will. Soon."

. . .

In the morning, I fed Rook and Tigger and prepared a tray of food for Rhett, who was exhausted and wisely staying in bed — meeting the contractors and seeing the scope of the renovations at Intime had taken its toll on him. Then I dressed and headed to the Cookbook Nook. Tuesday was our one day off each week, but I'd asked for all hands on deck today. We had a lot to prep. The Fourth of July festivities would be upon us soon, and I needed to do as much as I could to make things easier for my aunt and the others before I got wrapped up in the wedding brouhaha.

While dreaming of seeing myself walking to the altar at CC Vineyards, I gathered last year's boxes of red, white, and blue items for the display window.

"Someone's happy," Bailey said, pushing Brianna in her stroller through the front door. My pal had donned a white tunic shirt over red skinny jeans. Her daughter looked adorable in a duck-themed shorts outfit, and her knee was sporting a Big Bird bandage. "Your red, star-studded T-shirt is exactly right for today's activity."

I'd made my top at a crafting class I'd taken with Pepper last year and had decided it was the perfect seasonal T-shirt to wear over white capris. "You dressed for the occasion, too, I see."

"One can never go wrong with red-and-white anything, as you obviously know." She pirouetted. "By the way, I like the tune you were singing."

"Was I singing?"

"On key, too."

"What's not to be happy about? Rhett's on the mend. The DJ canceled but found us a worthy replacement." The YouTube video and the reel of his work that Harmony had forwarded had assuaged my concern. "And Harmony hasn't informed me of any more glitches. So I'm good."

"Why did Ilya Bakov need to see you yesterday?"

"Sarita had a life insurance policy."

"That's it? Big deal."

Bailey settled Brianna into her sit-to-stand play chair and then helped me unpack one of the boxes, withdrawing an adorable flag-themed cookie jar and some porcelain flag-shaped cookies. We wouldn't make the display window an exact replica of last year's, but some of the items were too good not to use.

"Ilya found it in a suitcase that she appropriated from the workroom at her jewelry store."

"*Appropriated?*"

"Stole. It had belonged to Sarita. Ilya took it to protect her friend's memory. There was something in it—not the policy—that she worried might implicate Sarita. She couldn't figure out how to tell the police what she'd found without pointing a finger at herself. I told her to go to the police anyway. If she gets caught for—"

"If *who* gets caught?" My aunt strolled into the shop in, of all things, jeans, hiking boots, and a long-sleeved Cookbook Nook T-shirt with the *I love to read . . . cookbooks* slogan. She locked the door behind her and stomped her feet on the mat by the door. Clumps of dirt fell off her boots.

"Look at you." I mimed a curvy figure. "I've never seen you in jeans. Or boots. You look va-va-voom!"

She twirled. "Marlon took me on an early morning hike. He likes me to wear jeans."

"I can see why." I wolf whistled. She'd been working out, and it showed.

"Look at the two of you. Almost twins." She deposited her small purse by the register and clapped her hands. "Now, if who gets caught?"

I repeated what I'd told Bailey and then recapped the entire conversation with Ilya.

"Hmm. Todd was still included on the policy?" My aunt raised an eyebrow. "That seems odd, considering the divorce. I suppose running off to New Orleans had occupied Sarita's thoughts."

"She probably hadn't peeked in the suitcase since she'd returned to town, either," Bailey said.

"True," my aunt replied.

I started disassembling the display case by removing all the bridal-themed items—the cookbooks, the white cookie jar with the cat's ears top, utensils, and plates—and setting them on the floor to my left. Then I pulled a few more items from the Fourth of July box, including long-handled barbecue utensils, barbecue sauce, and fake hot dogs in buns, and set them to my right.

"Jenna!" Pepper rapped on the locked front door.

I went to open it. "What's up?"

"Big favor. I hope you can help me out. Bucky dropped five kittens off with me because there's a fire on the upper ridge and winds are coming, and he and the other firefighters have to tame it. Not everyone has picked up his or her kitten yet. But now I've got to get my assistant to Mercy Urgent Care because, well" — she gestured to the parking lot, where her curly haired assistant was standing, her hand wrapped in gauze — "she had a glue gun accident."

"Is she okay?" I asked.

"She will be. I shouldn't be gone long, but even so, I hate to leave the little darlings alone. Can I bring them and my adorable Phoenix here in the crate? They shouldn't be any trouble."

"I'll come get them." I followed her to Beaders of Paradise.

In a matter of minutes, I returned to the Cookbook Nook with the wire crate that was holding Phoenix plus three more gingers and two gray kittens. I shuttled it inside — they whined their dissent as it bumped against the jamb — and locked the front door again. Then I placed the crate at the base of the kitty condo and reached inside to make sure the kittens' water and food bowls as well as litter box were properly positioned.

Tigger leaped to the floor to inspect the kittens in the crate and warbled loudly.

"They're merely visiting, pal. Relax. They're not staying."

Brianna eagerly wanted to hold one of the furballs, but Bailey reminded her their new kitty was at home.

A half hour later, Katie waltzed through the breezeway arch carrying a tray of canapés. "Yoo-hoo," she trilled. "Who's hungry? These little morsels are for your bridal shower, Jenna. I need your opinion."

Flora Fairchild trailed her, wiggling a hand overhead, her braided hair bouncing on her shoulder. "I want to be one of your official taste testers, too. I skipped breakfast." She patted her tummy. "I'm starved."

Katie pulled a face. "Flora, for heaven's sake, I told you no already. I even closed and locked the door to the breezeway."

"Yes, but I found a way in." Flora held up a long hairpin that she must have used as a lockpick. "Persistence will out."

Katie huffed. "Make yourself useful then and set up the children's table."

"Aye-aye, Chef." Flora saluted.

I inspected the choices of canapés. "What's on the menu, Katie?"

With her pinky, she pointed to one and then another. "Tabasco cheese bites. They set fire in your mouth. Mini bacon-and-apple quiches."

I nabbed one of those, popped it into my mouth, and hummed my approval.

"There's also goat cheese and pesto on crusty baguette slices," she continued.

"Mine!" Bailey chirped, and grabbed one.

"And roasted garlic with sun-dried tomatoes and melted brie."

"Be still my heart," Flora said as she was setting out the napkins Katie had brought along.

"I'll get some glasses of water," my aunt offered.

"Each one of those looks divine, Katie," I said, "and I approve of whatever you choose to serve."

Someone rapped on the door. I turned to see Tina unlocking it with her key. She sailed in, the tails of her white asymmetrical blouse flying behind her. "I won!"

"Won what?" I asked.

"The expo prize. I won ten thousand dollars plus a honeymoon cruise. I couldn't wait to tell you all. Whee!" She twirled and hurried to Brianna to kiss her nose. "I won, little girl."

Brianna cooed her delight.

"And you've graduated," Aunt Vera said. "Congratulations."

"Thank you."

"So will you tell us your beau's name now?" my aunt asked.

Tina rose to her full height and rocked on her heels while looking demurely from beneath her long lashes. "He's none other than . . . my baking teacher."

"Your teacher?" my aunt squawked. "Isn't that" — she glanced at me for corroboration — "against school protocol?"

"Not really. I'm of age. But we decided it wouldn't seem appropriate, so we kept it a secret and only dated on weekends."

"That doesn't fix it," my aunt argued.

"He didn't give me a better grade because of it. I got a B-plus."

"B-plus." Aunt Vera grumbled.

"Yeah, I thought I deserved an A, but it's okay." Words gushed out of Tina. "We wanted to wait until all my classes ended to announce our engagement. He is the most wonderful man in the world. He's taller than me, five years older, loves to play in the ocean, and he adores dogs. All kinds of dogs. And children."

She was reciting his qualities as if she'd met him online. I was glad to know she hadn't, although like my aunt, I was concerned that a teacher had made advances to a student. On the other hand, Tina was right. She was of age.

"And now with the grand prize," she said, "we can truly plan our wedding."

I hugged her and wished her the best. So did everyone else.

"Umm," she murmured, weighing her next words, "I should probably also tell you that I've taken a full-time job at the Pelican Brief."

I gulped.

"What?" Katie yelped. "Why? Why not the Nook Café? I told you there would be a position."

"Because . . ." Tina worked her tongue along the inside of her cheek. "Because I don't want to disappoint you. I want to learn the ropes before I work for you. Lola will teach me. She's really patient."

"And I'm not?" Katie pouted.

"You're my friend," Tina said. "I don't think you'll tell me the truth. And I want to be a good chef. Really good."

I gave Katie a squeeze. "Don't worry. She'll come back to you in time. Fried fish is not her lifelong goal." Not that the food at the Pelican Brief wasn't exquisite. I relished it. "She wants to learn haute cuisine."

"She's right. I do," Tina said. "And you're the teacher for that!" She kissed Katie on the cheek and tucked Brianna into her stroller. "Also, don't worry, Bailey, I'll still have time to watch Brianna. I worked that out with your mother."

"Phew," Bailey murmured.

"Well, goodbye, everyone," Tina crooned. "We're off for an afternoon of fun."

As she was exiting with Brianna, I noticed Pepper pulling into the parking lot, sans her assistant. She didn't come to the shop to retrieve the kittens. Instead, she opened the door to Beaders of Paradise and flew inside.

On her heels came Todd Strachline in his Ford Ranger. His younger daughter hopped from the truck and dashed into Beaders of Paradise, making me guess that she had a class with Pepper. Shay loped after her, happier than she'd seemed yesterday. Perhaps to appease her, Todd had taken his daughters to Hobby Fun first. He climbed out and trudged after them.

Moments later, Harmony pulled into the parking lot, exited her BMW, and bustled to the Cookbook Nook. Her face was drawn, her gaze intense. She worried the strap of her shoulder bag as she knocked on the front door.

I opened it.

"May I come in?" she asked, her voice strained.

My stomach plummeted. Even though I'd braced myself for more hiccups, the look on her face told me this one could be a doozy.

Chapter 35

I beckoned her inside. "Are you here about the wedding?"

"No. It's"—she gripped my elbow and lowered her voice—
"Gunther. You won't believe . . ." She looked to the others, making
sure they weren't listening. "You won't believe what Gunther
confessed to. He said a month ago that he and Todd were joking
around about blowing up Sarita."

"He said that to the police?"

"No. To the attorney because . . ." She waved a hand. "Let me
backtrack—I meant to tell you last night when we spoke, but I was
so frazzled—Todd came into the Nook Café after you left yesterday.
He was all hot and bothered about Matias Lajoie."

"I know. I saw him in the parking lot. He told me."

"But Cinnamon—I mean Chief Pritchett—nipped that in the bud.
A homeless person saw Matias under the pier smashing bottles that
night, which confirmed Matias's own account, and Matias's
neighbor saw him slogging into his house about fifteen minutes
before the explosion."

"But if the bomber used a timer—"

"No timer was used. That bomb was discharged using a radio
device, but the device was triggered within one mile of the
incident."

I gawked at her. "An explosives expert can determine that
distance with that much certainty?"

"Apparently so. Matias lives"—she hooked her thumb—"at the
top of the mountain, over ten miles away. When Todd learned that,
he left the café grumbling. He'd truly believed Matias was guilty."

I frowned. "So when . . . or rather *why* did Gunther confess to the
attorney about joking around with Todd?"

"Because he's worried Todd will remember their chat and tell the
police, and Cinnamon will come after him again."

"I don't think Todd will. He likes Gunther."

"But he pointed a finger at him on Sunday."

"Not really. He said Gunther had a motive, but he hadn't
expected that to turn into anything. He regrets that it did."
Reassuringly I patted her arm. "Relax. Joking around doesn't make
something real."

"But what about the map of the plan?"

Right. The map. "Did Gunther say whether anyone might have overheard him and Todd, like his son?"

"I didn't ask, but even if Ulrich did, he'll be completely in the clear of detonating the bomb because he was with his wife and kids, and they live close to Santa Cruz. That's miles away."

I guided her to the children's table and said, "Eat something. Take your mind off this. You can think better on a full stomach."

When our tasting party was over, Harmony was eager to help Gunther with his legal battle. I sent her off with a hug, and then everyone left except for Bailey, my aunt, and me.

After we finished up the display window, I told my aunt to go home. For an hour, Bailey and I went over the Fourth of July cookbook orders. We focused on ones from the list I'd made yesterday, those featuring grilling tips, burger recipes, and dry rubs. We also selected a couple of kid-friendly cookbooks, including one from The Kid Chef Bakes series.

"Harmony looked upset during the tasting," Bailey said as she filled out an order form.

"She was." I explained Harmony's concern about Gunther's possible guilt.

"What if Wren Weatherly was dining at California Catch that day and overheard Gunther and Todd talking?" Bailey asked. "Have you ruled her out?"

"She has a solid alibi. Tina was with her at group therapy."

"What about Wren's daughter?"

I shook my head. "Darinda was stealing photography equipment at the expo when Sarita's boat blew."

"What? Whoa, hold on." Bailey signaled for me to fill her in.

I indulged her and told her as much as I knew. "She was filching the stuff after the expo closed, which was nine p.m."

"I suppose it's better to be a thief than a murderer," Bailey quipped. "Have you considered Sarita's ex-husband as a suspect? After all, if he'll reap the benefits of Sarita's life insurance policy . . ."

"He has an alibi, too. He was home with his daughters."

Though now that I uttered it out loud, how could I be sure about that? He'd said his daughters were upstairs playing video games so loudly that he'd had to wear headphones. Was it possible he'd slipped out without them noticing? I couldn't see it. He'd already gone out in the rain to pick up pizza, and after that, he'd run into truck trouble. On the other hand, he could have deliberately devised having trouble with his truck so a knight in shining armor, like Eddie, would help out and corroborate Todd's intention to return home.

"Talk to me." Bailey twirled a finger. "Something is whirling in that brain of yours."

"Todd is a truck buff. He goes to rallies and such. He must know his way around them. He could have rigged his radiator to blow. And he loves science."

"Oka-ay," she said, dragging out the word, motioning for me to flesh out my answer.

I pulled my cell phone from my capris' pocket, pulled up an internet search engine, and typed in *Beyond Science.* "Todd used to work at this company as an accountant." I flashed my cell phone screen to her and then clicked on the company's *About* page. "But I remember him saying he'd always been interested in science. His daughter Shay loves science, too. I'm wondering if he could have learned how to make a bomb there."

"Does the company deal in explosives?"

I read the *About* page, scrolled down, and sagged when I realized I was barking up the wrong tree. "No. It makes science kits. Purely for kids."

"I'd guess the worst they'd sell would be those volcano experiments. Remember doing those in, like, third grade? They would erupt and froth and—"

"Sorry, ladies." Flora opened the front door. "I forgot my purse. May I come in?"

"Sure," I said.

She crossed to the children's table and retrieved it from one of the little stools.

"Someone"—I continued my account to Bailey—"possibly Sarita, ordered bomb supplies online and had them shipped to Gunther's restaurant." I told her about the delivery label affixed to the box with Gunther's address, which he claimed was bogus. He'd never ordered the supplies. "Whoever did must have intercepted them or sneaked into California Catch and swiped them and stored them in Ilya's workroom."

"To frame Sarita," Bailey stated.

"Or to frame Gunther since his name was on the label, but if Sarita didn't stash the box, and Ilya didn't do it—"

"Are you sure she didn't?" Bailey cocked her head.

"I can't imagine. She really loved Sarita." I pocketed my cell phone. "Who else could have done it, besides Gunther or his son?"

Flora stopped beside us as she slung the strap of her purse on her shoulder. "Have the police traced whoever made the order? I send packages to my nieces all the time. I make the purchases, but they're the recipients."

"I don't know if they have," I said. "Ilya told me if someone used a gift card, there would be no paper trail."

"Not so," Flora said. "All senders are in the system. And even if Sarita didn't send it to Gunther, someone close to her might have known her logon and password information. For example, Todd knows all my info. Given all the deliveries I have to receive at the shop, I have to rely on someone like him in case my computer glitches, or there's a snafu in the delivery, or any number of other nightmare scenarios. I swear, if I didn't have a fiancé, I'd be setting my sites on Todd. He's such a doll." She snapped her fingers. "He's there in a pinch if I need him."

"Hold on. You're engaged?" Bailey bounded to her feet and clasped Flora's hand. "Where's the ring?"

"Oh, my fiancé doesn't want us to wear rings," she said coyly. "He wants to keep it a secret until we set a date."

Bailey exchanged a look with me, clearly thinking what I was thinking, that this story sounded way too similar to Tina's. "Is he, um, married?"

"Heavens, no!"

"Is he a teacher?" I asked.

"No." Flora giggled. "Well, sort of. He's the assistant pastor at my church, and he does teach Bible school."

I breathed easier. Bailey, too.

"He doesn't want anyone spreading rumors among the flock. Nobody likes rumors."

Other than you, I mused.

"When we set a date, we'll make a formal announcement and get the license and blood tests and all the proper documents in order."

Documents. I flashed on the punch line to Eddie Milsap's joke. *Your name is written inside the cover.* Todd's name was on Sarita's insurance policy. Did he know that? Surely he wouldn't still have access to her logons and passwords after all this time. She'd have changed them and kept them private. Unless his daughters . . .

"Oh, must run!" Flora consulted her watch. "Ta-ta!" She hustled out, skidding slightly on the mat by the door.

As she did, I caught sight of the clumps of dirt left by my aunt's hiking boots and flashed on the wet and dirty clothes that I'd seen in Todd's truck. On top of the pants had been a pair of tennis shoes caked with mud. Upon reflection, I supposed it could have been tar.

Chapter 36

Todd might have guessed Sarita had stored things in Ilya's workroom. He could've been the person that had sent Gunther the items from Super Ship—using Sarita's account information—and then swiped them from Gunther's restaurant and stored them in the workroom after Sarita came back to town. To frame Gunther or to frame Sarita, did it matter which one? He most definitely would have remembered his conversation with Gunther about bombing Sarita. Maybe he'd even planted the map in Gunther's office.

I pulled my cell phone from my pocket and phoned our insurance agent.

"What's up?" Bailey asked.

"I have to ask Jim Daley a question."

Bailey's cell phone jangled. She skimmed the readout. "Oh, no. Tina texted. Brianna is running a fever. She's taking her home. I have to meet them there. I hope it doesn't have to do with her scraped knee."

"Kids don't run fevers because of a boo-boo. I'm sure she just has a little cold." I blew her a kiss and reminded her to drive carefully.

Daley answered after a few rings. "Hello, Jenna, what's up? Is everything alright with the Cookbook Nook? The café?" He posed the same standard questions he'd asked of Ilya. "Hope all is okay at Intime."

"This call has nothing to do with my businesses or the restaurant. I . . ." How could I get him to tell me what I needed to know? It had to be proprietary. *Jump in, Jenna. Don't procrastinate.* "I heard you talking to Ilya Bakov on the telephone earlier."

Daley grew quiet.

"She chatted with you about Sarita Strachline's life insurance policy."

He didn't deny it.

"Have you told Todd and his daughters about it?"

"Not yet," he replied. I could hear the tentativeness in his voice. "Why?"

"Because I know what's in the policy. Ilya told me." I paused for effect. "Is there any way that Todd would know that he's included on the policy?" I asked, then chuckled. "Silly me. Of course he would. Ilya said Todd and Sarita drafted their policies at the same time. The better question is did Todd realize that Sarita hadn't revised her policy?"

Daley remained silent. Was he being tight-lipped or didn't he know?

"Did Todd ever revise his policy to omit Sarita as a beneficiary?" I pressed. "If so, he might have asked if she had done the same."

"Jenna, this is very uncomfortable for me."

"Would you rather Chief Pritchett ask the questions?" I asked sweetly. I happened to know that Cinnamon, prior to meeting Bucky, had dated Jim Daley for a year. According to Pepper, at the time of the breakup, insults had been hurled. Cinnamon said Daley could be obstinate, and he'd said Cinnamon could be pigheaded.

"No. Fine. I'll answer you." He grumbled. "Yes, Todd revised his policy right after the divorce."

"But Sarita didn't." I paused. "Was that something you ought to have mentioned to her?"

"No. Each client is different. I presumed she wanted things to remain status quo."

I cleared my throat.

"Now hold on," Daley said. "Don't go judging me like that, Jenna. I didn't feel it was my place to advise Sarita, her being a savvy businesswoman and all. She steered the boat." He faltered. "Sorry for the analogy, seeing as she died on a—"

"Go on."

"If you must know, about a month ago, Todd was in the office. We were discussing the policy on his truck, and during the course of the conversation, he decided he wanted to up the amount of his life insurance policy. His girls were getting older, he said. If something happened to him, he wanted to make sure college was paid for, yada-yada."

"That makes sense."

"Halfway through our meeting, he asked me for a cup of coffee. My assistant was out, so I stepped out of the office for a moment. When I came back, he was going through my file cabinet."

"Whoa." My eyes widened.

"Yeah, it caught me off guard. Todd apologized and said he was simply making sure his client William Stevenson had paid for the coverage for his shop. William owns Friar Tux."

"I know his wife," I said. "She's a regular at the Cookbook Nook. Lovely woman. She does alterations and teaches occasional classes at Beaders of Paradise."

"According to Todd"—Daley made a smacking sound with his mouth—"William lies about getting things done sometimes, and Todd wanted to make sure William hadn't let that to-do item slip. Heaven forbid a fire start in one of the other businesses in the six-unit building, and Friar Tux goes up in smoke." Daley hummed. "After the arson at the Grotto, Todd has always been fire-safety conscious."

I found that tidbit interesting, given that he was out of the picture when the arson occurred.

"Did you believe him?" I asked.

"I had no reason not to, but now that you mention it, it did seem like, well, an overreach. I mean, he could have asked me about William. I'd have gladly made the search myself."

"Is William Stevenson's file close to Sarita Strachline's file?"

"Yeah." He heaved a sigh. "They abut one another."

"Is it possible that what Todd really wanted to check out was his ex-wife's policy, and by doing so, learned that he was still a beneficiary?"

Daley moaned. "Yes."

Money fueled by vengeance was motive for murder with a capital *M*.

Chapter 37

I thanked him, ended the call, and gazed at Todd's truck in the parking lot. Would the wet clothing and shoes with black mud — which was possibly tar — still be inside? I had to find out. From a distance, I spied Todd inside Beaders of Paradise, standing with his back to the window, supervising his daughters while they selected items from the racks holding colorful twine. Hoping I had enough time, I told Tigger I'd be right back and hustled to the passenger side of the vehicle. I cupped my hands around my face and peered in.

The items weren't there, but I knew what I'd seen. I hurried back to the Cookbook Nook and retreated to the storage room to call the precinct. I didn't know if Cinnamon would listen to my theory about Todd killing his ex-wife to get the life insurance payout, and my seeing the tar on his tennis shoes wouldn't confirm that he'd planted the box of bomb-making materials in the workroom at the Velvet Box, but it would lend credence to the idea. Even if he'd tossed the offending shoes into a Dumpster, if the toe of another pair of his tennis shoes matched the print in Ilya's workroom, that could be considered circumstantial evidence. Add in Jim Daley's account about catching Todd rifling through his file cabinets, and *bingo*.

The clerk that answered said she'd patch me through. I waited. And waited.

Unexpectedly Tigger yowled. I startled and bobbled my cell phone. It fell to the floor. I left it and raced out of the storage room to help my cat. I skidded to a halt when I saw Todd standing by the vintage table, hand in the air.

Shoot! I hadn't remembered to lock the door when I'd come back in.

Tigger was hovering by the crate of kittens. His eyes were as big as saucers, and his tail was sticking straight up behind him. Had Todd hurt him, or had Tigger darted there to protect the babies?

"Hello, Todd." I sounded cool, but I wasn't. My insides were thrumming with a mixture of anger and fear. I beckoned Tigger with my hand. He sprang into my arms. Poor little guy was shaking like crazy. "We're closed. Did you come by to pick up your kitten?"

"No. Maybe you forgot. We didn't get one."

"Right. Well, I'm afraid if you want to make a purchase, you'll have to come back tomorrow during regular hours."

Todd skulked to the bookshelves with the endcap filled with wedding cake cookbooks. His lips curled in a snarl. "I saw you peeking in my truck."

"It's a great vehicle. I've been thinking of investing in one." How was I keeping my voice so neutral? I was shivering as much as my cat. "It would be much easier to transport boxes of books and to make home deliveries than in something the size of my VW Beetle, don't you think?" If only I hadn't dropped my cell phone in the storage room. I set Tigger on the floor. "Go." I nudged his rump. He didn't budge, prepared to stand guard. "As it is now, I have to make multiple trips."

"Can it with the truck talk, Jenna. You've been asking about me."

"Says who?"

"Says Jim Daley."

Dang it. He'd reached out to Todd that quickly? He wouldn't get my business in the future, for sure. "I was asking him how many clients he had."

"Bull. I know you know."

"Know what?"

"That I knew."

"Knew what?" I tamped down a nervous laugh.

"About Sarita's life insurance policy," Todd said.

I peered past him at the parking lot. I didn't see his daughters. Were they occupied with Pepper? If only they would appear and divert their father's attention. In the meantime, if I could inch my way to the storage room for my cell phone —

"Stop!" Todd hissed.

Tigger mewled. The kittens echoed him.

Todd pulled a switchblade from his pocket, flicked it open, and aimed it at me. I squeaked in fear. I'd faced off a killer before but never one with a knife. The blade glinted in the fluorescent light.

"Move toward me," he ordered.

Reluctantly I obeyed. "So you killed Sarita for the money. Wow. Business must be bad."

"There was another reason."

"Really? Which was . . ."

"She divorced me."

I smirked. "C'mon. You're going with that old excuse? She broke your heart?"

"I loved her. I did. But the restaurant created such tension. I told her if she'd quit, we could have made a go of it, but she wouldn't. So you see? It was her fault. All she had to do was choose me over that dang restaurant. She blew up our marriage."

"So you blew her up."

"Yeah, she had it coming." His face turned into a snarl.

"Be honest, Todd. It irked you that after she divorced you, she came up with a way to reap a bunch of money and get away scot-free."

"Except she didn't get away. She went to prison. That was horrible . . ." His nostrils flared. "Not for her. I wanted her to get caught. But it was brutal for the girls. They not only lost their mother, but they were shunned by their friends for nearly six years. Their mother was a criminal. An arsonist. A thief. If only she'd loved them the way I did." He heaved a sigh. "They were just coming into their own and making new friends when we learned she got parole. Released early for being a model citizen. A model citizen," he repeated, and growled. "I couldn't take it. I couldn't let them be teased again. I couldn't let them suffer."

"When you found out about her parole, you began to plan her demise," I said, "but first you needed to set the stage." I searched for something at my fingertips that I could use to defend myself. A cookbook wouldn't cut it. Neither would a pair of porcelain salt and pepper shakers. I spotted the items I'd set on the floor for the Fourth of July display and quickly cut to the right. I skirted the bookshelf and made it to the display table before Todd bellowed at me.

"Stop right there. Don't move."

I raised my hands meekly in the air, trying to figure out how I could bend down without him striking out. "You knew Sarita harbored a grudge for Rhett and me," I said, stalling for time, "so you decided to blow up Intime and make it look like Sarita had done it. You didn't want to kill us. You hoped to show everyone that your ex-wife was unstable and send her back to jail. You put the bomb in place and stowed the bomb-making items in Ilya's storage room to frame Sarita."

He sniggered.

A theory niggled the edges of my mind. "But first, you lucked out when you heard Sarita had harangued me at the expo. Did your daughters tell you that she told me to back off?" I nodded. "Yeah, they must have. So you came up with the idea to hurl a brick through my window. To scare me. To put me on edge. To think Sarita was after me. After us. What I don't get is why you wanted to frame Gunther, too? Having the shipment sent to him has incriminated him."

"I forgot about the shipping label." He flourished the blade. "I never meant to hurt him. It was just easy for me to get in and out of his office. He's a trusting soul."

I held up a finger. "One more question. How did you know Rhett and I would be at the bistro by ourselves? On a regular night, dozens more people could have been injured."

"I'd just bought swimming gear for my girls at Swim and Fins and was heading to my truck when I overheard one of the kitchen staff talking on the phone to her boyfriend. She was standing on the sidewalk. Not whispering. It played perfectly into my plan."

Timing is everything, I mused as an idea of how to get to my cell phone came to me. Could I pull it off? "How did you plant the bomb in the kitchen?" I asked.

"One of the cleaning crew had propped the door open to take a cigarette break."

As I'd theorized.

"Thanks to my ex-wife, I knew my way around professional kitchens," he went on. "I was in and out inside two minutes."

"Two—" I cut myself off on purpose and winced. I clutched my abdomen. "Ooh." I moaned. "My stomach hurts. I need to use the restroom."

"Uh-uh. I can't let you."

"Please."

"No."

"What are you planning to do to me?" I asked. "You don't want to kill me. Think of your daughters."

Tigger slinked toward us, crouching stealthily like a tiger on the hunt.

"O-o-oh." I doubled over, milking my act. "I must've eaten

something bad, Todd. Please let me — "

"I don't care. Move to the rear of the store." Todd waggled the knife. "Now!"

In a split second, I reached for the cookie jar — the white one with the cat's ears top. The lid came off in my hand. I hurled it at Todd's face like a Frisbee, but it missed its mark. I grabbed the barbecue fork with the sharp prongs and charged Todd. He dodged right and flailed the knife. I swiped again, this time connecting with the knife. I'd never taken official fencing lessons, but I'd played Laertes in the high school production of *Hamlet*. I still knew the moves. Thrust, parry, lunge.

The barbecue fork and knife connected with a *clack.*

At the same time the front door opened, and Shay poked her head in. "Dad, I want to go home and — " She froze, her face wrenched with horror. "What's going on?"

"Shay, leave!" He lashed out at me again.

Tigger vaulted onto Todd's back and caterwauled. That made the kittens riotous. They whimpered and hissed in their crate, drawing Shay's attention. Todd shrieked in pain. He writhed, trying to shake Tigger off, but my brave cat clung to him. Todd pitched forward. His knife flew from his hand. He landed on his knees and hands. Tigger bounded away. Cursing, Todd scrambled for the knife. But I beat him to it and braced it with a foot.

"Uh-uh." I aimed the prongs of the barbecue fork at his eyes. "Don't move a muscle."

"What's going on, Dad?" Shay's voice skated upward. "Talk to me."

Todd glowered at me with pure hatred.

"Shay," I regarded the girl, "after your father brought the pizza home the night your mother . . ." I hesitated. "On the night your mother died, did you see your father again?"

"Sela and I ate upstairs and went to bed. Why?"

"Do you remember the wadded-up clothes that were in the truck the other day?" I asked.

"Uh-huh."

"Was that mud on your father's shoes?"

"I don't think so. It smelled bad." She wrinkled her nose. "Like gasoline or something."

"Darn it, stop talking, Shay," Todd commanded, finding his voice.

"Don't swear at me, Dad." Shay sounded like her mother, powerful and shrill. "Why did you attack her with a knife? Answer me!"

Todd shuddered, hearing the change in her.

I said, "He tried to hurt me, Shay, because I found out he killed your mother."

"It's a lie!" he hollered.

"He wanted to shut me up."

"No, no, no." Shay's gaze wavered between him and me. "Is it true?"

Todd peered up at her, tears flooding his eyes. He sputtered, "B-baby, I'm sorry. I . . ."

"Stop!" she shouted. "Just. Stop. OMG, I can't believe this!"

"Todd," I said, "did you once consider how your daughters would feel or how they would be shunned if you were tried for murder and sent to jail?"

He blubbered. "I'm so sorry. So sorry."

"Shay, call nine-one-one," I ordered. "There's a telephone by the cash register."

She did me one better. She pulled her cell phone from her purse and stabbed in the number.

Chapter 38

Cinnamon and Appleby showed up. Cinnamon had to pry my fingers from the barbecue fork. Appleby cuffed Todd.

When Todd was on his feet, Shay rushed to the front door. "I have to find my sister."

"She's right here." Pepper strode in with Sela. Seeing Todd in cuffs, she said to Cinnamon, "You'll fill me in. In the meantime, I'm assuming we'll need to find someone to take care of the girls."

"Our grandmother," Shay said. "She lives in San Jose."

Pepper nodded. "Let's go back to my shop, and we'll call her." Over her shoulder she said, "Jenna, I'll fetch the kittens in a bit."

"No rush." I'd been thankful for their noisy support.

Clasping my elbow and drawing me to one side, Cinnamon said, "Explain."

I did, quickly. The life insurance policy. The daughters eating pizza and playing games. The rain alibi, thanks to Eddie. Flora's idea regarding logons and such. Todd sending the items to Gunther anonymously. Seeing the dirty clothes in his truck the other day and wanting to verify that.

"Why didn't you call me?" she asked gently.

"I was doing so when Todd broke into the shop." I wriggled from her grasp. "Didn't your clerk tell you?"

"She said you ended the call. I figured you had yet another theory to share and decided it wasn't important. You're like the little boy who cried wolf, except when you aren't." She smiled supportively. "I apologize for dismissing you out of hand."

"It's okay. I didn't even know if my conjecture was correct until Todd showed up. Shay was amazing. A real force."

"Just like me at that age," Cinnamon quipped.

"Me, too."

"Ha! No, you weren't. Your father said you were an angel."

I snorted. "He doesn't know the half of it."

She gave me a sly glance. "After your honeymoon, you and I are sitting down with a big bottle of wine, and you're going to give me details."

"So you can blackmail me for the rest of my life? Not a chance. I'll do the wine, but no secrets. Hey"—I snapped my fingers as a notion struck me—"I'll bet Todd didn't go home after seeing Eddie. I'll bet he was the stranger the carny woman saw lurking by the pilings, eagerly watching his handiwork."

"That's enough conjecturing, Jenna. I've got this."

I grinned. "Yeah, you do."

Katie appeared through the breezeway. "What the heck is going on?" She glanced out the door. Appleby was helping Todd into the police cruiser. Pepper was guiding Todd's daughters into her shop.

"I'll fill you in," I said, and thanked Cinnamon for her speedy response.

• • •

On Friday night Bailey hosted the women-only bridal shower at her house, and it went off without a hitch. With games like How Well Do You Know the Groom? and What's in Your Purse?, it was a noisy and laughter-filled affair. Rhett and I had decided to register only a few items for our wedding. I had plenty of china and crystal from my first marriage. He had all the cookware a home chef could want. And we didn't need twelve of anything. So Bailey had landed on the idea of an all-white, wedding-night theme for the shower. I received a lacy white teddy, a sheer peignoir, rhinestone-studded sandals, fluffy white slippers, and comical pillowcases that said *Yes* and *Not tonight*. I'd never said *not tonight* to Rhett and doubted I ever would.

Katie's canapés were excellent. She'd also made white chocolate petit fours, in keeping with the white theme, that were divine. Keller had even pitched in and made a chocolate-peppermint ice cream bombe. He apologized profusely for having to use the word *bombe*, in view of recent events, but it was his favorite dessert to serve at a soiree. With Rhett fully healed, I told Keller it was fine that he'd used the term. Some even got a big kick out of it.

On Sunday, a group of us met at my aunt's house for dinner. We were on the patio, my father sitting next to Lola on the floral-and-wicker love seat and Rhett in one of the armchairs. I was standing at the railing gazing at the setting sun, the sky awash with dusky orange and soft gray clouds. The sound of the surf was soothing and made me believe everything going forward would be smooth sailing.

Bailey and Tito had decided to take a little walk while Brianna napped in the spare bedroom. Marlon Appleby was running late.

My aunt strolled out carrying a tray of tapas and a pitcher of margaritas. "Who needs me to top off their beverage?"

I wiggled my half-drunk glass. "I'll take a bit more. And don't forget, we need to discuss the Saturday brunch menu for the wedding weekend."

She said, "I was thinking of serving something similar to tonight's meal. Tapas, tacos, lots of guacamole, and margaritas."

"Sounds great," Rhett said. "You know I love your margaritas." He held up his glass for a top-off.

When my aunt had refreshed all the glasses, my father stood and raised his glass. "A toast to another crime that was solved by my relentless daughter."

"Pfft. I'm not relentless."

"It was a compliment." My father winked. "I might not have been a fan of your getting involved years ago, but you have proven your mettle. The apple doesn't fall far from the tree, young lady."

Lola elbowed him. "A show of modesty, my love."

He snickered. "Modesty? In my family?"

We all said, "Cheers," and sipped our drinks.

Dad added, "And may you never stumble across a dead body again!"

"Hear, hear," Rhett said.

My aunt said, "Speaking of *hear, hear,* did you hear Matias Lajoie is moving to Illinois to take care of his aging parents?"

"Losing Sarita broke his heart," I said. "For the life of me, I can't see what he saw in her, but then love can make you stupid."

"Not me," Rhett declared.

"Nor I," my father chimed.

"Who will buy Matias's boating business?" Lola asked.

"Eddie Milsap wants to," Rhett said.

"You've spoken to Eddie about the sale?" I gazed at him.

"Yep."

I crossed to him and put a hand on his shoulder. "You're still going to run Intime, right? You're not planning to manage Bait and Switch again."

He patted my hand. "I'm sticking with the restaurant, my love.

Don't worry. But I'm also a businessman. Eddie needs an investor. His parents are tapped out. Eddie's a good and decent man. I'd like to help."

I pecked him on the cheek.

"Are you done with your gossip, Vera?" Lola asked.

My aunt harrumphed. "It wasn't gossip. It was truth. But, yes, I'm finished. Why?"

"Okay, here's what I know," Lola said. "I heard Darinda Weatherly got probation. The owner of That's Amore Photography got wind of Darinda's story about how strapped she and her mother were, and she sympathized with her. She, too, had struggled to pay for a wedding. She said if Darinda would work for three months as her intern to learn the business—Darinda isn't just a dental technician; she's an aspiring documentary filmmaker and knows a lot about photography equipment—she won't press charges."

"Gee, that's noble of her." I hoped Wren Weatherly was happy with the outcome. Would Darinda's fiancé's frozen heart thaw and welcome her back into his life? Would she want him to?

Bailey and Tito climbed the stairs to the patio hand in hand and blissfully happy. Until Brianna started to cry.

"I've got this, my love," Tito said, and hustled into the house to tend to the whimpering child.

Bailey picked up a margarita, moseyed to me, and sipped. "Ah, I love walking on the beach. I'm envious that you live here."

"But you have your incredible view," I said. She and Tito lived in the hills like my father.

"Yes, but to walk right out the door onto the sand is heaven." She sipped again. "But it would be scary with a child. Like having a pool without a safeguard fence."

I laughed. "That's what backyards are for."

"So, daughter." My father got to his feet and went to the railing. He leaned against it. "Bring us up to date on wedding plans."

"My dress is ready. The DJ and I have agreed on a playlist." I ticked the list off on my fingertips. "I've approved the final floral arrangements. Katie has finalized the menu." Harmony had kept me hopping for the past few days. "And we've settled on the flavors for the cake. Have you rented your tux, Dad?"

"He has," Lola said. "I've seen to it."

"My dress is ready, too," Bailey said. "And I found the most adorable outfit for Brianna to wear."

The doorbell chimed.

"Come in, Marlon," Aunt Vera trilled, shaking her head. "Why would he ring the bell?"

Harmony emerged through the opened patio doors and came to a stop. "Oh, Jenna, Rhett." She pressed a hand to her heart. "I'm so sorry to barge in on the party, but I wanted to tell you in person." Her shoulders rose and fell. "The . . . The . . ." She could barely catch her breath. "CC Vineyards has to cancel the wedding. They've had a huge flood on the property."

"Oh, no!" I cried.

"Everything is under water."

I sagged. Tears flooded my eyes. I couldn't stem them this time.

"Hey." Rhett jumped to his feet and threw his arms around me. "It's okay. It'll be fine."

"It's a sign," I mumbled.

"It is not a sign. *This* is a sign." He pulled a turquoise blue box from his pocket and opened it. Within was a silver infinity heart bracelet. "This belonged to my grandmother. She and my grandfather were married for sixty-five years. I want you to consider this"—he pulled the bracelet from the box and clasped it around my left wrist—"a symbol of our future together."

My throat grew thick with emotion. "Rhett—"

"*Shh.* There are no omens. No evil signs. Just our love. You and me. Forevermore." He held me at arms' length and tipped up my chin with his forefinger. "We're getting married, Jenna Hart, and that's all there is to it."

"But not when we'd hoped." I fingered the bracelet.

He studied me, the love in his gaze intense. "Yes, when we'd hoped."

"Where? How? All other venues are booked. Even the Baldini and Storm vineyards are taken. I'm not going to Timbuktu to get married."

He turned me toward the ocean and said, "We're going to do it right here. On the beach. We have everything we need."

"It'll require a permit," Harmony said.

My father said, "Not a problem. We happen to know the mayor."

Chapter 39

Throughout all the preparations for the wedding on the beach, Harmony brought along her new kitten Firecracker, a gray cat with a white blaze on its forehead. Not wanting to spend a moment without him, she'd purchased a multi-striped pet carrier backpack to keep him comfortable and close.

My sister Whitney—witty, winsome Whitney—and her husband, Spencer, and their children came in a day early and were pleased with their accommodations at the Crystal Cove Inn. Whitney asked if there was anything she could do to help. I told her no and to simply enjoy herself. Considering her aptitude for organization, she could have done the whole wedding herself, which was why I'd hired Harmony. I hadn't wanted my sister hovering over me, telling me this was right and that was wrong.

My brother Mitchell had decided to lodge with his buddy, a fellow high-end home designer in Carmel, whose house had a view of the ocean. The commute wouldn't be too bad, he promised me. Knowing Mitchell could be loosey-goosey regarding time, I made him promise to get to each event a half hour early.

Rhett's parents and sisters arrived on Friday, right before the out-of-towners' dinner at Pelican Brief. In an instant, his parents were fast friends with my father and Lola. His sisters, who had opened a vineyard in Napa, were more than happy to talk shop with our friends and guests at the dinner, in particular Hannah Storm and her husband, Alan Baldini. Hannah was supplying all the wine for our wedding.

After the out-of-towners' dinner, which went off without a hitch—Lola had followed Rhett's menu to the letter—Rhett kissed me pristinely on the lips and went to spend the night in his cabin in the hills so that he wouldn't see me until the moment I walked down the aisle.

Sunday morning's festivities were nonstop. We'd closed the shop for the day so everyone could participate. We set up headquarters in my master bedroom. Bailey helped with my hair, giving me beautiful tendrils. My aunt fussed over my dress, an ecru, V-neck, lace sheath with a sweep train that fit me like a glove. The makeup artist turned out to be a wizard with eyeshadow. Lola had provided treats to keep our energy up. The willowy female in her twenties that In the Moment Photography had assigned to the wedding roamed taking photos of all the activities. She'd also worked the out-of-towners' dinner the night before and had already sent me a digital photo album to view. I was happy to say that Rhett and I had made quite a handsome couple. I'd worn a pale peach number, and he'd donned a white linen shirt and tan slacks.

An hour before I was supposed to head to the beach, my nerves kicked in. I started giggling. Bailey gripped my shoulders and reminded me to breathe. My aunt rubbed her amulet and babbled something that sounded like a prayer. Harmony put on soothing instrumental music and brought me a jigger of brandy. After one sip, I felt better, and Bailey and my aunt made their way to their respective places.

At six thirty p.m., Harmony said, "Here we go. Beautiful sunsets wait for no one."

She escorted me to my father, who was standing behind a blind of ficus out of sight of the wedding party, but we could see through the leaves. Also behind the blind were Bailey, Whitney, and Tito, who was holding Brianna and a basket of flower petals.

Near the water's edge at the far end of a burgundy carpet was the altar, a beautiful metal pergola adorned with burgundy and ecru flowers as well as soft green ferns. A pair of dwarf palms in white pots as well as two white speakers stood on either side of the arch. The ocean lay beyond. Guests were already seated in the folding white chairs that had been placed in rows on either side of the aisle. Bouquets of flowers adorned the end chair in each row. To the left of the seating was a wood-finish dance floor.

Beyond the floor were two bars and a vast array of buffet tables and food stations filled with Katie's inspirations. The wedding cake table stood apart from everything and featured four gorgeous tiers of cupcakes. The servers, a happy smiling bunch, were ready and waiting to begin. The DJ, a handsome man in his forties, had set up his audio mixing console near the dance floor and was already piping symphonic music through the speakers. Once the ceremony was concluded, he would launch into the oldies but goodies that Rhett adored.

Rhett and my brother moved into view and stood to the right of the altar. Both looked handsome in their ivory linen suits, but Rhett's eyes were aglow with anticipation. I felt my heart leap at the sight of him.

The sun was sinking lower in the sky, and the wisps of clouds turned golden and then the color of orange sherbet.

Suddenly the music stopped. Then it started up again with Pachelbel's "Canon in D."

The guests turned toward the blind of ficus trees. Harmony signaled for Tito to go first. Carrying Brianna, he prodded her to throw flower petals along the carpet. Bailey trailed them, step-pause, step-pause. Whitney followed her at the same pace.

My father offered me his elbow and whispered, "I've never seen you look more beautiful. Your mother would be so happy for you. I know she's watching."

"Don't, Dad. I'll cry." I bussed his cheek and said, "Okay, let's go."

Recipes

Banana Mocha Cupcakes + Gluten-free Version
Keller's Chocolate-Peppermint Bombe
Vanilla Ice Cream
Fennel-Feta Appetizers
Katie's Wedding Cookies
Lobster or White Fish Panini Sandwich
Margarita Cocktail
Peach or Pear Flambé
Perfect Bliss Cocktail
Salmon and Avocado Rolls
Scallops with Bacon Benedict + Gluten-free Biscuits with Chives
Spicy Fish Kebabs à la Katie
White Wine Risotto
Stir-fried Shrimp with Asparagus Tips

Banana Mocha Cupcakes
(Yield: 16 cupcakes)

From Katie:

Yes, some cakes take a lot of steps and a lot of time to prepare, but these little gems are worth it. I got the idea for this combination from Harmony Bold, who'd tasted the cake at the Naylors' youngest daughter's wedding. Thinking of Jenna, she'd slyly swiped a slice for me. Smart Harmony. The baker had made two six-inch cakes and had sprinkled cacao nibs on the filling as well. They added such a lovely crunch. But for Jenna, we thought a cupcake tower would make the perfect wedding cake for her guests. So many flavors and choices. Why choose just one? By the way, I'm including the gluten-free version below, too.

For the cake:
3 bananas, medium-sized
1½ cups flour
1½ teaspoons baking powder
¼ teaspoon baking soda
¼ teaspoon salt
½ cup vegetable oil (I used canola)
1 cup white sugar
2 eggs
1 teaspoon vanilla extract
½ cup sour cream

For the frosting:
1 cup unsalted butter, softened
16 ounces cream cheese, softened (full-fat kind)
1 tablespoon espresso powder
1 tablespoon cacao powder
4 cups powdered sugar, sifted

For the topping:
cacao nibs
chocolate-covered espresso beans
freeze-dried bananas

For the cake:
Preheat the oven to 350 degrees F. Fill cupcake tins with 16 liners. I like to spray mine lightly with nonstick spray.

In a small bowl, mash bananas. Set aside.

In another small bowl, combine the flour, baking powder, baking soda, and salt. Set aside.

In a stand mixer fitted with a whisk, combine oil and sugar. Beat until light and fluffy. Add eggs, then the vanilla. Mix to combine.

Add in the sour cream and mix. Then add the dry ingredients and mix lightly. Add in the mashed bananas and mix until just incorporated.

Divide the batter evenly between the cupcake liners, to about ⅔ full. Bake 15–20 minutes or until a toothpick inserted in the center of the cupcakes comes out clean. Check often. They should be lightly browned on top.

Remove the cupcakes from the oven and place them on a wire rack to cool completely.

For the frosting:
In the bowl of a stand mixer fitted with a paddle, combine the butter and cream cheese. Beat until smooth. Add the espresso powder and cacao powder. Mix to combine. Add the *sifted* powdered sugar and mix until combined. You will have to scrape down the sides of the bowl often.

To assemble the cupcakes:
Using a piping bag, top the cupcakes with frosting. Add an espresso bean at the top. Insert a few dried bananas for decoration into the frosting. Dust with the cacao nibs. Please note, add the freeze-dried banana decorations at the very end. They will get mushy if allowed to sit in the icing for too long.

Banana Mocha Cupcakes
Gluten-free Version
(Yield: 16 cupcakes)

For the gluten-free cake:
3 bananas, medium-sized
1½ cups gluten-free flour (I use a combo of sweet rice flour and tapioca starch)
2 teaspoons whey powder
½ teaspoon xanthan gum
1½ teaspoons baking powder
¼ teaspoon baking soda
¼ teaspoon salt
½ cup vegetable oil (I used canola)
1 cup white sugar
2 eggs
1 teaspoon vanilla extract
½ cup sour cream

For the frosting:
1 cup unsalted butter, softened
16 ounces cream cheese, softened (full-fat kind)
1 tablespoon espresso powder
1 tablespoon cacao powder
4 cups powdered sugar, sifted

For the topping:
cacao nibs
chocolate-covered espresso beans
freeze-dried bananas

For the cake:
Preheat the oven to 350 degrees F. Fill cupcake tins with 16 liners. I like to spray mine lightly with nonstick spray.

In a small bowl, mash bananas. Set aside.

In another small bowl, combine the gluten-free flour(s), whey powder, xanthan gum, baking powder, baking soda, and salt. Set aside.

In a stand mixer fitted with a whisk, combine oil and sugar. Beat until light and fluffy. Add eggs, then the vanilla. Mix to combine.

Add in the sour cream and mix. Then add the dry ingredients and mix lightly. Add in the mashed bananas and mix until just incorporated.

Divide the batter evenly between the cupcake liners, to about ⅔ full. Bake 15–20 minutes or until a toothpick inserted in the center of the cupcakes comes out clean. Check often. They should be lightly browned on top.

Remove the cupcakes from the oven and place them on a wire rack to cool completely.

For the frosting:
In the bowl of a stand mixer fitted with a paddle, combine the butter and cream cheese. Beat until smooth. Add the espresso powder and cacao powder. Mix to combine. Add the *sifted* powdered sugar and mix until combined. You will have to scrape down the sides of the bowl often.

To assemble the cupcakes:
Using a piping bag, top the cupcakes with frosting. Add an espresso bean at the top. Insert a few dried bananas for decoration into the frosting. Dust with the cacao nibs. Please note, add the freeze-dried banana decorations at the very end. They will get mushy if allowed to sit in the icing for too long.

Keller's Chocolate-Peppermint Bombe
(Serves 8–12)

From Keller:

*I love an easy recipe. And as everyone knows, I love ice cream. That's why I
"pedaled" it for so many years. Get it? Pedaled? On my bike? Heh-heh. An
ice cream bombe is one of my favorite treats, and, despite its name, in view
of recent events, I was excited to prepare it for Jenna's bridal shower. By
the way, I'm including my homemade vanilla ice cream recipe, too. It's nice
and rich and works well in this recipe, but you can use store-bought.*

2 pints chocolate ice cream, softened
1 pint peppermint ice cream, softened
1 pint vanilla ice cream, softened *(my homemade recipe to follow)*
crushed peppermint candy and chocolate sprinkles, for decoration,
if desired

Freeze an 8-inch bowl. When it's cold (about 1 hour), place the
softened chocolate ice cream in it and press it evenly up against the
sides. Then, cover a 6- to 6½ -inch bowl with Saran wrap and press it
into the chocolate ice cream. Freeze the ice cream (with the Saran-
wrapped bowl in place) for 30–60 minutes, until firm. Remove the
Saran-wrapped smaller bowl.

Spread an even layer of *softened* peppermint ice cream in the cavity
of the chocolate ice cream and then press a 4-inch bowl wrapped in
Saran wrap into the peppermint ice cream to make the layer even.
Freeze the ice cream for 30–60 minutes.

Remove the 4-inch Saran-wrapped bowl and spoon enough of the
softened vanilla ice cream to fill the remaining cavity in the
peppermint layer. Freeze the bombe until hard, at least 2–4 hours.

To unmold, fill a larger bowl about 2 inches high with warm water.
Dip the 8-inch bowl into the larger bowl. Don't let the water run
over the top onto the ice cream. Run a knife around the edges to
loosen the bombe. Unmold it onto a flat serving plate. You may need

to use a spatula to release it. Smooth the edges. Freeze the bombe until ready to serve.

If desired, decorate with crushed peppermint candies and chocolate sprinkles.

Vanilla Ice Cream
(Yield: 3½ cups)

1 cup whipping cream
¾ cup sugar, divided
⅛ teaspoon salt
2 teaspoons vanilla
1 (12-ounce) can evaporated low-fat milk*
3 large egg yolks

In a saucepan, over medium heat, cook whipping cream, ¼ cup of sugar, salt, vanilla, and evaporated milk. Cook for 3–5 minutes, until tiny bubbles form around the edges. DO NOT BOIL.

Remove from heat and let stand 10 minutes.

In a medium bowl, combine the remaining ½ cup sugar and egg yolks. Stir well. Gradually add the hot milk mixture to the egg mixture, stirring constantly.

Return the mixture to the saucepan. Cook over medium heat for 3–5 minutes, until tiny bubbles form again. DO NOT BOIL.

Remove the pan from the heat. Cool at room temperature (for about 30 minutes) and then set in refrigerator for 2 hours.

Pour chilled mixture into ice cream maker and churn according to manufacturer's instructions. My apparatus takes approximately 30 minutes.

If desired, during the last 5 minutes of churning, add in ¼ cup crushed candy or sauce of your choice.

Pour ice cream into a clean freezer-safe container. Cover and freeze for at least 2 hours.

The beauty of using the evaporated low-fat milk is that it reduces the extra moisture in homemade ice cream that can "ice up" when frozen.

Fennel-Feta Appetizer
(Yield: 24)

From Katie:

Appetizers shouldn't take all day to prepare. This one is super easy and very tasty. It has a nice bite and is a good balance for all the other sweet appetizers you might present. Be careful with the feta. It does not like to be roughly handled.

2 teaspoons fennel seeds
½ teaspoon lemon zest
3 tablespoons orange juice
1 teaspoon black pepper
4 ounces feta cheese, cut into 24 cubes
24 mint leaves
12 pitted green olives, cut in half
2 cucumbers, peeled, and cut into ½-inch chunks
6-inch skewers

In a medium bowl, combine the fennel seeds, lemon zest, juice, and pepper. Add the feta and coat, stirring gently. Marinate in refrigerator for at least 1 hour.

To assemble the skewers, pierce a mint leaf and string to lower end of skewer. Then add a half olive and cucumber chunk. Carefully (the cheese will break if you are too forceful), add a piece of the feta cheese. Keep refrigerated until ready to serve.

Katie's Wedding Cookies
(Yield: 30–36 cookies)

From Katie:

These are one of my favorite cookies. They're so easy to make, and they look so elegant on a platter because of the dusting of confectioners' sugar. Make sure you have plenty on hand. They go quickly.

1 cup unsalted butter, at room temperature
½ cup confectioners' sugar, plus more for coating baked cookies
1½ teaspoons vanilla extract
1¾ cups all-purpose flour
¼ teaspoon cinnamon
1 cup chopped cashews, chopped into very small pieces
add water if necessary

Preheat the oven to 275 degrees F.

Line cookie sheets with parchment paper.

Using an electric mixer, cream the butter and sugar at low speed until it is smooth. Beat in the vanilla.

At low speed, gradually add in the flour and cinnamon.

To chop the nuts, I used my food processer. You can also use a "whackah-whackah" (manual food chopper) or you can put them in a baggie and smash them with a meat tenderizer hammer.

Mix in the nuts into the flour mixture with a spatula.

For each cookie, use about 1 tablespoon of dough and shape it into a crescent. Dust hands with flour, if necessary, as you make more cookies.

Place cookies onto prepared cookie sheets. Bake for 40 minutes. When the cookies are cool enough to handle, but still warm, roll the cookies in additional confectioners' sugar to coat.

Cool entirely before eating. Store in an airtight container.

Chef's notes:

If you want, you may substitute your favorite nut for the cashews.
If you're not a cinnamon fan, remove it or switch it out with nutmeg.
If you'd like to make these gluten-free, substitute the all-purpose flour with sweet rice flour and add ¼ teaspoon xanthan gum to the mixture.

Lobster or White Fish Panini Sandwiches
(Yield: 1)

From Katie:

This seasoning can be tweaked however you like, but I'm really partial to the cumin and oregano combo. If you don't have a panini maker, you can make this like you would a typical grilled cheese sandwich. Just be careful as you flip the sandwich because the fish will want to spill out. Maybe, in order to avoid the spillage, cook the bread and cheese for one side, and separately cook the bread, cheese, and fish for the other. Take the cooked bread and cheese side and set it on top of the fish side and press down with a spatula so it all holds together. Cook over low heat.

For Katie's Special Seasoning:
½ teaspoon ground cumin
½ teaspoon ground oregano
½ teaspoon freshly ground black pepper
½ teaspoon ground salt or kosher salt

For the Lobster or White Fish Panini Sandwich:
2 ounces lobster meat or white fish, cooked
1–2 tablespoons butter
2 slices white bread (may be gluten-free)
3 slices deli-sliced Gruyère or Swiss cheese

In a small bowl, make Katie's special seasoning by combining all the ingredients. Sprinkle ½ teaspoon on the cooked lobster meat or white fish. Set the rest aside for another use.

To make the panini, heat the panini maker on medium. Butter two slices of bread. Place one slice butter-side down on the hot panini grill. Top with 1½ slices cheese. Top with the seasoned lobster or fish. Top with the remaining cheese and the other slice of buttered bread.

Close the panini maker, and cook the sandwich on medium for 4–5 minutes until the cheese is melted.

To precook the white fish, you may set it in a bowl and microwave for 2 minutes on low. Then toss with the seasoning.

Margarita Cocktail
(Yield: 1 nice-sized drink)

From Aunt Vera:

My mother's margaritas were legendary. She fell in love with the cocktail when she went to Mexico after she graduated college. She liked her margaritas on the rocks, and that's how I prefer them, too, but you may blend this cocktail, if you so desire. The recipe is pretty basic. It might even be written on a Rose's lime juice bottle. But that is the key, the bartender in Mexico told my mother. She had to use Rose's lime juice, not margarita mix. The lime juice has a hint of syrup in it, but not too much. Enjoy.

margarita salt, if desired
1 part Triple Sec
1 part Rose's Lime Juice
2 parts tequila
ice

If desired, rim a glass with margarita salt by wetting the rim of the glass and then dipping the rim into the salt.

In a measuring cup, mix the liquor and juices in this radio (1:1:2). If you're making for a group, mix ½ cup of Triple Sec, then ½ cup Rose's Lime Juice and 1 cup Tequila. Get it? (1:1:2)

Fill a margarita glass or wineglass or even a tumbler with ice cubes. Pour the liquid over the ice cubes.

FYI: This is potent. One is plenty. Two could, um, lay you flat.

Peach or Pear Flambé
(Serves 2)

From Katie:

This dish is perfect for two and may easily be doubled or tripled for a party. It's quite a crowd pleaser and so easy to make. Choose peaches or pears, depending on the season. They cook at the same rate. Is it messy to clean up? Well, yes, but that comes with the territory.

1 peach or pear, ripe but still firm
2 tablespoons butter
2 tablespoons brown sugar
2 tablespoons dark rum

Peel and cut fruit in half, removing pit or seeds, and slice each half into 2–3 slices.

In a deep skillet, melt the butter over medium heat. Add the brown sugar and stir.

Add the fruit slices and cook until the fruit is warm and starts to soften, about 1–2 minutes. Turn the fruit over and cook an additional 1 minute.

Turn off the heat and add the rum. Stir the liquor into the butter mixture. Turn the heat back on and, using a kitchen torch or a very long match, pass the flame over the mixture. Make sure you stand back and keep your face and hair away from the flame. Wait until the flame dies down, and then remove pan from heat and serve the fruit plain or over vanilla ice cream.

Perfect Bliss Cocktail
(Yield: 1 cocktail)

From Katie:

There's nothing that says "Your Wedding" like a signature cocktail. This was one of my mother's favorite drinks. She said she loved anything Hawaiian in flavor. Now, peaches aren't typically what I think of when I think Hawaiian, but I would never contradict my mother. If you want to switch out the peach nectar to make this more Hawaiian, try guava nectar or mango nectar. So refreshing.

3 ounces peach nectar juice
1 ounce vodka
dash of lime juice
½ cup club soda
4–6 ice cubes
lime wheel for garnish

In a tall glass, mix the nectar, vodka, lime juice and club soda. Add ice and garnish with a lime wheel.

Salmon and Avocado Rolls
(Yield: 4)

From Katie:

This is one of the easiest and tastiest appetizers. It can be a tad messy, but it will firm up and look beautiful on plates or serving platters. Make sure your guests are not allergic to sesame seeds. Sesame seeds are a sneaky allergy. PS: There will be ends of the salmon rolls that might not look beautiful on a plate. Those are for you to savor. Heh-heh.

4 tablespoons softened cream cheese
1 tablespoon chives
1 teaspoon lemon juice
1 avocado, sliced
½ cucumber, peeled, seeded, and diced
8 ounces smoked salmon, divided into 4 slices
4 tablespoons olive oil
2 tablespoons champagne or white wine vinegar
1 teaspoon sesame seeds

In a medium bowl, mix the cream cheese, chives, and lemon juice. Set aside.

Prepare the avocado and cucumber and set aside.

Lay the 4 slices of salmon out on a cutting board. Spread 1 tablespoon of the cream cheese mixture on each. Top with the avocado and cucumber. Roll gently. Cucumber chunks will slip out. That's okay. Cover and refrigerate for two hours to let the cheese firm up.

Before serving, combine the olive oil and vinegar in a small bowl and whisk until emulsified.

To serve the salmon, cut the rolls into 1-inch slices. Set on plates. Drizzle with the olive oil dressing and then sprinkle with sesame seeds.

Scallops with Bacon Benedict à la California Catch
(Yield: 6 sandwiches)

From Jenna:

So I took the card that California Catch offered at the front of their restaurant and had to try it. I'm not very deft with sauces, but this sounded fun and challenging. What I loved about it was the hollandaise sauce. So easy and so yummy.

For the biscuits (yields 12; you can freeze the extras) / (Gluten-free biscuit recipe below):
2 cups flour
3 teaspoons baking powder
¼ teaspoon baking soda
⅓ cup very cold salted butter, cut in small cubes
3 tablespoons chopped fresh chives
1 cup buttermilk

For the hollandaise sauce:
3 egg yolks
¼ teaspoon Dijon mustard
1 tablespoon lemon juice
1 dash hot pepper sauce, like Tabasco
¼ teaspoon white pepper
½ cup butter (one stick)

For the scallop mixture:
6 large fresh scallops
1 tablespoon butter
1 tablespoon olive oil
5 eggs scrambled and cooked
6 slices crisply cooked bacon, chopped

To prepare the biscuits:
Preheat oven to 400 degrees F.

In a food processor, pulse the flour, baking powder, and baking soda. Add in the cold butter and pulse a few more times—do not

242

over-pulse — until the mixture resembles small peas.

Transfer the mixture into a large mixing bowl and add the chives. Toss together and make a well in the center. Add the buttermilk. Work this together with a wooden spoon, folding the dry mixture into the buttermilk. Once it's combined, stop. You don't want to overmix.

Put the dough on a well-floured countertop. Sprinkle the top with additional flour and roll the dough into a flat round, about ½ inch thick. Cut out biscuits with a round cookie cutter or the top of a round glass.

Bake biscuits for 10 minutes, then lower the temperature to 375 degrees F and bake 10 minutes longer.

To make the hollandaise sauce:
In the blender, combine the egg yolks, mustard, lemon juice, hot pepper sauce, and white pepper. Blend for about 5–10 seconds.

Put the butter into a microwave-safe bowl or measuring cup and melt completely, about 30–45 seconds.

Set the blender on high speed and add the melted butter to the egg mixture in a thin stream. It will thicken up, fast.

Neat trick: You can keep the sauce warm until serving by placing the blender itself in a pan of hot water.

To make the scallops:
Season the scallops with salt and pepper and pan sear them in a hot pan with the butter and olive oil for 3 minutes a side.

Assembly for each sandwich:
Slice a biscuit in half and use one piece as the bottom. Set it on a plate. Add some scrambled eggs and top those with a seared scallop. Pour on some of the hollandaise sauce and sprinkle with chopped bacon and extra chives, for garnish.

If desired, top with the second half of the biscuit. Serve hot.

Gluten-free Biscuits with Chives
(Yield: 8 large or 12 small)

2 cups gluten-free flour
1 tablespoon whey powder
4 teaspoons baking powder
1½ teaspoons powdered psyllium husk
1 teaspoon sugar
½ teaspoon salt
¼ teaspoon baking soda
3 tablespoons unsalted butter, chilled and cut into ¼-inch pieces
¾ cup plain whole-milk yogurt (or sour cream)
1 large egg, lightly beaten
2 tablespoons vegetable oil
3 tablespoons chopped chives
2 teaspoons lemon juice

In a food processor, pulse gluten-free flour, whey powder, baking powder, psyllium husk, sugar, salt, and baking soda until combined. Add butter to gluten-free flour mixture, and pulse a few more times — do not over-pulse — until the mixture resembles small peas.

In a separate bowl, whisk together yogurt (or sour cream), egg, oil, chives, and lemon juice until combined. Add to the gluten-free flour mixture and pulse until thoroughly combined and no flour pockets remain, about 6–8 pulses. Transfer to a bowl. Cover bowl with plastic wrap and let batter rest at room temperature for 30 minutes.

Adjust oven rack to middle position and heat oven to 450 degrees F. Line rimmed baking sheet with parchment paper. Use greased ⅓-cup dry measure for large biscuits; use ¼-cup dry measure for small biscuits. Scoop heaping amount of batter and drop onto prepared sheet. It'll measure about 2½ inches in diameter and about 1½ inches high. Repeat with remaining batter. Space biscuits about ½ inch apart in center of prepared sheet.

Bake until gold and crisp, about 15 minutes, rotating sheet halfway through baking. Transfer baking sheet to wire rack and let biscuits cool for 5–10 minutes before serving.

Note: Do not omit the psyllium husk; it is crucial to the structure of the biscuits.
Resting time: Do not shortchange the 30-minute rest for the dough; if you do, the biscuits will be gritty and spread too much. You certainly don't want that.
These may be frozen. Wrap individually and freeze when completely cool.

Spicy Fish Kebabs à la Katie
(Yield: 12)

From Katie:

Okay, yes, I was inspired to make these kebabs because of the ones California Catch made. They are deliciously spicy. You may serve them with a sauce, but the olive oil, lemon, dill, and other spices create a lovely flavor that dresses the arugula. You decide.

1 teaspoon parsley flakes
1 teaspoon ground sage
1 teaspoon ground cumin
1 teaspoon kosher salt
1 teaspoon ground black pepper
1 pound thick fish fillet, like halibut or mahi-mahi, cut into 1-inch cubes
¼ cup extra-virgin olive oil
juice of 1 lemon (2–3 tablespoons)
1 teaspoon dill
arugula for serving
canola oil for prep pan
20 red cherry tomatoes

In a bowl, combine the parsley, sage, cumin, salt, and pepper. Add the fish cubes and toss to coat. Let stand for 10 minutes.

In a separate bowl, whisk the olive oil, lemon juice, and dill. Pour the mixture over the fish and toss to coat. Cover and refrigerate for at least 1 hour.

Meanwhile, submerge 12 long skewers (8 to 12 inches) in cold water. Let soak for 30 minutes. Line a platter with arugula. Set aside.

Coat a broiling tray with canola oil (or nonstick spray may be used). Preheat the broiler.

Thread the fish and tomatoes on the skewers, alternating. Set on the broiler pan and cook for 6–8 minutes, until the fish is cooked through. Turn on the kitchen vent fan. The skewers might start to smoke.

When done, transfer the kebabs to the arugula platter and serve immediately.

White Wine Risotto
(Serves 4–6)

From Rhett:

My parents taught me that the best part of risotto is the love and care that goes into it. You have to be patient as it cooks through and all the flavors meld. Adding the wine gives it a savory elegance. This dish may be served with any protein entrée. Add a sprig of parsley for garnish.

2 cups chicken stock, more if needed
½ sweet onion, diced
1 clove garlic, if desired (may use ½ teaspoon freeze-dried garlic)
4 stalks celery, trimmed and diced
2 tablespoons olive oil
2 tablespoons butter, divided
1¼ cup risotto rice
1 cup dry white wine, like Pinot Grigio
¼ teaspoon kosher salt
½ cup grated Parmesan cheese
parsley, for garnish

In a saucepan heat the stock and keep it warm.

Chop the onion, garlic, and celery.

In a sauté pan, heat the olive oil and 1 tablespoon of butter on low. Add the onion, garlic, and celery, and cook on low for about 15 minutes. Don't let it brown. When the vegetables have softened, add the rice. Turn the heat to medium.

The rice will lightly brown. Stir so it doesn't become too brown. It will start to get translucent. When it does, add the white wine and stir. Once the wine has cooked into the rice, add a ladle of hot stock and the sea salt. Turn the heat to simmer. Every few minutes add a ladle of stock and stir. Allow each ladleful to be absorbed before adding the next one. This will take about 15 minutes.

Taste the rice to see if it's cooked. If not, keep adding stock until it's soft but has a bit of a chewiness to it.

Remove the pan from the heat and add the remaining 1 tablespoon butter and the Parmesan. Stir well. Let sit for 2 minutes. Garnish with parsley and serve hot.

Stir-fried Shrimp with Asparagus Tips
(Serves 2)

From Rhett:

This is not a French dish typical of Intime, but it happens to be one of Jenna's favorite entrées, so I offer it on the menu and try to prepare it for her at least once a year. The trick is to cook everything quickly so the shrimp bites don't get tough. If you'd like to use raw shrimp, simply cook the shrimp longer before adding in the precooked asparagus tips.

20 asparagus spears, trimmed
2 tablespoons olive oil
½ teaspoon garlic, minced, if desired
½ pound cooked shrimp, diced into bite-sized pieces
2 green onions, julienned or diced
½ teaspoon salt
¼ teaspoon ginger
1 tablespoon tamari
1 tablespoon lemon juice

In a small saucepan, bring 2 inches of water to boil. Prepare the asparagus tips, reserving the remainder of the asparagus for another use, and add to boiling water. Boil 2 minutes. Remove from water and put into an ice bath to cool and stop the cooking process.

Meanwhile, in a large saucepan heat the olive oil over medium heat. Add the garlic, if desired, and cook for 1 minute. Add the diced shrimp, green onions, and salt. Add in the ginger, tamari, and lemon juice. Stir 1–2 minutes. Add the asparagus tips and stir until asparagus has heated through.

Serve hot over white or brown rice or alongside risotto.

About the Author

Agatha Award–winning, nationally bestselling author Daryl Wood Gerber writes suspense novels as well as cozy mysteries. She is best known for her Cookbook Nook Mysteries, featuring an admitted foodie and owner of a cookbook store in Crystal Cove, California, and her Fairy Garden Mysteries, featuring a fairy garden shop owner in Carmel, California. She also writes the French Bistro Mysteries, featuring a bistro owner in Napa Valley. Under the pen name Avery Aames, Daryl writes the Cheese Shop Mysteries, featuring a cheese shop owner in Providence, Ohio. Her suspense novels, including the Aspen Adams novels, *Girl on the Run,* and *Day of Secrets* have garnered solid reviews.

As a girl, Daryl considered becoming a writer, but she was dissuaded by a seventh-grade teacher. It wasn't until she was in her twenties that she had the temerity to try her hand at writing again . . . for TV and screen. Why? Because she was an actress in Hollywood. A fun tidbit for mystery buffs: Daryl co-starred on *Murder, She Wrote* as well as other TV shows. As a writer, she created the format for the popular sitcom *Out of This World.* When she moved across the country with her husband, she returned to writing what she loved to read: mysteries and suspense.

Daryl is originally from the Bay Area and graduated from Stanford University. She loves to cook, read, golf, swim, and garden. She also likes adventure and has been known to jump out of a perfectly good airplane. She adores Lake Tahoe, and she has a frisky Goldendoodle named Sparky who keeps her in line.

Visit Daryl at www.darylwoodgerber.com, and follow her on Bookbub at http://bookbub.com/authors/daryl-wood-gerber, on Goodreads at http://goodreads.com/darylwoodgerber, and on Amazon at http://bit.ly/Daryl_Wood_Gerber_page.

Made in the USA
Monee, IL
18 April 2022

94955299R00152